MUCH MORE INTO AFRICA

WITH KIDS, DOGS, HORSES AND A HUSBAND

ANN PATRAS

Ann
Press

.

The continuing adventures of a young family who went to live and work in Zambia for two years – and stayed much longer.

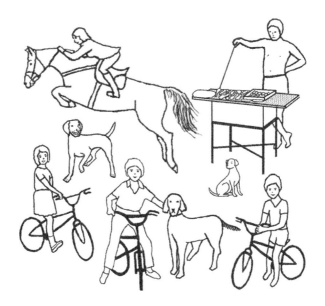

Book 3 of the 'Africa' Series
Available in Large Print, paperback and ebook.

AUTHOR'S NOTE

This book should not be considered as a regular travel guide, nor does it delve deeply into Africa culture. It describes the life of myself and my family living in Zambia, based on letters written at the time to family and friends in the UK.

I have what I consider to be a typically dry, British sense of humour and do, on occasion, use mild swear words.

It should be noted that in the interest of authenticity, conversations and observations contained in this book reflect what was said, assumed or apparent to me *at that time*.

To BRAD, VICTORIA AND LEON,
the Superstars in my life
xxx

CONTENTS

GLOSSARY

OF AFRICAN WORDS OR EXPRESSIONS AS WELL AS A FEW
OTHER WORDS WHICH CHANGE AFTER CROSSING THE
ATLANTIC.

BAKKIE open-backed van; pickup truck.

BILTONG cured meat snack, similar to beef jerky.

BOEREWORS a long sausage an inch or more in diameter, made of beef (or game) with spices added to varying degrees. It is about a yard long and is wound in a tight circle to be cooked on the braai whole. After being cooked on both sides it is then cut into shorter lengths for individual consumption.

BRAAI (item) this is a barbeque (equipment and event). A traditional braai would be made out of an oil-drum sliced in half lengthwise. It would have holes punched in the curved base and often legs made for it, though it could be supported by bricks or rocks. A large expanded-metal grid would be placed on top, on which to braai the meat.

(event) at a traditional braai, all the men would stand around the braai with their beers, chatting away and laughing raucously as they watched the meat burn. Beer would be chucked over the coals (and meat) if flames got high. The men would shuffle around the braai box as necessary to avoid being 'smoked out'. Meanwhile the wives would be making all the salads, garlic bread, and suchlike, or sitting in the shade with a G&T.

BUNDU open countryside (the bundu). Bundu bashing – going off track, into the countryside.

BUSH similar to bundu. Most wild animals in Africa live in the bush, not in the jungle, though I understand why this became a popular word. It doesn't sound nearly so impressive to say a lion is 'the king of the bush', does it?

CHIPS fries/French fries.

CHONGOLOLO a lovely, harmless creepy-crawly in the form of a black/brown, very long (up to 25cm/10") millipede.

DONGA a narrow steep-sided ravine formed by water erosion but usually dry except in the rainy season; a man-made storm-water ditch found either side of a road.

EISH! an expression, usually exclaimed in surprise, dismay or regret at something. Is frequently accompanied by a slow shaking of the head.

KATUNDU possessions; baggage.

MEALLIES maize; sweetcorn; corn-on-the-cob.

MEALLIE MEAL powder ground from maize, when mixed with water and cooked to a stiff paste, forms the staple diet of many African nations. Otherwise known as nshima; pap (South Africa); grits (USA).

MNINGI lots and lots of something.

MUTI medicine or remedy for some ailment.

NSHIMA staple diet in Zambia (see meallie meal above) generally served with relish.

PICCANINS young children.

PLAITING hair braiding.

RELISH a sauce, or stew of vegetables and meat (if income allows) served with nshima.

SHEBEEN illegal drinking establishment usually found in townships, compounds or out in the bundu.

TAP a faucet.

VELD pronounced 'felt': open countryside or grassland.

VLEI pronounced 'flay': veld which is usually marshy in the wet season.

VOETSAK pronounced 'futsak': an Afrikaans word meaning 'go away', and mostly directed at a dog (or other creatures).

ZAIRE now (as at December 2019) called the DRC (Democratic Republic of Congo).

CERTAIN EXPRESSIONS or AFRICAN IDIOMS

NOW

'Now' takes on a whole new meaning in Africa. If someone says something will happen 'now' it can likely be within the hour, today, this week, or this year, depending on the subject matter. If you are making a request for something to be done, the timeframe of effective action is mostly dependent on the number of now's given in the instruction. So if you want something attended to immediately it would be best followed by, "…and can you please do this now, now, now?"

SORRY

'Sorry' took some getting used to, when I first arrived in Zambia. It can be uttered by a complete stranger, who is in no way connected to the mishap which provoked the 'sorry'. I recall my first encounter with the sorry syndrome:

I was walking in Kitwe city centre and was so absorbed by the random contents in a hardware store window I was passing that I failed to notice the broken pavement and duly tripped on a jutting paving slab. As I stumbled to remain upright a Zambian gentleman walking towards me said, "Ah, sorry madam!" in a most concerned way. I wondered whether perhaps it was his job to have levelled the slab but saw no sign of work clothes or tools for such a project. Being a bit unsure I muttered, "Oh, that's okay" and continued on my somewhat confused way.

It was only after I had elicited the same response from a barman after bumping into an unoccupied chair, and from my house servant when *I* dropped and broke a glass jar in the kitchen at home, that I realised apologies were not being proffered because *they* had done anything wrong. It was rather a way of saying, "I'm sorry that happened to you." Which, of course, is a very nice gesture.

Naturally 'sorry' was also used in the normal manner when someone actually *had* done something wrong, except in that case it would be more like, "Oh, sorry madam. Sorry, sorry, sorry. I am sorry madam." This would be repeated as much as the severity of the offence demanded.

WHAT YOU NEED TO KNOW

(Unless you have read the previous two books, in which case you might want to skip this bit.)

Back in 1980 my husband Ziggy and I upped sticks and went, with our three very young children (Brad, Vicki and Leon), to live and work in Zambia. Being in the days before the informative World Wide Web, when the only rare documentaries on British TV were about lions and elephants, we had no idea what to expect life would be like in Africa, but it wasn't like anything we would have expected if we had.

Shortages of basic food and household consumables abounded, and other commodities seemed to consist only of items that could be made out·of copper or crimplene. It appeared the only things we could guarantee getting on a regular basis were sunshine and mosquito bites. I love sunshine…

Having spent my early years in my family's busy corner grocery shop, and later ones in their lively public house, the lack of essential groceries and pubs came as a bit of a shock to my system. But we soon found that there was a plethora of sports and social clubs, and these were the places to go to learn from the friendly expat community how to live an enjoyable, if somewhat unusual at times, life in Africa.

Allow me to expand a little:

When we first arrived basic commodities like sugar, butter, salt, flour, cooking oil, rice, washing powder, soap, shampoo and toilet rolls would never make it to the supermarket shelves. When they arrived at a store they were rationed out to the queuing shoppers straight from the box. Tinned food was limited to baked beans and corned beef, and packet items (soups, cake mixes, pasta, sauce mixes, cereals, all that sort of stuff) were simply non-existent. 'Convenience' items like jams, dried fruit, ketchups, pickles and frozen foods were stuff dreams were made of, and if you wanted hamburgers or sausages you made your own from scratch - when you could get the meat.

Beef and chicken were available most of the time, as was pork when it was the right season. They didn't appear to have heard of sheep in Zambia so the nearest you could get to a leg of lamb was a scrawny goat. For some reason most expats tended to avoid the goat option. Fresh vegetables and fruit were always available, if somewhat limited in their variety.

We adjusted our culinary habits accordingly.

If you had dogs (and 98% of expats did) their meals were something else altogether, as dry dog biscuits (kibbles) were unheard of. Instead they ate mealie meal mixed with chicken (just the bits humans didn't want to eat - beaks, feet, eyeballs), or kapenta (miniature dried fish). Just recalling the stench that permeated the air when the dog food was being cooked makes me want to vomit.

Beyond the culinary concerns, other scarcities came in the form of electrical items, kids' toys, sporting equipment, vehicles and clothes. There were a few shops selling clothes, but they seemed mostly to be made from crimplene.

After three or four years the variety of available goods improved somewhat as produce became more readily imported from South Africa. At a price!

One of the things which initially took some getting used to was the use of 'house servants'. Like it or not, that is what the home help was called. I initially balked at the idea of employing a house servant, but soon realised that given the lack of *convenience anything,* they were essential to any household. It was expected for expats to employ house servants. Many of the better-off Zambians did too. Far from being demeaning, vast numbers of the community relied on these jobs and would be out of work and starving if it weren't for house servant positions, as well as those of garden help (no lawnmowers) and security guards (lots of thieving).

In the majority of cases only the expat husbands worked; mostly being employed by the copper mines or their affiliated companies. On our initial contract, Ziggy worked as Site Manager for a private company building the new cobalt processing plant for the government-owned Zambia Consolidated Copper Mine (ZCCM) in Kitwe.

Very few expat wives were employed, as they were unlikely to be given work permits because most jobs suitable for women had been 'Zambianised', i.e. a post *had* to be given to a Zambian national. Some exceptions could be found among doctors and teachers.

Our first four years in Zambia were spent in Kitwe and we became heavily involved with the Kitwe Little Theatre (not that we had previous experience of such a hobby), and there we made many wonderful friends. Our second social area was the Cricket Club; our interest and knowledge of the game was minimal to say the least, but the people were fun.

All things considered, any minor drawbacks to living in the middle of Africa were outweighed by the many things there were to enjoy, and we soon grew to love the vagaries of life in Zambia.

1

IN THE BEGINNING

"**M**ummy, there's a big hole in the garden," called Vicki.
"It's huge!" Leon cried.

"I'm going to climb down it." That was Brad, racing towards the enormous crater which sat in the front garden of our new home in Lusaka.

We had driven down the day before, from Kitwe on Zambia's Copperbelt to live in the capital city. Allow me to enlighten you.

In August of 1984 Ziggy was coming to the end of his second two-year contract with Rhinestone, the company which instigated our move to Zambia when he, together with about half the expatriate population of Kitwe, came down with hepatitis.

In the last few months of this contract Ziggy had become quite disenamoured with the company's (mis)management, so directed his boredom whilst recovering from the hepatitis to looking for another job. It didn't take long for him to be offered a position by a man who owned several companies in Zambia. Ziggy was offered three jobs actually and was asked to decide which one he'd like to take. The one he chose, General Manager of Management Services for the Mutende Group, saw us moving to Lusaka, giving us a very fresh start.

So it was that, at the end of the first week in September, Ziggy and

I, together with Brad, almost eight, and Vicki and Leon, six-and-a-half years old, said a sad goodbye to the wonderful bunch of very dear friends we had made over the past four years, and headed 225 miles south to Lusaka.

Before we knew we'd be leaving Kitwe we had arranged for my parents, Nancy and Mev, to come out to us for a holiday. My mum had visited in 1981, but my parents hadn't been able to come out together until now because they ran a pub which couldn't do without both of them for longer than a week. Sadly my dad had developed a serious back problem necessitating surgery, which caused them to take early retirement. The upside was that now he was all sorted, they were now both able to visit us in our adopted country. It was just a pity that we would be moving house in the middle of their stay. So the first part of their holiday was based in Kitwe and they then travelled with us down to Lusaka.

My mum hadn't been feeling too good during the few days leading up to our Kitwe departure, with no obvious cause, but the long drive south to Lusaka really took its toll. We had to stop several times on the roadside as she felt nauseous. When we eventually hit the capital we made our way to the Intercontinental Hotel where we were supposed to stay overnight while we awaited the arrival of all our katundu in the removals truck.

Unfortunately the hotel booking which should have been made for us by Ziggy's new employers had somehow been forgotten, and the hotel was fully booked. Ziggy phoned one of his new colleagues, and asked for help in the matter. After some substantial and protracted negotiation, he managed to get us squashed into a couple of box-rooms in the 4-Star Ridgeway Hotel. How it had ever been classified as a four-star establishment I do not know. In my younger life I had stayed at boarding houses in Skegness with better facilities than were offered at the Ridgeway. Fortunately this cramped accommodation was only needed for one night so we muddled through, with Ziggy and I and the three kids sharing two single beds. In their room, three floors higher and at the other end of the hotel, my mum and dad had the luxury of a small single bed each and thankfully, by the time they were settled in, my mum was feeling a lot better.

The next day we were up bright and early, anxious to see our new home.

Situated on a corner of Lukanga Road, it looked very nice from the outside; a spacious house with a large garden, but what a disappointment it was when I walked inside or, more specifically, when I first walked into the kitchen where I would naturally spend a lot of my time. I almost wept. It was tiny. Wherever I'd lived throughout my life there had always been a spacious kitchen.

In comparison to anything in my past, this one was minute. With the cooker, sink and drainer taking up most of the space along one wall, there were only a couple of small cupboards with counters at right angles at either end, and the oven door fell off when I tried to open it. On the upside, there was a small pantry for storage, about the size of half a toilet cubicle.

The single-storey house contained four bedrooms and a bathroom at one end of the house, and at the other end a large bedroom with bathroom en suite as well as a kitchenette sort of area. In between were the lounge and dining room, which were separated by a central fireplace facing the lounge, and a small bar which faced the dining room.

An advantage to the place was the large covered patio leading off the lounge and dining room which looked out onto the garden, which is where the crater was that caused so much excitement for the kids. This, it appeared, was the beginnings of a swimming pool. Rather on the large side, and not just a conventional rectangular pool with steps at one end like those we had previously experienced, it was an irregular octagonal shape. As it developed, it revealed submerged 'seats' on two sides and a small paddling pool leading off the centre. It was all very fancy, though it took a few weeks to complete.

Once it was finished and painted we had two meagre hosepipes running into it during the night (water was needed during the day for household use). We were taking bets on how long the pool would take to fill, but no-one expected the eleven days it took! By the ninth day it was also becoming obvious that the builder hadn't been too bothered about levels. As the water level rose it revealed that one side of the pool was four inches lower than the other, and that was only across the width! So when you stood at the end of the pool you had a tendency to lean slightly to one side, which could make diving in quite a hazardous affair. Unfortunately my parents never had the chance to dip their toes in it as they had to leave us before the pool was complete.

As usual, goodbyes at the airport were quite tearful, but we promised to do our best to spend Christmas with them in England. In the meantime letters would continue to flow, keeping them well updated about our new life in Lusaka.

A few days after us, Benton and his family arrived and settled into their new home on the other side of the driveway on our property. Benton was our house servant.

As I mentioned in my earlier books, items like washing machines and tumble dryers were not readily available in Zambia at the time. All washing had to be done by hand, and every single item of clothing, bedding and even towels had to be ironed. This was necessary to kill off putzi fly larvae.

The putzi fly, which goes by various names in different parts of Africa, lays its eggs into areas of damp washing on the line and then, as you wear or use the infested fabric, they infiltrate the skin and turn into fat wriggly grubs which cause sores which are itchy and painful and continue to grow under your skin until they are 'extracted'. To avoid a serious backlog, washing and ironing had to be done on a daily basis, along with all other household chores.

Benton had started working for us after we'd had a couple of 'former employee disasters' in 1980/81. One of the perks of his job was that he and his wife with their two small children were also provided with free accommodation in a purpose-built building known as a kya.

As soon as I knew we were moving to Lusaka we had offered Benton a generous redundancy package, as well as help in seeking alternative employment, as I assumed he would want to remain in Kitwe. He surprised us by turning that down, saying that he would like to move to Lusaka so that he could continue to work for us. Naturally we were delighted as from past experience we knew finding another trustworthy house servant like Benton was not going to be easy. So Benton, his wife Catrina, and their now *five* children were given train tickets so that they could join us.

The day after my parents left saw the commencement of other arrivals. Our dogs. We had left them in the care of the Kitwe SPCA, which also had boarding kennels. They helped us tremendously with the travel arrangements, organised a large crate and sent it down, complete with dog, via Zambia Railways.

Bass, our huge Rhodesian Ridgeback, and youngest of our dogs, was the first to arrive. He was so happy to see us, his long tail whiplashed from left to right, knocking things off tables and leaving us with red welts on our legs. We returned the crate on the next available train and three days later Coke, our Irish Red Setter arrived. He too was clearly delighted to see us and soon resumed his role as top dog over young Bass. Finally Sally arrived, our smaller black-and-tan-something-crossed-with-something-else dog we had adopted from friends when they left Zambia. She seemed totally unfazed by any of this and resumed her laid-back life.

Ziggy had been very busy since joining the new company, only finishing work at six or later and coming straight home. A vast change from the 'finish at four and sit drinking at one of the social clubs until seven' situation he had become accustomed to in Kitwe. And now he was thoroughly enjoying himself.

While they were with us we had housed my mum and dad in our bedroom, but once they returned to England I moved all of mine and Ziggy's stuff into there. It was large enough to be able to set up a good sewing area where there was plenty of light.

Once I had the house in order I managed to find a street map of Lusaka and tentatively drove around in Lizzie, our Land Rover, sourcing the various shopping and other facilities. The shops were a little more plentiful and varied than in Kitwe. I checked out the location of the retailers selling fabrics and a few accessories, but to what end? My client base for sewing had all been left behind in Kitwe.

And already I missed my friends terribly.

Everything had happened so quickly and with so much stuff going on I hadn't given much thought to what I would do once the dust settled on our new Lusaka life. For the first time since leaving England in 1980 I actually felt alone.

When we had first arrived in Kitwe people went out of their way to get us integrated into the system but now, being *experienced expats* who had simply moved location, there was no welcoming committee.

Expats were very spread out around the capital city, which was a fair bit larger than Kitwe. There was more variation in the expat workplace too, with many smaller companies as well as the larger international ones and, of course, the embassies. So from what I could see at that time, Lusaka did not seem to have an expatriate 'community' like I had been used to in Kitwe.

The company Ziggy worked for was wholly Zambian-owned and didn't employ all that many expats, but that was of little consequence anyway, as Ziggy had never been a big fan of mixing his social and working lives. A few exceptions to this in Kitwe had mostly come about because we belonged to the same clubs.

I didn't know where to go to find any new friends for myself, apart from the kids' school. The kids had settled well into their new school, Lake Road Primary. They started school at 9:00 and finished at 1:30, with me ferrying them back and forth each day in Lizzie. Unfortunately it was the norm for many families to have a driver deliver and collect their kids, so that was a bit of a non-starter for meeting people too.

Apart from that, I was at a loss. My chief hobby in Kitwe had been sewing, whether it had been for the Kitwe Little Theatre Club in which we had been heavily involved during our first three years in Zambia, or sewing for friends and acquaintances to earn a few kwacha (the local currency). Now I didn't have anyone to sew for; the kids and I had more than enough clothes until the kids outgrew theirs.

As I write this I do wonder what on earth I did to occupy my time right then. Whereas letter-writing used to take up a lot of my time in Kitwe, when you are not doing anything of interest what is there to write home about? I do know that I was rapidly sinking into a quagmire of boredom and self-pity at having no friends nearby, nor any idea of how or where to make new ones.

Of course I did have the winemaking. I had decided to take up that hobby when I found we had a very productive grapevine at our last house in Kitwe. So when I had been in the UK on leave, just prior to moving to Lusaka, I bought all the assorted paraphernalia appropriate for winemaking.

It goes without saying that I didn't buy the large glass demijohns which were normally used for the job - could you imagine transporting them in a suitcase? However it was possible to get substitutes in the way of Coca-Cola concentrate bottles which were about the same size but had a wider top opening and didn't sport those strange little loopy handles found on demijohns. The biggest difficulty was trying to buy cork stoppers big enough for the tops, but a couple of Kitwe winemakers had put me onto a source.

While my folks had still been with us I had stripped the vine at our old Kitwe home and brought buckets-full of grapes to Lusaka. Nancy and I'd had great fun treading grapes in the bath, though I can't say that I was all that enamoured by the grapes squidging between my toes. At one point we were giggling so much at one small errant bunch of grapes which succeeded in avoiding our four feet that my mum had to get out of our primitive press before she wet herself laughing. That would have given our home brew a very distinctive and, I am sure, not-so-pleasant flavour.

The kitchenette in our bedroom was the perfect site for my new vinicultural activities, and I was amazed to find that we also had a grapevine at this house, attached to the patio roof. Over the months I tried various fruits on this production line including pineapple, which came out far too sweet; passion fruit -you know, the one which looks like someone has puked in it, which was quite insipid; and guava, which for some reason went mouldy so got thrown away. By far the best wine I ever made came from our huge, constantly fruiting lemon tree. And it didn't taste at all lemony. It was very more-ish!

The lemon tree was located fairly close to the corner of our house and had a 24-hour light source from sunshine nearly all year round during the day, and our outside security lights which illuminated it throughout the night. So we always had lemons for Africa!

Have you ever heard that expression, "*such-n-such* for Africa"? It's a very common expression that we have used for as long as I can remember. Basically if you had an excess of something you had enough for Africa - it being a big place with hordes of people. It could be anything, even totally irrelevant to Africa, but if you had a lot of it, you 'had it for Africa'.

Just thought I'd throw that in. Anyway, where was I?

Oh yes, viniculture. A new hobby this might be, but it was hardly a time-consuming affair - unless you enjoyed watching a single bubble rise through an airlock every three or four hours.

I definitely needed something else to occupy my time.

But I'm getting in front of myself.

2

HAPPY OCTOBER

September turned into October and Brad's eighth birthday was fast approaching and had us in a bit of a dilemma what to do. Having only recently started at their new school, the kids hadn't yet had time to make many friends. A gang of our Kitwe pals were going to Mfuwe Lodge for the Zambian Independence Day long weekend and we agreed that if we could join them Brad would have an 'official birthday', just like the Queen, whilst we were there.

On Brad's actual birthday we just had a special meal at home followed by games of cards and dominoes between the five of us. However, he did get one really special surprise for his birthday:

Ziggy had been down to Johannesburg in South Africa on business the previous week and had bought Brad a special birthday present, a BMX bike. And it was not just any ordinary BMX bike. Whilst the frame and forks were chrome, the tyres, seat, chain, pedals, grips and brakes were all red. His favourite colour.

Ziggy could hardly contain himself from revealing it when he got in from the airport, but I made him wait until Brad's actual birthday. Brad was absolutely thrilled to bits, the only trouble was the tyres needed pumping up and Ziggy had forgotten to buy a pump. Benton had a bike pump but alas the fitting was different, so Brad had to wait until we could track down one which would fit.

The day after his birthday I was sitting on the patio when I spotted Brad pushing his bike.

"What are you doing?" I asked.

"Oh, I'm just taking my bike for a walk," he said.

He continued to take his bike for walks until we managed to get some air into the tyres three days later, after which he could be seen bombing around the garden on it like a thing possessed.

The following Saturday was quite an eventful day for us. We had been invited out to Musa Siame's house (Ziggy's boss) for pre-dinner cocktails (minus the dinner). Of course, kids weren't invited so we left ours under the watchful eye of Benton.

It was a very pleasant affair with about half a dozen other senior employees, with spouses, being invited. It was nice to put faces to the names Ziggy had mentioned, and for me to meet Mr Siame for only the second time. Chatting to him, he was so unassuming you would never guess he was the owner of such a huge business empire.

Trays of savouries and sweets had been brought in from one of the large hotels, and Mr Siame's bar stock could have given my parents' pub serious competition. What little I saw of his house - phew, impressive!

On the Friday we had received a call from our very good friend Nandy, up in the Copperbelt. He was coming to Lusaka and asked if he could stay with us. Naturally we said yes and expected him on Saturday evening.

We got quite a surprise when we returned home from our little cocktail soiree at about 7:15 to find Nandy sitting behind our bar supping beer and eating biltong while trying to entertain the kids with various tales of Kitwe events. He had a Hungarian accent and laryngectomy. Despite the fact that it was over four years since his surgery, and he had now re-accomplished the art of speech, the kids still occasionally battled to understand him.

Before he travelled down he'd phoned me to ask if there was anything I wanted bringing from the Copperbelt. Knowing he had great contacts in the butchery business I asked him if he could get me some fillet steak. He brought us four huge fillets and an enormous bag of his biltong.

Nandy was Zambia's King of Biltong so we were thrilled with this gift (he refused point bank to accept money for anything). He also had the back of his Land Cruiser filled to bursting with crates of Ndola beer.

Perhaps I should explain about Zambian beer in case you haven't read my first book, *Into Africa with 3 kids, 13 crates and a husband.* (And NO, those weren't crates of beer!)

When we first arrived in Zambia there was only one brand of beer available. We didn't even realise it had a name for a year or so because the bottles never bore labels. Made by Zambia Breweries it turned out to be called Mosi and was supplied by two breweries, one in Ndola on the Copperbelt, the other in Lusaka. Although the name was the same, you would never guess that it was supposed to be the same drink.

A year or so previoiusly the Ndola brewery had a crisis which temporary halted production, so supplies were sent up to the Kitwe bottle stores from Lusaka. To our horror, we found the stuff brewed in Lusaka bore a close resemblance to liquid horse manure. Not that I have ever drunk any of that you understand, but the taste reminded me of the smell which emanated from a galvanised bucket of luminous, greenish-brown slop which sat in our yard when I was a kid. It was a concoction my grandmother Doris brewed with which to water her tomato plants in our conservatory, and consisted of water to which manure from my pony was added.

The poor sods who lived in Lusaka must have got used to this vile taste, but us 'northerners' were more discerning. Knowing what awaited him on his trip to Lusaka, Nandy had taken the precaution of bringing sufficient beers to supply any friends he might be visiting here so they could offer him a decent drink! We were thrilled about this, as our own supplies of Ndola beer (which we'd also taken the precaution of bringing down) were almost depleted.

Once we had stored all our goodies, Nandy took us out to the Flying Club at City Airport, which is a place he frequented when in Lusaka. One of the many people he introduced us to there was Dan, who was the manager of a place called the City Free Shop. Located in the city centre the layout was along the lines of a duty-free shop, where you could get innumerous imported luxuries, including things such as chocolate, cereals, biscuits and cans of South African beer at a price which certainly wasn't free of duty! During the course of conversation I asked Dan if he had any connection with the shop next door, City Radio, which was part of the same group. He did.

I asked him if he knew when the new ovens were arriving from South Africa and he said they'd been in for a week but were now all sold. I was furious. I'd had a conversation with a manager in that shop who said he would let me know the instant the cookers arrived so that we could buy one. At this our new friend said he could organise it if I wanted one, saying that he was expecting a consignment of ten for someone and he would now sell one to me and the other customer would have to make do with the nine. *What a nice man*! I thought it was very decent of him, given that he didn't know us from a bar of soap until an hour ago.

During Nandy's four-day stay we visited more places than we had during the previous five weeks. When he departed he still managed to leave us with twelve full crates of Ndola beer.

A nice new, gleaming-white cooker was delivered a week later by City Radio. It was bigger than the door-falls-off one we had, which was fantastic except that the door to the cupboard where I kept my baking tins could now only be opened half way, so finding stuff could be a tad hit and miss but, hey, I like surprises.

Of course the new oven was crying out to be used, so the next day I simply had to do some baking. One of the things my mum had brought out with her from England was a sponge cake mix. I'm not sure if she was trying to make (un)subtle hints about my baking or what, anyway I decided to use the packet, adding some instant coffee to the mix to make it a more interesting coffee cake. I also decided to make a malt loaf.

I started with the malt loaf, but when I came to put the mixture into the loaf tin it turned out to be too small. I fumbled around blindly in the baking cupboard until I located a larger pan and, after greasing it suitably, transferred all the mixture into that. Even then I only just managed to fit the mixture in. With a cooking time of an hour I decided not to start on the sponge cake until the malt loaf was nearly cooked, as they needed different temperature settings. The glass door and inside light of my new cooker, being quite a novelty after the old ovens I had been used to, ten minutes into baking time I bent down to see how it was doing.

Oh my dog! I watched in horror as the sticky, pale brown mixture slowly erupted out of the tin and slithered down the sides like volcanic lava. It then dribbled in slimy curtains through the rack below to form a pool of gook on the base of my brand new oven! And I had to leave it there until the loaf was cooked. The smell of burnt cake (on the hot base) pervaded the house for nearly an hour.

After I'd scraped and cleaned up the mess in the oven I was delighted (and amazed) to find that the malt loaf had actually turned out very well. I then moved on to the coffee cake. That was a very simple process, and it wasn't long before two sponges were baking nicely in the oven.

As I'd been preparing this, our friend Robin phoned from Kitwe and each of the kids had a natter with him before I got my chance to converse. We had a good catch-up of news before signing off. Ten minutes later I remembered that my sponge cakes were still in the oven. Needless to say, they weren't very spongy by this time, but more resembled two large, thick, coffee-flavoured biscuits!

All in all my first experience with the new cooker wasn't really the resounding success that it should have been, and the experience did not help my already very pissed-off state of mind.

We had been living in Lusaka for several weeks by now and I still hadn't made any progress with the local social scene. I was feeling very sorry for myself. Apart from one couple who worked for Rhinestone and who had moved to Lusaka twelve months earlier, we didn't know anyone. And this couple were not known for their socialising tendencies, so there was no point asking them about such things.

As a pick-me-up I decided it was time I got us booked into Mfuwe Lodge in the South Luangwa National Park for our few days with the Kitwe mob.

3

SOUTH LUANGWA

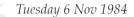

Tuesday 6 Nov 1984

Dear All,

Time for a little update. First of all thanks for the phone call. It was a lovely surprise. I don't know if you could tell from the cacophony in the background, but at the time we had a houseful of folk, like in the good old days.

We had just landed in Lusaka after our game park trip and the Kitwe crowd had a three-hour wait for their connecting flight home, and as our house is only a 25-minute drive from the airport we suggested they all came back to ours for some decent beer and a steak sandwich. Everyone was suitably impressed with the house (I wish I was) and with the pool. When we had left to fly to Mfuwe, the pool had been almost full and turning a bright shade of green. Fortunately, in our absence, Barfig (a pool maintenance company) had been along and lobbed a load of chemicals into it, so by the time we got back it was beautifully blue and crystal clear.

While they were enjoying their quick lunch I was able to play back some of the video footage I'd shot at the game park,

and everyone agreed that a video camera was an absolute must
for future trips to Luangwa.

Personal video cameras were still very new to the UK marketplace in the early 1980s. We had been lucky enough to be able to kit ourselves out with a JVC setup at the end of our first contract. But what a piece of equipment it was! Well, three pieces to be precise.

This was real state-of-the-art stuff in those days, but the size of it was something else. The camera alone must have weighed over 3lb. Then a 6ft cable was used to attach it to the 'portable' video recorder/player, which must have weighed in at about 7lb, being about a foot square and four inches deep (a full-size VHS video tape was housed inside it). The setup wasn't complete without the tuner/power-unit/charger, which was the same size as the recorder/player. For safety and security, when we travelled all this had to be carried in our hand baggage on flights. It also needed almost a seat to itself on the Land Rover when we took it game viewing!

On the upside it lasted us for many years, only being replaced by a small Sony camcorder in 2003!

But back to the game park trip:

When I first heard that our Kitwe friends were going there for the long Independence weekend in October I suggested to Ziggy that it would be great to join them, so he sent a memo to his new boss asking for leave time. He got a reply the next day saying "Your leave requests are noted and granted. Have a good holiday." Not only had Ziggy requested three days off to make up this long weekend, he had also put in for leave at Christmas to go to the UK. Such a rapid and nice response would never have happened with his previous employers, especially with the later management.

Mfuwe Lodge is situated on the edge of a lagoon close to the Luangwa River on the eastern side of the South Luangwa National Park. I went along to a local travel agent to make the booking.

"Would you like an all-inclusive package with National Hotels, or do you want to book the tours with Norman Carr Safaris?" the agent asked.

I quickly used her phone to call my friend Jenny in Kitwe and asked her what they had booked. She said all their tours were included in the price so I went ahead and booked with National Hotels. We were to meet up with our pals at Lusaka airport on Wednesday the 24th.

On the day, our rendezvous was delayed due to the fact that a whole load of military paraphernalia was monopolising the airport, and all normal air traffic ceased for a couple of hours.

You would have thought that the airport authorities would have known well beforehand that military planes and choppers would be taking off and landing like fury at Lusaka airport during the morning of Independence Day. After all, Independence Day is on the same date each year, so even if the President's office hasn't told you to keep your diary open, it doesn't take a mastermind to have plans in place 'just in case' the celebrations *did* happen as usual. It would appear they didn't do planning.

Only after the ETA was long passed did the arrivals board post that the Copperbelt flight had been delayed for two hours! If that wasn't bad enough, the Lusaka authorities didn't appear to have told other airports about Lusaka's commercial closure until the last minute. It transpired our friends had been sitting in the plane, on the tarmac, at Ndola airport since their original boarding time as no-one had mentioned the reason for the delay to them.

It must have been an absolute nightmare. Jenny and John had their two children, Richard and Sarah aged about eight and three. Also Peter and Karen had their baby. Thankfully the plane which was to fly us up to Mfuwe had waited as they knew several of their passengers were arriving on the Ndola flight. As soon as their plane landed we all boarded the waiting one and headed to our destination.

After we tumbled out of the small plane at Mfuwe we milled around the airport building until a driver called for all those who were booked on Norman Carr safaris to board his bus. All our friends piled in! What? Bang went Jenny's assumption that they were with National Hotels. When it looked as though we were about to be left stranded I stopped a passing bloke who looked like a driver (whatever they are supposed to look like) and asked him if anyone was going to take us to Mfuwe Lodge.

"Yes, me. Hop in that Land Rover," he said, pointing beyond the bus.

It was a typical khaki-coloured, game-viewing Land Rover, with three tiers of seats. The lower level had two seats alongside the driver, the second tier was a higher three-seater bench, and behind that was another threesome bench, raised even higher. As was the norm for National, there was no roof.

If you discounted being tossed about like balls in a lottery barrel when going over potholes, and up and down rough terrain, we had always found these vehicles to be relatively comfortable for such a basic mode of transport, even though the padded upholstery was plastic, presumably to enable easy cleaning after passengers were gored or savaged by the varied wildlife. We took our luggage and hopped on board. This would be much more fun than sitting in a boring bus!

By the time our driver joined us, the bus containing our friends had already left, but we caught up with it at the bridge over the Luangwa River, and entrance to the game park. And there we saw our first game.

Standing right by the riverbank, not more than 100 yards away, were several giraffe. This was the first time we had seen giraffe so we were delighted when the driver stopped for us to ooh and aah at them. Then something startled them and they took flight. I couldn't believe how graceful such a large and odd-shaped animal could be.

This bridge was the point where all tarred roads ended, and the considerate bus driver had waited to let us overtake him so that we wouldn't be eating his dust on the dirt road. Another advantage to being in front was that we were first at the Mfuwe Lodge's reception desk to book our chalets. I asked the nice man behind the desk if he would be so kind as to give us a chalet near to the Coote/Heath party, as they were friends of ours. He said he would.

Ziggy and I rounded up the kids, who had disappeared around a corner chasing monkeys, then headed for the bar as we were gasping for a nice cold beer (there had been no cabin service on the flight). Two beers were put before us and we each took a long slurp. They were Lusaka beers at their very worst. However they went down almost without touching the sides. It was only when I came to drink a second one that it almost made me throw up! Not only did it taste vile, but the fact that it was barely cold made it even worse, if that were possible.

When the Heath/Coote crowd joined us they were horrified when they tasted theirs, asking how we could possibly cope with drinking this muck in our new location. They took some convincing that this was only the second time we'd drank Lusaka Mosi since moving to that city.

Shortly after this, the receptionist arrived to give us our keys. As he described the location of the rooms it was clear we were on the opposite side of the camp to our friends.

"Ah, but madam," he apologised, "I did not know what people you meant." (I wondered how many guests by the name of Coote and Heath he had.)

As it turned out, we got the better end of the deal as our cabins were situated between the main bar area and the swimming pool, whereas our friends were past the kitchen and at the furthest end of their block of cabins.

We had discussed the possibility of changing our game trips to be on the Norman Carr ones like our pals until we realised we would never all fit in one Land Rover anyway. In the event it was for the best, as (had we been with them) the kids would doubtless have been chattering to each other instead of enjoying the wildlife.

It also meant we had more space for our video equipment. We went on our first game drive that afternoon.

I had made sure the recorder unit was fully charged before leaving home, so everything was ready to go. The first thing we came across was an enormous herd of buffalo, but having seen loads of them on a previous visit I didn't bother to record them. Next we came across some elephant, so I decided to get them on film, only to find that the damn battery was as flat as a pancake. Whilst it had been carried and jostled about, the unit must have been knocked into the 'play' position, and used up all the power. I was as sick as a parrot.

Have you ever thought what an odd expression that is? I mean, how many people have actually seen sick parrots? Certainly not me, nor anyone I know. I wonder where that saying originated? Anyway, where was I? Oh yes, elephants.

The frustration got worse as, a few minutes later, we came across another small herd which was spread either side of the road. After stopping for a quite a length of time for us to observe them, the ranger eventually decided to drive through. As he did so, one of the elephants on the left side started to move closer, and I was sitting on the left side of the Land Rover. As we slowly passed, it was less than two yards away. I was crapping myself! Once we were safely out of reach I was livid that I hadn't been able to get any footage of it - until I realised that if I had, the screen would simply have been full of grey as the elephant was so close. And my hands would have been shaking too much to record anything discernible anyway!

On swapping stories with our pals when we enjoyed sundowners that evening, we discovered we had been in completely different areas. They bemoaned the fact that their honourable driver, Norman Carr himself (quite a celebrity in Zambia) had a tendency to stop and look at obscure things which most tourists weren't too interested in. It was only on their way home that they came across a tremendous find. A buffalo had got stuck in the mud on the edge of the river. All the experts predicted that it would be dead within hours, if not from natural causes, then assisted along the way by lions.

Of course, next morning everyone had the same idea. To get out there as early as possible and try to catch the lion at the kill. Being a more disciplined party than the Kitwe rabble, we managed, with batteries charged, to be first on the scene, arriving just as a pride of lions were leaving the riverbed. If they hadn't been moving, the lions' presence might have been missed, as they were covered from head to tail in mud and blended perfectly with the background.

As they walked onto the road our excellent ranger could tell where they were headed, and going off-road ("This is only bumpy, man" whispered Vicki) he drove past them and beyond so that we were between the lions and their obvious destination, some shady bushland. Here our driver turned off his engine and we simply sat, and admired.

It was so quiet. There was absolutely no air movement so grass and trees remained motionless and silent, though a variety of birds could be heard. The familiar call of the cape turtle dove, crying "Where's FAther, where's FAther" was ever present, but that just seemed to enhance the overall tranquillity.

As the three females with their five cubs walked slowly but purposefully in our direction this was no time for fear, this was time to video! I couldn't believe the great shots I was getting and the children, bless 'em, were remarkably quiet, being equally entranced by this amazing experience.

After a couple of stops to rest their (thankfully) full bellies, and for the cubs to frolic a little, they continued down the road parallel to where we were parked, but once having walked past us the leading lioness cut across right in front of our vehicle. They were so close now that we could easily differentiate between the caked mud and the dried blood on their faces, evidence of their recent feast. At this point the driver muttered, "I think maybe we're a little bit *too* close" and promptly, with our full blessing, switched on the engine and reversed a few yards. The procession continued to the shaded area, and flopped down to rest.

We had been so absorbed that we hadn't noticed that two other vehicles, one containing our pals, had arrived.

Then a male and female were spotted further away to our left, so we moved in for a closer view of them. We soon discovered these were part of the same pride, as the females with cubs rose from their resting place and trotted out to join them. Once again we were blocking their path, but this time our driver moved out of the way in good time, as the lead female was becoming quite vocal and might be getting a bit irritated by all these unwanted visitors.

I had taken some excellent video of all this, and when I replayed it to our Kitwe friends on our return to Lusaka they confessed to having been extremely envious of our prime position that morning.

At this time of year, when we normally went to Mfuwe, we were at the end of the dry season. This is strategically an excellent time for game viewing because the limited availability of water meant the assorted game would, at some point,congregate at what few waterholes there were. All you had to do was find a waterhole and wait.

One of the things which had always fascinated me was the Luangwa River itself, which varied along its course between wet and dry. In some areas it had water which still seemed to flow very slightly, where in others it was bone dry to the extent that when pursuing game, as we did one afternoon, our Land Rover would drive straight across the dry river bed, the ground so hard that it barely left a track. This was quite a contrast to the muddy area where the buffalo had been stuck, even though that was only half a mile away. As the river snaked through the land the inner bank of a bend was a gentle slope, while the outer bank could be anything between one and four yards high.

In the areas where the outer bank was particularly high and vertical, thus prohibiting the bank being used as a crossing point, the wall would be pocked with dozens of holes. These were the nests of scores of beautifully-colourful bee-eaters which swooped and swirled around nearby areas, expertly catching the various flying insects.

One recollection I have of birdlife at Mfuwe Lodge was at night. While we unfortunately did not manage to see it, we heard something in very close proximity.

"Wonder what that was?" several of us chorused. I think it was Pete Heath who replied, "It's a Pels fishing owl."

"How do you know?"

"Because, listen to how distinctive it is. It sounds like a man crying out as he's falling down a deep well. I'm telling you, *that is the call of Pel's fishing owl.*"

Since there weren't too many wells in the vicinity into which a man could fall and cry out, and could thus be confused with this bird, we were compelled to believe him.

We thoroughly enjoyed the rest of our stay, during which time we saw all of the Big Five: Elephant, Rhinoceros, Buffalo, Lion and Leopard although, in the case of the latter, it was only a distant glimpse of the rump and tail of one leopard as it lay between the foliage on the branch of a tree. Even with binoculars, I could only just make it out. How on earth the game ranger had spotted it as he was driving along I shall never know. Over the years I continued to take my hat off to their remarkable observation skills in the bush.

We were not without plenty of antelope either, with impala by the hundreds, puku, waterbuck, bush buck, kudu and roan antelope. Then there were zebras and warthogs, hippopotami and crocodiles, baboons and vervet monkeys. We even saw a lone hyena, an unusual event in my past experience.

There were plenty of vervets hanging around the lodge (the males with their unbelievably bright blue testicles on display) on the off-chance of being able to steal food out of someone's hand, or off their breakfast plate (as they did to my mum back in 1981). For this reason they were constantly being chased away by members of staff, who also dissuaded guests from encouraging them.

On the second night of our stay we had Brad's 'Official Birthday Party'. He received gifts from his friends, as well as from Vicki and Leon and us, of course. I had brought along two small birthday cakes I'd made, complete with candles. One was for Brad and the other for me, as it was going to be my birthday in a couple of days. There proceeded a rousing rendition of the 'Happy Birthday' song from everyone in the dining room, and a jolly night was had by all.

I was always sad to leave Mfuwe, and no matter how many times I visited a game park I left with the greatest respect and love for nature and all its diversities.

Except mosquitos, of course! Mosquitos were a pain in the butt - and everywhere else. You could plaster yourself with every kind of mosquito repellent known to man, but the little buggers would always manage to find a spot you'd missed.

4

BACK INTO RIDING

For the first five weeks of the school term, Lake Road School had been collecting items for the summer fête, which was to take place on Saturday 3rd November. They also had planned a Halloween Party for the 31st October. This was a fancy dress event which commenced at 6:30 and included a disco. Of course the kids wanted to go so I set-to making them costumes. Rather than be one of the dozens of witches or ghosts which were bound to appear, we decided on something a little more original.

I turned Brad into a toad with a costume in a yukky mud colour, complete with knobbly warts and a hood bearing the face of a toad, with golf-ball eyes. Vicki became a bat, all grey with bat wings, and huge ears on her hood. And Leon just *had* to be a spider. (He'd been given the nickname 'spiderbum' by his Nannan when he was little, as when he first started crawling he did it on hands and feet, with his bum sticking up in the air, like a spider.) His costume was all black, with black spindly arms and legs, and I made four extra 'legs' which were stuffed and stitched to the side of the body. I then connected these with black thread to his wrists so that when he waved his 'arm-legs' the others moved too. I was quite chuffed with that outfit in particular. None of them won prizes, but they had a wonderful time.

The witch's cauldron contents gathered around our (at that time)
gruesomely green swimming pool.

Unfortunately another thing to happen on the 31st October in 1984 was the assassination of Indira Gandhi, the Prime Minister of India. As is his wont on such grave occasions, our President Kenneth Kaunda declared three days of national mourning, which demanded the cessation of all social functions within Zambia during that time. Bang went the school fête.

As it turned out it was better for us. The whole family had planned to go to the fête, but Ziggy had to go away unexpectedly on business on the Friday.

Via Larnaca in Cyprus he flew to Athens for a meeting, then on Monday went to Amsterdam via Zurich for another, before returning via London on Wednesday to Lusaka. When he returned we were all able to go to the fête which had been rescheduled for the following weekend.

Before he left on his little trip Ziggy gave me a stern talking to. He was rapidly losing patience with my constantly miserable-looking face when he came home from work at night. He told me to get my arse into gear in regard to organising some sort of social life by the time he got back. Yes, SIR!

THE VERY NEXT DAY MY SCOTTISH FRIEND KARIN CALLED ME FROM KITWE. I was feeling a bit down so was having a little moan. She pulled me up: "Oh no, not you! I just can't believe it." She said in her soft Edinburgh accent. "You, of all people!"

I could imagine the 'look' she was giving me.

"You've never been backwards at coming forwards, so what's your problem?"

"I just don't know where to start." I mumbled.

"What did I tell you before you left here?"

"I don't know, what did you tell me?"

"Didn't you say you used to do a lot of horse riding when you were a kid?"

"Yes."

"And didn't I tell you to get yourself straight to the Gymkhana Club when you got to Lusaka?"

"Oh, yes. I forgot."

"You forgot? For goodness sakes woman!"

"Well, there was so much going on when….."

"I want to hear no more excuses. I told you that they are a very nice bunch of people there. I know, because some of them come up to the Copperbelt for the major shows, so I've met them when Andrew's been riding."

"Okay. I'll check it out. But where is it?"

"I'm not sure because I haven't been there, but I think it's on the Great East Road, but it should be big enough for you to find it."

"Oh, our house is off the Great East Road so I guess it can't be far away."

"Right," she said, "the next time I talk to you I want you to tell me the name of the horse you are riding."

"Okay."

"And one more thing."

"What?"

"Don't fall off!" And with that she was gone.

I must confess I was quite keen to get back into the saddle again. My grandmother Doris bought me a pony when I turned eleven. I used to ride just about every day, mostly by myself. During school holidays I'd be riding all day, going to local gymkhanas when I could. In the winter I even went fox hunting in the days before it became a 'dirty' sport. My greatest thrill was when, on my little 13.2 hands high pony, we soared over a five-bar gate as he was so caught up in the excitement of the chase. I had loved horse riding, though never had any formal riding lessons.

So we piled into Lizzie and I found my way to the Lusaka Gymkhana Club. There was a guy about to drive out of the car park as I pulled in, so I flagged him down and asked where I should go to see about joining. He directed me to the clubhouse, saying I should speak to a chap named David McCleeery, who was the Chairman of the club. So I did.

There were only about half a dozen or so people in the bar, and they all took a keen interest in the arrival of a strange woman hauling three kids behind her.

I was told that it was very difficult to get membership there as they were trying to keep it strictly as an active riding club as opposed to simply a social bar. To become a member one needed to own a horse or at least ride someone else's on a regular basis.

Regardless of this, someone bought us drinks and after a while I was asked if I played darts. I acknowledged that I had thrown the odd dart (I didn't think it prudent to mention that my parents' pub's ladies team, of which I was a member, had won the league championship a few years back). I was then challenged to a game of darts by one of the chaps who, to be fair, was not at his soberest, so I won the first game of 501. He won the next game and I thrashed him in the decider.

During the course of my conversation with David he mentioned, in reply to my query about availability of horses, that there was a notice up on the club board asking for someone to help exercise polo ponies. In view of the fact that he'd also told me all the horses at the Gymkhana Club were privately owned and I'd be unlikely to find anything to ride there, I decided to give the guy a call so took down the details.

It was Monday by the time I eventually managed to get hold of the polo player, Otmar, a German gentleman, and arranged to see him on the Tuesday evening at 5:30. I made a point of saying as little as possible on the phone in case my lack of 'proper' experience put him off.

As Ziggy was still in Europe I took the kids with me on Tuesday. We arrived on time but unfortunately Otmar was running late.

While we were waiting for him his wife Barbara, who was very pregnant, told us how her husband had only got interested in horses since moving to Zambia, and with the cost of stabling at the Polo Club steadily increasing he'd decided to buy a smallholding on the outskirts of Lusaka on which to keep them. Now not only did they have horses, but they also kept eleven milk cows and 30 sheep, as well as some ducks and geese. The kids had loved being introduced to all these animals.

Otmar eventually arrived and it was almost dark by the time he had me seated on a horse. The kids stayed behind with his wife while we rode out onto his land.

As we rode he explained that he had four thoroughbreds - polo ponies - and as his wife was clearly unable to ride at the moment, needed help exercising them. In order to see how I rode he put me on his most tried and trusted 16-year-old horse, and as we rode along the tracks he told me a bit more about the way he used the horses and the sort of commands he gave.

I, in turn, explained that it had been years since I'd ridden regularly, and that I'd never been properly trained in riding, but that I 'just rode'. He was actually delighted at this, saying that I clearly had 'a natural seat' and that he was glad I hadn't been 'properly trained' because it meant he could get me to ride his horses the way he wanted, which was quite different to what most people were taught.

When we returned to his house the kids were full of enthusiasm about the place. We agreed to meet again on Wednesday for another evening ride. It was a lovely clear night and riding by moonlight was an amazing experience for me.

I had expressed my surprise to Otmar at going out riding in the dark. No-one in Kitwe would venture out far on their own, even during the daytime for fear of robberies (steal your wallet, watch, rings, fillings from your teeth…) or kids throwing stones. Otmar assured me it was very different in Lusaka.

I was thrilled when he said he'd like me to ride his horses on a daily basis and, "Yes", I could do it in the mornings when the kids were at school if I wished. The horses had been rested for two months after the end of the previous polo season, which coincided with the annual treatment (imposing minimal exercise) for prevention of African Horse Sickness, a virulent problem in Zambia. They all now needed to be slowly brought up to full fitness.

Ziggy's flight was only landing at 11:45 on Thursday morning and he had sent a telex to say I should collect him from the airport after the kids finished school, so I was able to go riding that morning. Did he ever get a surprise with all I had to tell him on his return!

Thankfully, another event which Ziggy did not miss was the kids' school Open Day. The first one was held a couple of months into the start of the school year so we went to the school, along with half of Lusaka's expat population, to check out our offspring's progress. We had glowing reports from Vicki and Leon's teacher.

On talking with Brad's teacher we found that she was quite new on the scene. Mrs Oliver explained that in her absence at the beginning of the new school term a temporary teacher had taken Brad's class and that his efforts were obviously satisfactory as she hadn't been given any reports which required comments on his classwork. She did say, however, that he had already made his mark in the class as far as she was concerned, in the personality stakes.

"*What this time?*" I wondered, and held my breath.

She explained that just a few days after taking over, she had asked the class monitors to distribute the English books, at the end of which Brad remarked that he hadn't been given his. He said he'd definitely handed it in the day before, so much questioning of helpers and searching of the classroom ensued, with no sign of the elusive book.

Having spent quite some time only half an hour earlier stressing the importance of keeping desks tidy, Mrs Oliver eventually decided to look inside Brad's and immediately found his English book. She tore him off a strip for wasting ten minutes of the class time, whereupon he immediately stood up from his desk and solemnly walked out to the front of the classroom. With a deadpan expression he turned to face the class and said, "I'm sorry!" then promptly walked back to his desk, drew out his seat, and sat down as if his actions were nothing out of the ordinary.

Mrs Oliver said she had so much trouble trying not to laugh that she had to turn away from view for a goodly while.

It was nice to know that our eldest son was now at least renowned for his *good* manners rather than the 'hit 'em back first' attitude he had when he was little more than a toddler (see my first book *Into Africa*).

So our life in Lusaka established a more normal 'everyone's happy with their lot' format.

The next thing to start thinking about was Christmas.

5

THE CHRISTMAS OF '84

S o we headed back to England.

It was cold, but only in outside temperature. The warmth generated by our family on our arrival more than made up for that. Grandparents and great-grandmother were delighted at the prospect of having the children around for Christmas. Of course, the kids were just *so* excited at the thought that Santa would be visiting them in England this year.

"How will he know we're here, Mummy?" asked Vicki.

"Santa knows *everything* you silly girl," responded Brad sagely to his sister, who was only 17 months younger than he.

"Yeah. And he'll know just how naughty *you've* been, Brad Patras," said Leon, "so *you* won't be getting any presents!"

It was actually amazing that all three still believed that it was Santa who brought their presents in the early hours of Christmas Day. This was going to be so much fun.

Then on walking into the kitchen I had instantly noticed that something was amiss when I spotted a cage containing a blue budgerigar in the kitchen counter. I knew my Nannan Johnson (my dad's mum) had one, so this did not bode well. Sure enough, my dad came into the room and closed the door, when he told me that my

Nannan had quietly passed away just a week earlier. This was one year and three days after my granddad, her husband, had died of cancer. To lose two dearly loved grandparents in such a short space of time was quite a shock to the system, though thankfully they'd had a good shot at life, both having reached their eightieth birthdays. They would both be sadly missed this Christmas.

Apart from what we had planned to buy for them, we knew the kids would be spoilt rotten by the rest of our family who would be making up for the fact that we hadn't spent Christmas in England for four years.

The nights, of course, got darker much earlier in UK winter than the 6:30pm we were used to each day throughout the year in Zambia, so the kids were thrilled when we took them into town and streets were alive with lights. Whopping strings of lightbulbs sent Santa and reindeer flying towards the roofs, bright red and green holly flashed before our eyes and golden bells swayed between the buildings.

Inside all the stores were further delights of masses of colourful decorations hanging from the ceilings, the likes of which the kids had never seen in Africa. They were all too young to remember their last Christmas in England back in 1979, so this was a truly awesome experience for them.

And of course they went to Santa's Grotto. A much grander set-up than had been managed by the Kitwe Cricket Club; in Burton's Co-op in High Street they approached in awe as a larger than life Santa sat on a giant-size chair.

I strained my ears to hear what each one was telling Santa they would like for Christmas. I was very surprised when Vicki said she'd like a dolls' pram. If he granted her wish, how on earth would we pack *that* to get it home to Zambia in a suitcase, I wondered.

Christmas in England was so much more exciting for the children than in Zambia. There was much more hype, much more glamour and, oh, so much more choice. The small amount of TV our kids were able or allowed to watch was also geared up to Christmas. Alas, I was astounded at the increased commercialism which appeared at every opportunity on the television and radio. This was one aspect of Christmas I was delighted had not filtered through to Zambia yet.

Christmastime was more than a little crowded in my parents' home, with the tripling of bodies to be accommodated overnight. Nannan (my grandmother Doris) had her own room which she refused to share on account of her snoring. She said she'd be so fixated with trying not to keep others awake that she would get no sleep herself. The small single-bed boxroom was given over to my mum's sister Betty, who was here to enjoy the merriments too. Ziggy and I and the kids were allocated my parents' room, whilst they relegated themselves to using our kids' previously-stored bunkbeds, temporarily resurrected in the garage.

It had taken us some considerable time and effort, after a long day spent preparing for the big day, to place all the presents around the tree after the kids had gone to bed on Christmas Eve. The overspill took up almost half the living room floor space. As we all turned in for the night, I'm not sure who had been the more excited, the kids or the grown-ups.

Early on Christmas morning our kids did us proud. As soon as the first one stirred at the foot of our bed all three were instantly awake, trying not to wake us. Talking in whispers they quietly tiptoed out of the bedroom and closed the door. But even with the hushed voices, I could catch some of their conversations.

As they huddled at the top of the stairs I could hear, "Do you think he's been?"

"I don't know."

"Look over the rail."

"I can't see anything from up here."

"Well is the lounge door open?"

"I can't see. I'm going for a look."

I could envisage Brad the Bold now taking tentative steps down the stairs.

"NO, DON'T GO DOWN," came a pair of shouted whispers. "If he's still there putting the presents out, and he sees you, he'll take them all away!"

Of course, none of them had a clue what the time was. It was still well dark even though it was past seven o'clock, their normal wakeup time. At this latest behest Brad must have come back up the stairs and all three disappeared into the bathroom, from where I could hear less clearly.

However, now that they were moving about on an uncarpeted floor, they must have been heard in the bowels of the garage because next came the sound of the connecting door to the garage being opened by my dad.

"It must be about time for a cup of tea, I reckon." He said, in an exaggerated voice.

The kids were then fighting their way through the bathroom door to shout from the top of the stairs,

"Can we come down Branbrand?" (Branbrand was the way Brad pronounce Grandad when he was a toddler, and it had stuck.)

"Has Santa been?"

"Branbrand, we're here, can we get up yet?"

I shook a very unenthusiastic Ziggy to force him out of bed. "Come on, it's after seven, we can't make them wait any longer."

By the time we had put some clothes on and made our way downstairs, Nancy and Mev were in the kitchen with the kids, handing out tea. The door to the lounge and its secret hoard was still firmly closed.

"Well this is a pretty party we have going on in here," said Ziggy, always so bright and chirpy first thing in the morning. "What's going on then?"

"Oh, *come on* Daddy, we're dying to see if Santa's been."

"But what about Nannan? She's not here yet."

"NO, no, no!" shouted the junior masses "we can't wait for Nannan, she doesn't get up until dinnertime."

This was true. For as long as I could remember, Doris had suffered from terrible insomnia, usually going to sleep when everyone is about to get up, then sleeping until half the day is gone.

"Okay," said Nanny, "let's go and have a look then."

She led the short few steps from kitchen to lounge door and opened it just a crack to look through. Three anxious bodies squeezed between her and the bottom of the door until, "He's been."

"I can see presents."

"Yay, Nanny *please* let us go in."

She flung open the door and three bodies fell tumbling in in front of her and all four of them nearly finished up in a heap on the floor.

What delight!

They stood in awe, looking from a distance and trying to guess the contents of all the parcels and who they were for, because I had persuaded them to wait until we'd managed to prise Betty out of bed with a cup of tea so that she could be party to all the excitement too.

Then the great unwrap began.

I have no recollection of what gifts were received other than that there were a helluva lot of them including a dolls' pram, Lego sets and enough chocolate to choke a donkey.

We had a fabulous time with visits from many relatives and friends over Christmas and Boxing days.

We also had a party at home to see in the New Year. Neighbours from either side were invited, as well as friends who were prepared to run to the expense of a taxi home. Jane and Robin, ex-Zambia, as well as their daughter Amanda and her current boyfriend joined us, driving up from their home in Solihull and staying overnight. Having been forewarned about our shortage of beds they came prepared to sleep on the floor. Being seasoned expats this was no big deal for them, though many of our 'normal' Burtonian friends and relatives were absolutely horrified by their willingness to sink to such a primitive exercise.

The night before we were due to fly back to Zambia, the kids had just been put to bed when my dad put on his coat to go to the local pub for his usual pint. He dashed back into the lounge, "Would you believe it's snowing?" he said. "What a shame the kids have gone to bed already."

I couldn't let them miss this, their first sight of snow since they were toddlers, and which they couldn't remember. I dashed upstairs and into our bedroom.

"Is there anyone still awake in here?" I said. There was no answer.

But I knew that ruse, as I recalled ignoring such a question when I was a small kid, only to find the next morning that my parents were going to invite me back down to their party to sing in the New Year. I never lied about being asleep after that.

"What a pity," I said as I walked out the door, "because it's snowing outside and I would have let them get up to see it."

"I'M AWAKE!" came a loud chorus of three as they leapt up in bed.

I led them through to Nannan's bedroom. Here they could look out onto the front garden, where the street lights would illuminate the snowflakes. I left them oo-ing and ah-ing for ten minutes before putting them back to bed, with the promise they could play in it the next morning if the snow settled. Much to their disappointment, it did not.

While the next morning didn't bring snow, it did bring another problem.

When she got up, my mum complained that she wasn't feeling too good. She looked awful. My dad and Ziggy had gone out with the kids to do some last minute shopping so I tried to help my mum.

"I'm feeling really rotten" she said as she dropped down onto the sofa.

I knew my mum. It was not like her to complain about any illness. She ignored head colds and I had even known her to continue working with a severe bout of flu. She was very strong willed. So this current situation was some cause for concern.

I got the phone and called Mum's GP's surgery. I explained to the receptionist that it was VERY urgent and miraculously got put through to the doctor. I told him how I thought she was very ill as she had collapsed on the sofa. He said he would come straight away to see her.

When I told my mum this she mumbled, and insisted on my helping her up the stairs to her bed. It wasn't an easy transfer as she could barely stand.

Fifteen minutes later the doctor arrived. When I began to lead him up the stairs he stopped me.

"I thought you said she had collapsed on the sofa!" he said, harshly.

"She had, but we struggled and I managed to get her upstairs to her bed.

"Then she couldn't have been in a state of collapse. You have called me out urgently under false presences when I have a surgery full of patients!" He raged.

I was furious. I said I knew my mother well enough to know that something was very wrong and that he must go up the stairs to see her. He grudgingly stomped up.

He entered the room and walked up to the bed and took one look at my mother, "Oh, yes, this is not good," he muttered, "she is seriously jaundiced. I'll arrange for her admission into hospital and an ambulance to get her there, though it may not be until tomorrow. In the meantime, keep her in bed and get her to drink plenty of water."

I was still furious with him as we went back downstairs.

"So I *was* right to call you out then?" I asked, looking him straight in the eye.

"Yes," was all he said. No "sorry", nor "kiss my ass" or bugger-all. The bastard, I thought!

The next few hours were not good, as I worried about leaving my mum in this state. But my dad insisted that we must still return to Zambia as planned, and that he would take good care of her and keep me posted on progress.

So it was that in the afternoon a very despondent group of five said our farewells to my bedridden mother and took a taxi to the first airport of our trip as we headed back to Zambia.

Back 'home' in Zambia things soon settled down into some semblance of normality.

As promised my dad kept us in the picture, advising that my mum had an operation where they found and removed a lot of gallstones, which explained the jaundice. Within a couple of weeks she was home and feeling much better.

6

THE TROUBLE WITH EXERCISE

I had been getting some strange experiences at mealtimes. After a few mouthfuls of food, especially if I was particularly hungry, I would get a 'blockage' where I couldn't swallow. It felt as though food was getting stuck in my gullet in the area around the middle of my breastbone. When this happened nothing would shift it. Some bright spark suggested I take a drink of water to move it along, but that didn't work. If anything it made it worse as the water backed up behind the food, so I removed that from my remedial list. I would try burping it out of the way, but could not instigate a burp. Leaning against a wall and stretching my arms up felt like it ought to do the trick, but it didn't. I just had to wait it out.

People suggested that perhaps I wasn't chewing my food enough but I knew it wasn't that, confirmed by the fact that it could happen when I ate a forkful of rice, which hardly needed a lot of chewing.

The worse thing was that, when I got a blockage, not only could I not swallow food, but I couldn't swallow anything, saliva included. Over some months it got so bad that I spent the beginning of most meals in the bathroom. On one occasion, after eating two mouthfuls of chicken curry and rice I stood by the wash basin for over half an hour, as I had to spit out the constant build-up of saliva.

The odd thing was, once the blockage disappeared I was able to continue my meal as if nothing had happened. The only trouble was, by the time I reached that point the food on my plate had inevitably gone stone cold. This is okay if your meal is a salad, but not so appealing if it's a Sunday roast.

One day I had been out early exercising Otmar's polo ponics. I had taken with me a cold roast beef sandwich as a belated breakfast and chowed on this as I was driving home after my ride.

Yes, you've guessed it, I got a blockage. I figured it was time to do something about this and as the route home took me through the city, I decided to call in at our local clinic. By the time I'd parked and made my way up the stairs to the reception I first had to dash to the Ladies for a spit-out. Once at their reception area I managed to explain my urgent need to see a doctor before dashing back for another spit. Fortunately one of the doctors on duty was free quite soon and I was able to see him. After standing spitting into a stainless steel receptacle for five minutes I was able to tell him what the problem was. Once the blockage cleared we were able to converse more naturally, which concluded with Dr West organising an appointment for me at the Lusaka University Teaching Hospital with Dr Gupta, a specialist.

Oh what fun *that* was - not!

Dr Gupta's first directive was for me to have x-rays taken. The means of disclosing my condition was to have a 'barium swallow'. I had heard of a barium meal before, and been told by a couple of victims how unpleasant that was, so guessed a barium swallow wasn't going to be as pleasant as, say, attending a wine tasting.

I had been ordered to fast on the day in question, and pitched up at the hospital for my afternoon appointment starving hungry. When my time came I duly stripped and put on the assigned ~~blue ball gown~~ hospital robe. You know, the one which ties at the back as far as your shoulder blades and shows off your bum to all and sundry.

Then I was made to stand against a flat board where I stood watching as the radiographer prepared my first drink of the day. As I observed him, it reminded me very much of Ziggy mixing Polyfilla, but with just a little too much water added.

The radiologist presented me with the metal flask of gunk before positioning a mobile contraption in front of me into which he slid an x-ray plate. He then explained that I must take a large mouthful of the Polyfilla and hold it in my mouth until he had walked behind his protective screen. Only then, on his signal, must I swallow this potion as he clicked away at the machine *ad nauseam*.

Despite my very best efforts, I do not think I can adequately describe this experience. But I was forced to swallow, without pausing, a mouth full of a vile-tasting substance which had the consistency of a freshly hatched cow pat. I'm feeling *ad nauseam* just thinking about it.

The bastard came out of his closet and inserted a new plate in the x-ray-mobile in front of me, then muttered at me to take another mouthful. This I did and he disappeared to take another snapshot.

Take three, he was back again for another plate swap. This time he just nodded his directive for me to repeat the process. I had left filling my mouth as long as possible, until he was facing me through the glass screen. As soon as my mouth was full of the abominable abdominal concoction he decided something wasn't right and came out to adjust the x-ray machine.

Just as he finished he looked up at me with a sick grin to indicate all was ready now, but it was too much for me. With a heave which made my entire body shudder, I threw up the entire contents of my mouth (and probably stomach too) all over him.

Still with a mouthful of slime, I tried to apologise for my mishap. To give him his due, the poor sod did say that it was OK, "he understood". Watching him trying to manoeuvre the x-ray machine, which was also dripping barium over the floor, was like watching someone try to push-start a car on an ice rink. It took a while.

He eventually managed to move it far enough for me to (carefully) skate my way out of the room, as he said he thought he'd got sufficient info from the first two x-rays, not to bother with any more.

I was happy for him.

Four days down the line I was back in LUTH, this time to enjoy my first ever endoscopy. And I thought the barium swallow had been *fun*?

For those of you who have not had the pleasure of one, or in the unlikely event you do not even know what an endoscopy is, I shall enlighten you:

First you lay on a paper-covered examination table. Then a doctor, or in my case two, wedge a bottomless plastic bowl in your mouth, to keep it open wide enough to swallow a juvenile barracuda. In the lack of any obliging fish they take a Nikon camera and attach it to the end of a hosepipe, which is then fed through your gaping mouth, down your throat and along the oesophagus to look at your insides. Simple.

This was during the early days in the development of the endoscope because instead of the images from the camera being projected onto a screen, it was viewed through an eyepiece on the other end of the hosepipe.

Dr Gupta and his sidekick took turns looking at my insides, pulling, pushing and twisting the pipe this way and that as I lay on my back and quietly retched and heaved. To take my mind off the procedure, which was being performed *sans anaesthetic*, I fixed my gaze on the ceiling and tried to calculate how much of its flaking white paint was likely to drift down onto the pates of the medics, or into the plastic bowl in my mouth.

They jabbered away happily to each other in Hindi as they performed this clearly fascinating procedure before asking me if I'd like to take a look.

As my head seemed to be clamped in place by a vice worthy of my grandad's workshop bench, it was impossible for me to shake my head in decline of the pleasure, and they took my "UGH, EUR, AGH, OECH's" as a sign of enthusiasm and stuck the viewfinder to my right eye. They then jiggled the camera around a little more so that I could clearly identify (OR NOT!) the gap in my pulsating gut which was causing all the trouble. I continued to retch and heave as they searched around for any other problems in the region.

Eventually satisfied that they had seen everything of interest (like the roots of my toenails I shouldn't wonder) they hauled on the hosepipe, pulled out the camera and removed the jaw-aching plastic mouthpiece before encouraging me to sit up.

"Very good, Mrs Patras," said Dr Gupta, "I will send the results through to Dr West at the clinic."

Then they walked out of the room, abandoning all their plumbing tools, presumably for some minion to tidy up and sterilise before the next unsuspecting victim was called in.

I gathered up my chattels and tried to find my way out of the hospital's maze of corridors, while suffering the worst sore throat I had EVER had in my life. It was two and a half days before I felt able to eat anything solid, relying mostly on ice cream and cold beers for nourishment in the meantime.

An appointment had already been made with Dr West for the following week, so I trundled along to see him.

"First of all Mrs Patras," he said "I am delighted to tell you that there is no sign of cancer."

Cancer? He hadn't mentioned that being a possibility at all, and it shook me up a bit. Being a born optimist, the possibility of my blockages being caused by cancer hadn't even entered my head.

"It would appear that you have a hiatus hernia."

"Oh, that's alright then," I thought to myself, "what the hell is one of those?" I never studied biology at school beyond the second year of my senior education, and in the first two years we'd only covered a few plants and frogs. At least, that was all I could remember (and not much of that).

"So what's one of those?" I dared to ask.

"Very simply put, the hiatus is an opening in the diaphragm - the muscular wall separating the chest cavity from the abdomen. Normally, the oesophagus goes through the hiatus and attaches to the stomach. In a hiatus hernia a section of the stomach bulges up into the chest through that opening. In your case, when that happens it becomes agitated and then it expands and prevents the food from passing through into your stomach until it has relaxed/settled again."

"Well, I shall try my hardest not to agitate it in future," I said solemnly. I knew I could agitate Ziggy sometimes, but I wondered what I could possibly have said to agitate my stomach so.

"Don't worry," said the very patient doc, "I'll give you some medication which you must take twenty minutes before eating and that will sort it out."

And so it did, more or less. But the rest of me was more than agitated when I forgot to take my medication before food was served, and I had to wait twenty minutes before I could eat it. Then the only difference to what I had previously been experiencing was that at least now I didn't have to stand in the bathroom spitting into the toilet while I waited to commence a cold meal.

On one of my subsequent visits to Dr West I asked about the possible cause of the hernia, and told him about a situation which had occurred about 15 months previously when we lived in Kitwe.

A lady member of the Cricket Club, which was one of our regular socialising venues, started holding exercise classes twice a week. As my waistline had been steadily expanding I decided it would be a good idea to attend and try to reduce it by a few inches. During one of the sessions she had us divide up into pairs. One lady would lie flat on the floor whilst the other sat on her feet, then at a command from our esteemed leader the lying-down one would sit up. Simple.

Except when I sat up I felt something tear.

If you would just care to take a piece of material, make a small snip in the middle of one edge then, pulling on either side, tear the fabric into two pieces, the *sound* which that makes is what I *felt* inside. And it didn't feel at all nice. In fact after a couple of days I went to see my Kitwe doctor, who said I had likely torn a muscle and I would just have to wait out the healing process.

I asked Dr West if it was possible that this could have been what caused my hiatus hernia and he said it certainly was not beyond the bounds of possibility.

And keep-fit is supposed to be good for you?

I had also found out, after the event, that the exercise routines we had been doing at the Cricket Club were not exactly your trendy Jane Fonda workouts (which came bouncing onto the keep-fit scene in Zambia shortly afterwards) but were those favoured by the Canadian Air Force!

Over thirty years later I am still popping a little pill each morning to keep my hiatus hernia from getting agitated. Alas, there don't seem to be any pills I can take to stop me from agitating Ziggy!

7

NANCY

A t the beginning of March I received a sad letter from my mum, telling me that her brother Gerald had died.

Gerald had never really enjoyed good health, and he suffered quite badly with asthma. It appeared he had been in hospital on oxygen for a while and became very emotional about being away from his family so they sent him home. After a short while he was having other problems and the doctor was called, who confessed to my cousin that his dad was actually riddled with cancer and would be unlikely to last for more than a couple of weeks. In the event, Gerald died a few days later.

We had barely recovered from this news when in the middle of March we received another letter from my mum. On the outside of the plain writing paper she had written "very private, could you please read it both together".

This sounded very ominous.

 Dear Ann and Ziggy,

This is not going to be an ordinary "run of the mill" letter, so I suggest you get yourselves a stiff drink and sit down somewhere nice and quiet to read it.

We did as we were bid and, each with a drink, we sat together on the sofa and read...

>
> Actually I don't know quite how to start, but I suppose as Betty says I should start at the beginning and tell you everything.
>
> Well, I'm afraid I haven't been telling you the truth right from the start so I will now do so.
>
> The day I came out of hospital your Dad received an appointment to go and see my surgeon, Mr Glick. Mr Glick sent the request two days before, so I knew then that something was wrong, and when Mev came home I said "what did he have to say". He said "well you will be a long time recovering and he said I have to keep you happy and do what you want to do".
>
> So then I asked him to tell me the truth and that is, I'm sorry to tell you this, I have cancer of the liver. He told Mev it could be 2 or 3 months or it could be 2 or 3 years, it just depends how fast the cancer gallops or if it stays dormant for a while.
>
> Now I don't want you to get too upset about this because as you know I've always said when your number is up it's up and there is nothing you can do about it. I have taken it quite well and I am not afraid, just a little sorry.
>
> The reason I haven't told you before was my decision. I don't want it to spoil your lives over there and in any case there is nothing you can do. If I do get any warning signs then Bernard is going to telex you and let you know.
>
> I do hope I've done the right thing in letting you know. It was a very hard decision, but Betty persuaded me as she says if you hadn't known you might never forgive your Dad and the others for not telling you and I wouldn't want that to happen.
>
> Everyone thinks I am looking much better and I suppose I do really, I have a better colour and am eating well and going out a bit more now, especially since we have changed the car. We've bought a Metro, would you believe, quite the

opposite to the Rover as far as size goes but much better on petrol and insurance, and it's quite comfortable and easy to drive.

Well will close now, I hope this hasn't been too much of a shock to you, my loves, but keep your chins up like we are, as you have your own lives to lead and the children to consider.

I don't want Mev to see this so will sign off now before he comes in, as it would only upset him again.

All my love, Nancy and all my love to Brad, Leon & Vicki
xxxxxxxxxxxxxx

SHE HOPED IT HADN'T BEEN "TOO MUCH OF A SHOCK"?

We were both stunned into tearful silence.

My mum, dying of cancer! She was only 59 years old!

My first reaction was to get straight down the travel agents and book a ticket to the UK, but Ziggy persuaded me to think it through first so that my trip would be the most beneficial. To be honest, I found it difficult to think logically about anything right then. One thing was for sure though, I wasn't going to wait until she was drawing her last breaths before I went to see my mum!

The next day I took stock. Easter was coming up and the kids would be off school for three weeks. I would take them with me so that Nancy could enjoy her grandchildren as much as possible. Ziggy of course would have to stay to work as it was only 10 weeks since we'd returned from our UK Christmas trip.

Memories of the ending to that trip had me thinking about the build up to my mum's illness, and I couldn't help but think that all this might have kicked off when she was with us, taking a malarial prophylactic. [I have since read that mefloquine can have serious effects upon the liver.]

Naturally we didn't tell the kids the full story, only that nanny had been 'feeling poorly again', and we were going to visit to cheer her up. They, of course, were thrilled with the prospect of another trip. Two weeks later we flew back to England.

When our taxi pulled up outside my parents' home the kids raced up the drive while the driver helped me with our luggage.

"Branbrand, we're here!" they called through the letterbox.

I turned to see my dad as he opened the door to the brood. Whilst delighted to see his grandchildren, he looked haggard and drained.

"Go inside and find Nannan," I called to the kids. In the doorway I hugged my dad, and for a while we clung to each other and silently sobbed.

We eventually moved inside, drying our eyes before the kids could ask about the reason for this.

"Nancy's in hospital," my dad said, "they admitted her earlier in the week to do some tests. We'll go and see her in an hour or so, give the doctor chance to do his rounds."

When we arrived at Burton General Hospital the ward sister kindly agreed that having travelled all the way from Africa, the children could go and see their nanny, as long as they were quiet.

My mum was in the large general ward, which was sectioned off into groups of four beds. As we turned the corner I could see her lying in the first bed; it looked like she was asleep. She looked thinner and paler and so much older than she had at that happy Christmas, only twelve weeks earlier.

The kids crept up to the bed then in unison, in a shouted whisper cried, "Hello nanny".

My mum's eyes flew open and a look of incredulity and happiness spread across her face.

"What are *you* all doing here?"

"Branbrand said you weren't very well..."

"So we've come to cheer you up."

"Why are you in here?"

"What's this tube in your arm for?" asked Brad, forever the technical one.

We sat and chatted for a while until I excused myself to go and speak to the ward sister.

"The doctor attending your mum will be finishing his rounds soon. I'm sure he'll want to have a word with you," she said.

So I went back to the bed and observed as my mum listened to the kids rant about what they'd been doing in Lusaka and places they would show her when she next visited them there. I saw a fleeting look of deep sadness cross her face before she smiled and continued to enjoy their excitement. But gone was the cheery, vibrant Nancy who had been my mother for 35 years.

The doctor appeared at the bedside and chatted briefly to my mum before moving off, indicating that I should follow him. We entered a consulting room and he closed the door.

Hitching himself onto the edge of the examining table he looked me in the eye.

"I'm sorry to have to tell you that the prognosis is not good for your mother. When surgery was performed to remove the gall bladder we found cancer in several areas - the liver, the pancreas and the duodenum. I am afraid this is very serious.

"I see," I responded. "Isn't there *anything* you can do?"

"We have discussed the possibility of chemotherapy but feel the cancer is so extensive that it would be pointless, and is not worth the discomfort you mother would go through. Rather she should try and enjoy what remains of her life as best she can."

"And which is likely to be… how long?"

"Unfortunately we are unable to be specific as to how much time your mum has left, as we don't know at what point we have observed this. It's rather like switching on the television which is showing a film you have never seen or heard about, after it has started. You don't know whether you joined it at the beginning, in the middle or near the end."

He went on to say that they had completed all the required tests, and there was no need for my mum to stay in hospital any longer. She could go home later that day.

Once we got her home she perked up considerably.

"How long are you staying?" was one of her first questions.

"Well, we have an open-ended ticket, which lasts for three months, so we shall see," I said.

She thoroughly enjoyed having her grandchildren around, though she did have her 'bad days'. Then I could see why my dad looked so haggard. It was terrible to watch her suffer so, knowing there was going to be no happy ending.

It was during one of these days that I phoned Ziggy.

"It hurts so much to say this, but if you don't come over on a visit soon you may never see my mum again," I told him.

"My cousin Mark and Helen are getting married in two weeks and a bus has been organised to take all the Burtonians of the family through to the wedding in Wolverhampton. Why don't you see if you can get time off work to come over for that at the same time?" He duly did.

I used my mum's sewing machine to make outfits for the kids for the wedding, then Nancy and I went out shopping and bought new dresses for ourselves. Ziggy duly arrived and my mum was thrilled to see him. They had always enjoyed a good relationship.

On the day of the wedding a mini coach took a party of 15 of us through to my uncle's house at Seisdon and lots of photographs were taken before heading off to the church.

The weather treated us to all seasons during that day, giving us wind and rain as we arrived at the church, sunshine as we came out and snow when we were at the reception. It was a wonderful affair.

Nancy really enjoyed herself, even getting up to do a few dances. Alas, on the journey home in the bus she was not at all well.

Ziggy's time with us went all too fast, and after ten days he had to say a very difficult goodbye to his much loved mother-in-law.

Before he left we had discussed the situation with the kids, and decided that we should try and get them into a local school for the duration of our stay. Once the summer term commenced I went along to the school which covered the area we lived in, explaining the situation and that the property my parents were living in was actually ours, and would be where we lived if we were here permanently. They were very understanding and agreed to allow the kids attendance.

It was only then that I realised the school system we had been enjoying in Zambia was different to England. Where in Zambia there had been only one school year separating Brad from the twins, in the UK system there was a two year difference, causing Vicki and Leon to be in the Infants whilst Brad was placed in the Junior school.

They easily integrated into their temporary schools but it didn't take long for me to realise that the level of schooling was way behind what they received in Zambia. Brad, in the higher year was being taught English and Maths which he, *and even Vicki and Leon*, had already learnt in their classes in Zambia. If I kept them in Burton they would be way behind their classmates on returning home. It was decided the kids must return to Lusaka a.s.a.p. Without me.

This of course created great excitement for them. First we had to equip each of them with their own passports, as they had all travelled on mine. Again, the authorities were incredibly accommodating and we were all ready for them to leave within two weeks.

Unfortunately they left very much as they arrived, with my mum in hospital. She had been suffering greatly with a massive build-up of fluid on the abdomen, so had been admitted to hospital to have a tap inserted and was still being monitored before being allowed home. Although the finality of their goodbyes wasn't known to the children, it was heart-breaking to watch. I try desperately not to think what it must have felt like for my mum.

Quite a few of my friends in Zambia had children who attended boarding school in the UK, so I was familiar with the procedure of them being transported as unaccompanied minors. As we met the lady at the airport who would be looking after my children on the first leg of their journey, from East Midlands airport to Heathrow, they promised me most sincerely that they would be perfect little angels throughout the trip. I knew they would be. Well, almost perfect anyway.

The report that filtered back was that they had behaved extremely well, particularly when they were told by their carer on the long 10-hour flight from London to Lusaka that they could stay awake to watch the in-flight film. From what I could gather they all fell asleep watching it.

Once back at school they soon caught up with the work they had missed. Home-wise things were quite hectic, especially in the afternoons when it was necessary for Ziggy to leave them in Benton's charge. To say they had free rein would, I think, be an understatement, and I was probably better off not knowing some of the antics they got up to.

Back in Burton I spent all the waking hours I could with my mum. We would go out for a drive to anywhere she wanted when she was feeling well enough. It was good that in those days traffic was considerably lighter, making a drive around the countryside a pleasure instead of the frustrating hassle it became in later years. In the evening we would watch television together or have a game of cards.

The days seemed to fly by and it didn't seem long before it was time for me to make my return flight to Zambia before my ticket expired. Fortunately on the day I left my mum was having one of her better days and she was able to come with my dad to East Midlands airport.

EMA was quite small in those days, so with my mum in a wheelchair my folks were able to accompany me right to the point where I left the building to cross the tarmac and mount the steps to the jet which would take me to Heathrow.

As we said our goodbyes I promised my mum that I would return after I had got the kids settled into school at the end of the (southern hemisphere) winter holiday. By then I would have been able to arrange for them to stay with friends during the afternoons until Ziggy could pick them up after work, and I would be able to return to Burton.

"And don't you go doing anything silly while I'm away!" I admonished her, as we all tried to fight back the tears.

Once aboard the aircraft I could see them at the building's window, waving goodbye to me. I don't think they would have been able to pick me out through the small aircraft window as I sat there returning their waves, weeping. I was distraught that I might not see my mother again.

TIME PASSED BY SO QUICKLY AS THERE WAS ALWAYS SOMETHING GOING ON in Lusaka now. I made weekly calls to England to check on my mum. We were over halfway through August when I phoned one evening. My dad said that my mum hadn't been feeling so good lately. When I asked to speak to her he said that wasn't possible as she spent most of her time in bed now. This was long before mobile phones and even before cordless phones were common in the UK. You had to physically go to the phone.

"Well, perhaps one day you could arrange for someone to help you carry her down the stairs sitting in one of the dining-room chairs." I suggested, desperate to talk to my mother.

"I'll see what I can do," said my dad, "call us back on Sunday in the early evening."

I stressed terribly for the next three days.

Sunday arrived and I dialled home. As usual my dad answered, "Ok, we've managed to get your mum downstairs, here she is."

When I heard my mother's voice I almost broke down. It was all I could do to sound cheerful to speak with her. Her voice was terribly weak and I could hardly tell a word she was saying.

After a short while my dad came back on the phone, saying that he thought mum had had enough now. "I'm coming back!" I told him, before cutting the connection and breaking down in floods of tears.

Ziggy had been standing with his head close to mine, trying to listen in to our conversation.

"We'll get you on the next flight out," Ziggy said, once he was able to speak.

The following day, while I started to make all the necessary preparations for my absence, Ziggy went to the travel agents and organised a ticket for me. The flight was fully booked so I was on standby.

A three-hour wait at the airport that night saw me returning to Lukanga Road. There were no cancellations on that flight. The next UK flight was two days later and this time I was lucky.

After he got home from dropping me at the airport Ziggy had phoned my dad to tell him I was on my way. I arrived at our Burton house and, after an emotional reunion, my dad asked me not to go dashing upstairs yet.

"The district nurse is here with your mum, going through the ablutions and getting your mum dressed", he said, "best you wait to see her until after she's had her hair brushed."

About half an hour later the nurse came into the lounge.

"She's all sorted now and sitting in her chair," she said, "I told her she had a visitor but I didn't say who. She'll be so happy to see you."

As I reached the top of the stairs I fixed a smile on my face before opening the bedroom door.

The difference in the few weeks since I had seen my mum was unbelievable. She was so thin.

The instant she saw me she burst into tears.

"Oh thank God you've come," she said, "I can go now."

I knelt on the carpet in front of her and just held her skeletal hands in mine.

Eventually she managed a smile.

"Just look at my finger nails, our Ann, they've never been so long. Your dad doesn't know how to cut nails 'cause he bites his. You can do them for me."

My mum had always had beautiful nails so I sat on the edge of the bed and we slowly chatted as I carefully trimmed and filed them.

That was the last day my mum spent out of her bed, as she went into meltdown.

Since she'd known about her condition she was under no illusions.

She knew she was going to die, and soon. But she was now at the point where she wanted the 'soon' to happen. Unfortunately one cannot simply decide when one is going to die.

I was sitting with her on Sunday lunchtime and she asked me to help her up. I thought she wanted to go to the toilet and began to ease her up in bed.

"No," she said lifting her arm slowly and with difficulty above her head, "help me up. Help me up to God."

I didn't know what to say. I felt so helpless.

I told her I was sorry but I couldn't do anything to help in that line.

"I'll give Frank a call and ask him to come round. Perhaps he can help."

Frank was our local vicar. Although my mum had never been big into religion, a couple of weeks before I had returned to Zambia she had asked me to contact the nearby church. Frank, a young and very compassionate clergyman, had been a great comfort to her since then, visiting her many times.

Naturally he came around as soon as he'd finished his lunch and sat with her for several hours, returning again after he'd conducted his evening service at St Peter's Church.

Although my mum was getting weaker she was still aware of what was going on when she was awake. In a way that made things worse for her because she wasn't strong enough to say what she wanted to. I could see her words were getting mixed up between being thought and being said. It must have been so frustrating for her and, I felt, humiliating.

Two days later she slipped into a coma and in the early evening of Tuesday 27th August my darling mother passed away.

R.I.P. Nancy.

8

A BIT OF SPORT

When I had returned to Zambia back in June the welcome was a tad casual. As I stepped out of the plane I scanned the building windows for sight of His Lordship. It wasn't until I was about 15 yards away from the passageway which extends out from the buildings to the tarmac that I spotted him. He stood in its doorway, through which the arriving passengers were officially entering the country.

He wasn't looking all that 'official' either, standing there with a bright green thermos flask tucked under his arm which was wearing, along with the rest of him, a very colourful red and blue tracksuit. As we walked down the passageway I was showered with hugs and kisses and words of welcome home. All I could think about was how obvious it was that he really shouldn't have been where he was, and I walked in dread of someone tapping us on the shoulder to arrest Ziggy for being in a restricted area.

Of course, he didn't give a toss. He just walked me on through, completely bypassing the health control desk and jumping the queue at Passport Control. What if someone asked to see *his* passport? I was absolutely crapping myself, I can tell you.

Handing me the green flask, he suggested that I went and sat in our car and enjoyed a coffee whilst he waited around for my suitcase. My pleasure, I'm sure - until I saw the car. Apart from the fact that it was a spanking brand new Nissan Skyline GL which the company had got for him in my absence (very nice), it was also parked in an *authorised parking only* zone. Apparently the parking watchdog had asked Ziggy to move it, but he had retorted that he didn't believe the department which laid claim to the parking spaces had that many cars, so he refused. I was now terrified I'd get towed away while drinking my coffee!

He returned relatively quickly (for Africa) and told me he had soon located my luggage, which he loaded onto a trolley, of which there were plenty since he was amongst the first on the scene. He then confessed that he had extracted a piece of white chalk from his pocket and surreptitiously swiped a large X onto the side of my suitcase. As he strolled past the customs pay desk, catching the eye of the official who takes the money, he nodded towards the chalked X then shook his head, intimating that there was nothing to pay. The official acknowledged him, and so he walked out.

We took a leisurely drive the short distance home and though I was itching to see the children I listened patiently to Ziggy as he told me what he had been doing at work. A lot of this involved his presence in government buildings, which accounted for his confidence in doing as he pleased at the airport.

A toot outside our house soon had the guard opening the gates. As we drove in I could see Vicki riding about on Brad's bike at the bottom of the drive. I did receive an acknowledgement of my presence by way of "Hello Mummy" as she rode past the car.

Leon made a point of coming to the front door to meet me and give me a big hug and a kiss before dashing off somewhere. I eventually had to ask if Brad was actually at home when up came a shout, "Yes, I'm in here!". He was in his bedroom playing with his Lego.

As you can tell, after over a month of not having me around, their excitement (or lack thereof) at seeing me was truly overwhelming!

Once inside I trundled my luggage through to the bedroom and began to unpack. After a few minutes Ziggy poked his head round the door,

"Since you didn't notice when you arrived, can you come in here a minute?" he said, motioning towards the lounge.

"Didn't notice what?" I asked, as I did as I was bid.

"How I smartened up the kids," he said.

I looked up to see my three children standing to attention in a row and my jaw dropped.

"Good, eh? I decided they needed a haircut before they went back to school and I figured if you can do it, so can I. What do you think?"

Speechlessness is not a condition I am too familiar with, but it struck me violently at that moment.

The kids weren't saying too much either, standing there with their little poker faces. I don't think they had the guts to say what they really thought of their new haircuts.

"So which basin did you use?"

"What?"

"Which of my basins did you put on their heads to cut around? You couldn't have got that look any other way."

"I don't know what you mean. I think they look pretty good. I just got your haircutting scissors and cut all the way round," he said, clearly offended by my remark.

"Well you've clearly never really been watching when I've given them a haircut, or you'd have realised a lot more goes into it than that. But never mind, you did try. And I heard somewhere that the difference between a bad haircut and a good one is only about two weeks!"

"Don't worry, I'll soon sort it out for you," I whispered to the kids as Ziggy went off in a sulk. I got a quiet "Thanks, mummy" from Brad and Vicki. But I think Leon liked his. Strange child.

ANOTHER SHOCK ON MY RETURN WAS HOW COLD IT WAS IN LUSAKA. THIS was late June, mid-winter in the southern hemisphere. While nights

had been a bit chilly in Kitwe at that time of year, it felt a lot colder in Lusaka.

Given that winter is relatively short, the houses are not built for cold weather. One wall of our lounge/dining room was given over almost entirely to glass, be it fixed or sliding doors. And there was none of your double glazing here. But even worse, the top couple of feet was made of adjustable louvres which, even when fully closed, were not draught proof, so the cold air would sneak through the gaps between the glass and, gaining momentum as it slid down the cold patio windows, spread out across the room like a chilly, invisible, swirling pool.

Of course, nights were the pits. Ziggy had taken to going to bed at about 8:30 because it was the only place to keep warm, other than sitting directly in front of our one and only small electric fan heater, which I laid claim to. My worst experience of this weather was a special day in itself, when Brad's school had their Sports Day.

We had to take him there on the Saturday morning at 8:30, then stay to watch the races.

As we drove to the school we could see huge curtains of dust sweeping across the open veld. It looked like there was a gale-force wind blowing out there, but we weren't prepared for what hit us when we stepped out of the car. It was bitterly cold!

Standing in the African sunshine, even though I was wearing jeans, t-shirt and jumper, I was still freezing from that biting wind. Moving into the shelter of the buildings was no advantage as you were then in the shade. Of course the perfect option was to be in the sunshine, and sheltered from the wind, but the only place where you could do this and still see the racetrack (remember, we were here to watch races) was incredibly crowded, with a regular multi-shuffle of bodies to the left as the sunny area slowly shifted as the rays moved.

Some very plucky parents were really braving the weather by sitting in the chairs which had been thoughtfully placed alongside the track, but they spent most of their time picking up the unoccupied chairs which were constantly being blown over.

Fortunately I had brought with me a small flask of hot coffee to drink, but that was consumed before the races even started. Ah yes, the races.

I have never seen such disorganisation at a school sports day in my life. All the parents were complaining about it.

To begin with, the races were 35 minutes late starting, or at least we thought they were. No-one seemed to know exactly when the start was supposed to be. Then for some unaccountable reason there was a twenty-minute delay between the third and fourth races.

By the time half the races had taken place, most of the kids were missing, either because they were standing in line waiting to have the results of a previous race written down, or because they'd just wandered off in all the confusion to get hotdogs or a drink. About thirty kids were eventually tracked down behind one of the classrooms. Accompanied by music from a lad's personal stereo, they were watching an exhibition of break-dancing which some enterprising kids had started doing to relieve the boredom. They were quite good.

Just for a change, Brad had volunteered for four races, including the last one, so like it or not we had to stay to the (incredibly) bitter end. And although he didn't get placed in any of them, he did try hard so we were very pleased with him.

Ziggy had previously promised Brad that if he did well at school during the week, on Sunday he would take him to Munda Wanga Zoo just outside Lusaka, so of course we all copped for that treat. I must admit that I wasn't too hopeful of the contents if Kitwe Zoo had been anything to go by, but have to say I was pleasantly surprised.

As we drove in, the first thing we saw was a young elephant, only about two years old, wandering around freely, accompanied by two camels.

We comparatively rich expats tended to forget that the majority of the Zambian people were unlikely to have seen much of the wildlife which inhabited their country. Here at the zoo they would have the opportunity to see some of what we had already seen scores of in the national game parks.

Impala and puku wandered around untended and there was a huge female kudu, though we were surprised to see only one zebra, in a fenced enclosure along with some warthogs and bush pigs. The predators were kept in huge, sturdily-fenced enclosures, each with a well-built brick building for shelter from whichever element they needed shelter from at the time. There was a lion and lioness in one area, both looked quite young. Three leopards occupied another, one of which was pregnant, and a third pen held a male and female tiger. I was very surprised at this. They must have been imported into the country during one of Zambia's more financially-fluid phases. All the animals looked in excellent condition.

On our way to check out the bear pit on the far side of the zoo we went past a building which comprised several large glass-fronted rooms containing mostly snakes. I was fascinated to see a black mamba, which isn't actually black but is rather brownish-olive-grey in colour, with a paler belly. The 'black' aspect comes from the coloration of the inside of its mouth, which is a deep, inky black. When threatened, a mamba will open its mouth to show the black lining as a warning signal. These are known to be the deadliest snakes in Africa; apparently it is not unknown for one to chase an enemy if it feels it is under threat, and they can move *very* fast!

I studied this one quite closely, as one can from behind plate glass. It was all coiled up in a corner and wasn't a very wide-girthed snake, and I reckoned it must have been about five feet long when stretched out.

Anyway, we eventually moved off in our search of bears, as well as crocodiles. On our way back, once again passing the reptile house, I persuaded Ziggy to accompany me to show him the mamba but couldn't believe my eyes when we looked inside. The snake was no longer tucked up in its corner but was stretched across the tank. My five feet length had been somewhat of a miscalculation. This guy must have been eight feet long if he were an inch!

Further around the zoo were enormous cages containing a varied assortment of monkeys, as well as some containing birds. Throughout there had been various birds just wandering around: peacocks, maribou storks and some very nice-looking (at that point unidentified by us) creatures, which stood quite tall and had spiky feathers on the top of their heads as if they had a punk haircut (they were crowned cranes).

We strolled over a footbridge which spanned a ravine that contained a children's playground under a mass of trees. As well as an assortment of roundabouts and swings, there was a huge slide set against the side of the ravine so that you had to climb the hill to get onto it. The kids spent ages playing there while we tracked down a hut which offered cool drinks and a limited range of snacks. There was also a large, very nice swimming pool, though it was empty, presumably for the winter months.

All in all we agreed that they had made a very nice job of the place given the country's limited resources.

But the highlight of our visit came as we were on our way to the exit. We came across another large brick building which I thought had been empty. To our surprise it contained two gigantic male lions. And they didn't seem very happy.

They prowled back and forth on the other side of the sturdy bars. I couldn't believe the size of their feet, and the thickness of their legs was incredible.

A crowd of about twenty people had gathered to look at them. Eventually one of the lions lay down as if bored by the whole display thing. There was a young couple towards the front of the crowd with two small children, and the bloke wasn't happy that the one lion had abandoned his audience.

This excuse for a man picked up and began to throw stones at the recumbent lion. He even handed a couple of stones to his wife to throw, though instead she managed to hit his prowling cellmate, who emitted a guttural sound of displeasure. The bigger lion eventually stood up and walked right up to the bars. There he turned his back to his audience and lifting his tail until the black tip of it almost reached the roof, suddenly ejected half a dozen short, sharp, but very far-reaching jets of urine - straight onto the aggravating couple.

I don't know who made the most noise; the man who received one of the jets full in the face, his wife screaming at the stinking mess down the front of her dress, or the audience in the background as we all cheered at the successful comeuppance the lion had inflicted.

We giggled our way back to our car having had a most enjoyable few hours at Munda Wanga Zoo.

Our other sporting event came a week later.

Although they attended the same school, the grades up to Vicki and Leon's age group were located at different premises to Brad, and they held their own Sports Day. During my absence in the UK Vicki had kindly offered my help at the event to her form teacher. I sent a note to school with Vicki asking when she would like me to attend.

"Thank you for offering to help. Could you be at the school staff-room at 11:30, please."

On the due day I dropped Ziggy at work so that I could have the use of the car, and took the kids to school. Later in the morning I donned a white print dress and jacket that my aunt had given to me, and my new red shoes and looked in the mirror to see if I passed muster.

I looked as if I were about to hand out the prizes at Speech Day rather than assist in organising fun races for a group of six and seven year olds! So the lot came off and I threw on my track suit and a pair of takkies instead. It looked far more appropriate.

I arrived in time for the coffee break before the festivities began, and as I walked into the staff room was delighted to see Lynnette, one of the few people I'd got to know so far, as she was the mother of one of Vicki's friends. She too had been 'volunteered'.

At the end of break the teachers went off to collect their classes as all the helpers sought out the PE teacher. It transpired that Lynnette often got involved in school activities and so was given the task of helping one of the teachers with the score sheets. The PE teacher allocated jobs to the remaining four helpers and I was given the task of 'props lady', i.e. laying out the skipping ropes, hoola hoops, bean bags and egg 'n spoons. The others were asked to assist in judging by agreeing who came first, second and third.

Was I ever handed the bum steer on *that* one! For each race category I had to fetch the ropes and stuff back from the finishing line and run back to the start for them to be used for the next heat. By the time the kids had run all their individual races I was absolutely knackered, having run all of them myself!

I was thinking what a good job it was that I hadn't pitched up wearing the two-piece suit and high-heeled shoes, but then thought about it. Dressed like that I would probably have been given a more sedentary job. Note for next year…!

BETWEEN MY STAYS IN THE UK I HAD WANTED TO KEEP MY MUM AS entertained as possible, so it wasn't long before I was back into the habit of writing home, but this was not without complications.

I had bought a new typewriter, which presented me with a few problems, as you will see from the following letter I wrote to my folks:

 Dear Nancy, Mev, Doris and others,

It's letter-writing time again and what a bloody job I've had getting it started. First I decided to write a letter to Thorn Electrical as the bottom dropped off my liquidiser last night. I soon found that sitting at the dining table with my hands tucked under my chin to reach this new typewriter was not one of the most comfortable positions to type in, so something had to be done.

I searched around for a higher chair, or a lower table, but found that the only chair higher was the bar stool, which would put me about two feet above the typewriter which didn't seem like such a good idea either. Then I thought perhaps I could put the typewriter up onto the bar where it would be at the perfect height.

I shoved the bar a bit to make sure it was sturdy enough to be able to take the weight of a typewriter and couldn't budge it so decided it was. Then I tried to lift the typewriter onto the bar. Holy crap. The bloody thing must weigh nearly half a hundredweight, and it's not exactly the most liftable shape either. At this point I would normally have asked Benton to lift it for me but he was out at the hospital and only Catrina was here and I could hardly ask her as she is pregnant again.

Anyway I eventually got it onto the bar together with all

my paperwork when I decided it would be a good idea to read through the copies of letters I'd sent to you since I got back to see what I'd already told you about. That took up a good fifteen minutes as I got carried away re-reading letters.

I eventually got the typewriter and bar stool in place, rolled in the paper and starting typing the address. Dear god, the typewriter was jumping about on the narrow bar as if it were on a set of springs and every time I hit the carriage return I thought the bloody thing was going to shoot off the end of the bar, not to mention all the bottles inside it that were rattling so much you'd think there was a bloody earthquake! So I had to work up all my strength again and lift it off the bar, back onto the table. At this point I decided it was time for a beer.

I arranged all my papers around the machine, Tipp-ex and, of course, the beer. But then I looked at my watch and decided it was time I put the dinner on. I was doing a rolled sirloin and wanted it to cook slowly and it was already 10:05. I know! 10:05 is a bit early for the first beer but you have to admit, I deserved it by now. So I floured the outside of the still half frozen beef and put it in the oven.

But I still had the issue of the typewriter.

As you know, I always use a cushion on my chair when I'm at my sewing desk so I decided to use that, together with a cushion off the patio furniture. That should make me high enough to type. It did, but the cushion was also so big that it extended over the front of the chair so my legs wouldn't go down to the floor. Typing with your legs sticking out in front of you under the table is a no-no, just take my word for it.

I have now fetched my bedroom stool, put my cushion on that, topped it with the patio cushion and it looks just right. The only trouble is, the top of the cushion mound is almost level with the underside of the table until you sit on it. I've had to push down on the cushion mountain with both hands and as much weight as possible at the same time as sliding onto it.

So here I am, ensconced in front of my typewriter, beer at arm's reach, sitting at a good height for typing except that now I am the one who is bouncing around as I type, as if I were on a set of springs.

An hour and a half, and almost two pages of words later I am finally ready to tell you what we've been up to lately. Knowing my luck the bloody phone'll ring now!"

9

A MATTER OF DUTY

My final flight from the UK was a doddle, so I figured that things were going too well and that the officials at Lusaka airport would probably make up for that.

As you may know if you read my first two books, security was somewhat of a problem in Zambia. Add to that the general reputation that most airports had for theft out of baggage, and we were presented with quite a challenge when it came to securing the contents of our bags.

In order to cram as many goodies into our cases as possible the bags had to be as large as was allowable, and flexible. So we always had the soft ones with zips. The padlocks with which one could secure the two zipper tabs together were so small that even our dog would be able to break through it. But I had a special trick.

Instead of a padlock I got some spare electric cable and stripped it down to the three single wires. Then I threaded that wire through the holes in the two zip tabs and bases as many times as there was space for and knotted it, a lot. Next I bound insulating tape around the wired zip-ends until there was a bundle almost the size of a golf ball. Finally I wound several layers of packaging tape around the suitcase which hid the zip-bundle even further. It was very effective because we never had any interference with our suitcases as would-be thieves obviously decided it was easier to breach something a little less challenging.

As I arrived in the customs hall with my retrieved suitcase I was asked by an official to place it onto his counter. (Fortunately these were low level wooden benches so I didn't need a forklift.) Then he asked if I had anything to declare.

I told him I had about £14 worth of chocolates and toys. Clearly he didn't believe me and asked to look inside the case. I told him to be my guest. I wasn't worried that I had more than I'd claimed, as all the expensive stuff had been boxed and sent separately as unaccompanied baggage.

First he had to take several turns to pull off the tape around the suitcase. Then he was presented with the golf ball of insulating tape. This was, of course, very tightly bound so he couldn't get his scissors into it. He eventually found the end of the tape and began unwrapping. When that came off he found yet more tape to take off. He worked his way down the layers until a portion of the sturdily-wired zip tabs appeared. He looked pretty cheesed off by now and asked, "If you are sure you have nothing further to declare, maybe I won't bother looking in your case. Just pay the cashier K28 in duty."

So I loaded my case back onto the trolley and made my way towards the exit where Ziggy waited. (Security must have been upped a bit since his previous airport wanderings.) He gave me K28 and I went back to pay my dues.

At the cash desk I told the guy that I had to pay K28 and handed over three K10 notes. But after a little thought he said he would only charge me K17 and gave me K13 change and a receipt for K14. Of course he knew full well that you would not complain about getting a K3-below-value receipt if you'd actually paid less than you should have. Nice number he'd got going there.

It was only when I was taking stock of this period in my life for the purpose of writing this book that it occurred to me I seemed to have done an awful lot of things in a very short space of time. I can only put this down to one thing, my rather unnerving ability to adapt to change very quickly.

I think I'll blame my granddad, Harold Johnson, DCM. He was a Regimental Sergeant Major in the British Army, North Staffordshire Regiment and he travelled extensively during his army career, which started well before the Second World War. He and my nan had four sons, all born in different locations.

As I tend to adapt so easily it soon feels like I've been part of the new locations I'm in for absolutely ages, and I quickly get involved in all sorts of activities. I had rapidly integrated into the Kitwe Little Theatre activities, and so it happened now with the horse fraternity in Lusaka.

What an incredibly friendly bunch of people they were.

Ziggy and the kids had spent quite a lot of time at the Lusaka Gymkhana Club while I'd been in England and were now well accepted in its community. The kids loved it there because several members had kids of similar ages, some of whom they already knew from school.

Perhaps I should explain more about the place in general:

The Lusaka Gymkhana Club (LGC) was situated within the boundaries of the Lusaka Agricultural Showgrounds (LAS) which covered just under a square mile (by my rough calculation). It was a sort of triangular shape and consisted of three different organisations, four if you count the Veterinarian.

Accessed from the Great East Road, the LAS itself comprised dozens of brick buildings which accommodated the various businesses participating in the annual agricultural show. As well as these buildings, there was a large grassed arena where assorted equestrian and other events would take place during the week of the annual Lusaka Agricultural and Commercial Show. For the remainder of the year, 95% of this area was unused.

To the south of the showgrounds area lay the Polo Club, comprising the polo field, stable blocks and a large paddock. With plenty of parking and a highly regarded restaurant they were completely self-contained.

The western area of the showgrounds was given over to the Lusaka Gymkhana Club. Close to the entrance from the Great East Road sat the pulsing heart of the LGC, the clubhouse. Being the vendor of alcoholic beverages this was always well attended!

There was an open grassy area in front of the clubhouse and beyond that was LGC's own show jumping arena. Next to it was the 'collecting ring' which led on through to the stable yards and other facilities including a lunging ring, a small rectangular schooling arena, and a couple of grassed dressage arenas which were only used during competitions.

Then, past all these, you would find another stable block and small sand arena used mostly by the riding school, run by Lorraine Chalcraft. Every child in the place was absolutely terrified of her. She had a whole herd of ponies/horses which she used for giving riding lessons.

She would hold classes for children of various ages and stages of ability, and no matter which class they belonged to they were treated the same. She screamed at them at the top of her voice.

Standing in the centre of her schooling paddock she would watch every move they made, regardless of whether they were in front, to the sides of, or behind her. She never missed a thing.

"Eyes front, all of you!"

"Push those heels down"

"Tighten up those reins Sandra, before the bloody pony trips over them," this when the child loosened her grip a fraction.

"Sit up straight Gerald, who do you think you are, the bloody Hunchback of Notre Dame?"

"Now let's see you all trot on." Two seconds later, "Come on! What are you waiting for, Christmas?"

"Nice position Steven, good boy!"

"Catch up at the back there."

And so she went on, at full volume. And it didn't stop there. The voluminous instructions continued when they were doing the necessary pre- or post-lesson stable chores.

Fortunately all this was well away from the clubhouse though on a really bad day, as you sat outside enjoying a cold beer, you could still hear her shouting. I used to cringe as I pitied the poor little sod on the receiving end of her wrath. But she was very fair about it. She shouted at everyone, including the grooms. I think that is why her students consisted almost entirely of children. Adults didn't *dare* go to her. But she certainly got results, churning out many excellent young riders.

Lorraine became a good friend of mine down the line.

A remaining large area consisted of the disused (by any racing fraternity) rectangular racetrack, and inside the confines of that there was a substantial cross-country course. Cross-country was one of my favourites but alas we were not allowed to use the course except during competitions, except as a place for the horses to graze.

The racetrack however was in regular use by members wanting to exercise their horses. Not in the racing sense I hasten to add, but just for walking, trotting or cantering around. A strict code of conduct was actually adhered to, preventing 'fast' riders from disturbing slower horses as they passed.

Between the LGC clubhouse and the exit to the Great East Road lay the carpark and building used by the local Veterinarian, Chris Oparaocha.

A couple who soon became good friends were Heather and David McCleery (the first person I'd met at the LGC). David was part of an Overseas Aid Scheme and was a lecturer at Lusaka's Natural Resources Development College (NRDC - agricultural college). He and Heather lived on the college ranch where they had plenty of space for their horses. Although there were more, I particularly remember four of them. Two bays, being David's Double French (or Frenchie) and Heather's Rumtum (not his real name) and two greys, a beautiful gelding named Waterford and another (more white) called Big Boy.

Big Boy was the most amazing horse, and while I don't think he won many prizes for his looks (I always thought he bore a slight resemblance to a carthorse), he could manage quite a pace when he'd a mind to, could jump a fair bit and had a wonderful temperament.

Like our house, the ranch was also off the Great East Road, just a mile or so before the turnoff to Lusaka airport.

A short while after I returned from my mum's funeral we were at LGC having a game of darts when Heather asked me if I'd be interested in leasing Big Boy while her lads were away at boarding school in the UK. *Would I?*

I hadn't ridden much since before we went to England at the end of March as the polo season was in full swing, so I wasn't needed to help exercise Otmar's polo ponies. I did occasionally get the chance to ride other folks' horses at the LGC but would love to ride more regularly.

While Big Boy would remain at the McCleery ranch as opposed to being at the LGC stables, there was plenty of lovely riding space around there, which was fine for me. My biggest problem was going to be transport.

Lizzy Land Rover had been having engine troubles.

She spent a lot of time in and out of a garage which charged a lot of money for knowing next to nothing about how to fix Land Rovers. Apart from that, she guzzled fuel like a drunk at a wedding so had been costing a fortune in petrol as a town run-around. As we weren't planning on doing any bundu bashing around our new location she seemed to be a pointless luxury - if you can use such a term for a long-wheel-based vehicle with a loud engine and no rear seats.

When we did eventually manage to sell her I had become quite accustomed to being without my own wheels. Now I needed some.

While I had been away Ziggy kept a lookout for a car for me.

With amazing luck he heard that an expat who worked at one of the group's companies would soon be leaving the country so immediately jumped in and asked if he had a car for sale. He did, a Fiat 132 GL about five years old which had a very low mileage and within a price we could manage. Ziggy took a look at it and said it was in pretty good nick, its only downfall being that it had the regular fake leather seats. Hands were shaken on the sale deal and Ziggy suggested that all I needed to do was buy some seat covers while I was in the UK. I did.

A few weeks later I couldn't believe my eyes when I actually saw it; the car was exactly the pale yellow colour I had wanted (but failed to get) for our custom-built Land Rover. Unfortunately it had a tan interior which didn't fit too well with the blue seat covers I had managed to buy, but that was the least of my worries. Having previously accepted Lizzie's greeny-yellow exterior, black interior and sugar-pink dralon seats, I wasn't going to complain!

So now I had the wheels to go with the horse. Perfect.

10

TAILS ABOUT THE KITCHEN

Since we arrived in Zambia four years earlier, shopping facilities had improved quite substantially, but were still far from what we had been used to in England. Certain items were still only periodically available and/or difficult to obtain. One of those was butter.

Before my last trip to the UK I found that we were getting rather short of it. One of Ziggy's office workers, Patrick, used to work for the Dairy Produce Board and still had connections with folk there. He said that any time we wanted butter to ask him and he would put us in touch with one of his friends. So I left instructions for Ziggy to try and purchase two cases of butter during my absence. Of course, he didn't, so when I went to get some out of the freezer and saw our very depleted stocks I was not impressed. In Zambia you do not run yourself down to the last six blocks. The last time I had done that we ate jam on dry toast for a fortnight!

Ziggy assured me that he would be able to get some okay so he went along on the Thursday to the Dairy Produce Board factory, armed with a note from Patrick to the manager of the place, and asked for two cases of their finest butter. He was told they didn't have any right then, but that there would be some on Monday. He was advised to arrive no later than 9:00-10:00 otherwise it might all be gone, but not to go earlier as they wouldn't have cut it up and wrapped it by then.

On Monday morning he duly left the house complete with half my month's grocery allowance to pay for the butter. To be safe I phoned his office at nine o'clock and left a message with someone to remind him.

At about 11:00 I heard the car arrive and in walked Ziggy, proud as punch at having been able to acquire two boxes of butter. He brought them into the kitchen. Each box contained one solid block of butter weighing in at 10 kg (22 ½ lbs).

It immediately made me think of my mum, who had told me that when she first left school she went to work at a shop in Burton town centre called Oakhams where they sold butter 'off the block'. It was her job to cut it to the required weight and pat it into a rectangular shape with special wooden paddles. I really wished that I had a pair of her butter paddles at that moment!

It would seem I'd just have to use a large knife and cut it into blocks, then wrap it in greaseproof paper, plastic wrap or tin foil depending upon what stocks of those I had. This was all very well, but when I opened the boxes I found that the butter had been put into a large plastic bag before being shoved into the narrow cardboard box. When removed from the box it was shaped like a gigantic mango.

After I'd cut off the rounded outsides and cut the big block into butter-dish-sized pieces, I was left with six 'outer' slabs of odd shapes.

I searched the pantry and kitchen cupboards to find a suitable butter-dish-sized plastic container into which I could squash it to form a block, I found one. I rammed wedges of butter into the rectangular box then tried to shake it out.

Was I serious, or what?

I tapped it and shook it and banged it on the counter but the bloody stuff wouldn't come out. Eventually I loosened the edges with a knife then still had to prise it out of the box with a couple of spoon handles. By the time the mutilated block was on the counter it more resembled a distorted yellow sponge than a slab of butter!

Honestly, this was almost as bad as making pork pies!

(And if you haven't heard about *that* amazing performance, check out *More Into Africa*.)

ONE THURSDAY WHEN I HAD BEEN WITHOUT TRANSPORT I REALISED I HAD nothing for the kids to take for a snack to school the next day so thought I'd better do a bit of baking. A couple of days earlier I had been scanning my recipe books for something or other and came across a recipe for Swiss roll which sounded quite simple so thought, "why not? anything for a laugh."

I organised my three eggs, 3oz caster sugar and 3oz flour. The recipe told me to place the eggs and sugar into a large bowl and put it over a saucepan of hot water then whisk until stiff enough to leave a trail. Child's play!

So I whisked. And I whisked some more. I whisked with my right hand, then with my left hand, then with the right... Whisk, whisk, whisk! My wrists were aching so much after ten minutes of this that I'd have tried whisking with my feet if it had been feasible. After twenty minutes I had it looking something like it was meant to be.

After carefully (as instructed) folding in the flour I poured the mixture into my lined Swiss roll tin (which had been used many times before for all things except making a Swiss roll) and placed it in the oven.

After a few minutes I checked it through the oven's glass door and was horrified to see that the damn thing was rising so much it was about to start flowing over the side of the tin. There was nothing I could do that wouldn't ruin the sponge even further so I left it to its own devices for the full 15 minutes.

After removing it from the oven and carefully transferring it to some sugared greaseproof paper I did a quick flurry with some strawberry jam and then proceeded to roll it up. Except 'roll' isn't exactly the term I should use to describe the action, as 'roll' it did not! It ended up looking like a rectangular Victoria sponge cake with a kinky bend in it. Fortunately it tasted delicious so we had no trouble polishing it off.

The following afternoon for want of anything better to do I was thumbing through some different recipe books and came across another recipe for Swiss roll. It was identical to the one I had used previously except at the bottom of the recipe there was a 'quick tip'. It said *if your tin size is so-and-so then use only two eggs, 2oz sugar and 2oz flour*. Just out of curiosity I got out my tape measure and measured my tin. There lay the problem. The quantities I'd used the first time had been intended for a larger baking tin!

About a week later, a great amount of pestering by the kids resulted in me making another one, only this time I used the correct quantities. Perfection!

ONCE UPON A TIME I WENT INTO OUR PANTRY FOR SOMETHING AND thought I heard a rustle. I assumed it was a small salamander or gecko scurrying about behind one of the bags. That night I went to the pantry again and heard still more rustling. I thought it was a bit odd for either a salamander or gecko to be so out-of-sight active so I looked around. It didn't take me long to find some bags had corners missing with positive signs of having been nibbled on by something with sharp pointy teeth. Geckos might have sharp little teeth but they're not pointy.

As I didn't fancy coming into contact with whatever had those sharp pointy teeth I called Ziggy and asked him to do a thorough search of the pantry. This resulted in the removal of all nibble-able items, which of course was eighty percent of the contents of the pantry. With the price and lack of availability of so much of the stuff I couldn't just throw it all away. It took me the rest of the night to transfer all items which might be of interest to our little intruder into plastic containers, tins or jars, (discarding the food surrounding the nibbled corners, of course). I was pretty sure that whatever was taking an interest in our goodies would soon sod off when it couldn't get at anything to eat.

A couple of days later I was in the middle of clearing up after a baking session as well as making the kids' teas when a friend arrived.

We chatted in the kitchen as I completed my tasks and I was telling her about our little visitor as I opened the pantry door to put something away only to catch sight of, albeit very briefly, a tail disappearing into a hole in the ceiling where a water pipe went. The tail looked awfully long. So much for my hopes that it was only a mouse!

At that time Ziggy was out of town for a couple of days so it was only at the weekend that I talked to him of my friend's visit and the 'sighting' of the intruder. In explaining what had happened I opened the pantry door to point out the hole and was saying, "…and as I looked in, there was a…" before I could say "tail disappearing into the roof" a bloody great rat leapt from the back of a shelf, shot up the wall and disappeared through the hole into the roof.

Talk about an action replay. The BBC couldn't have done any better. At least now Ziggy couldn't dispute what I was telling him. By the following week he'd sourced some rat poison, chucked it in the loft and totally sealed up the hole accessing the pantry.

That seemed to do the trick because we saw no signs of the rat again.

11

ZIGGY SAFARI AND HOME ALONE

One of the things that we'd agreed upon before I went to say farewell to my dear mum was that on my return Ziggy should take a little holiday by himself. He decided he'd go game viewing, only this time game viewing with a difference. He booked with Norman Carr Safaris to go on a walking safari.

He chose to go during the week that included the Independence Day holiday. This year the holiday fell on a Thursday and, as so many workers would be unlikely to pitch up for work on the Friday, many companies gave that day off too. This meant Ziggy could take a ten-day holiday yet only take five days off work.

For a change he did all his own bookings, chose which type of game viewing he wanted as well as where to stay. The last three days of his holiday were to be spent at Mfuwe Lodge, where we would join him.

In the meantime I would be left home alone.

Well I wasn't exactly alone, was I? I was surrounded by three kids, three dogs, a house servant, his wife, their five children and the security guard.

I had no intention of sitting around on my backside doing nothing while he was lording it up in South Luangwa. I dropped him at the airport so had the use of his 'free petrol' company car for the week, and talk about 'make the most of it'. What an incredibly hectic week it was.

On the Friday night, Lake Road School was holding a braai as well as a disco for the kids. I phoned around to make sure there would be a few people there I knew, and so the kids and I went along to it. It was all very pleasant.

At two in the morning I woke up with terrible stomach cramps. After a second trip to the toilet I began to feel nauseous too. I was up and down all night, so got little sleep. When the kids got up I told them to get Benton to make breakfast. I took two paracetamols and went back to bed. I managed to sleep until noon.

Before he'd gone away Ziggy had told me things had been buzzing at the top of the business world. Some of the big boys were not happy about the way things were going since the introduction of the forex auction (hold tight, and I'll explain this in more depth for you") and wouldn't be surprised if there weren't a coup over the Independence Day holiday weekend.

Very nice! Here's him sodding off into the bush and leaving me and the kids in Lusaka with the possibility of a bloody coup taking place! I clearly remember the curfew imposed for several weeks after an attempted coup just after Independence Day in 1980, when we'd only been in the country for a couple of months. It was bad enough then up in the Copperbelt, but security would likely be much more heightened here in the capital. I hoped they were wrong.

In any event I managed to get well stocked up with meat, veg and beers, not that I was drinking any of those on Saturday, feeling so ill.

Sunday morning I was right as rain. After a late and hearty breakfast the kids and I went to the LGC where a few of the friends I had there had gathered. At precisely two o'clock we had our first shower of the season. Everyone went outside to stand and welcome those warm raindrops. It was nothing too hectic but nonetheless enough to put a damper on several folks' plans, who moaned that their charcoal would now be too wet to light.

"It doesn't bother me," I said "my charcoal is under cover, so is the braai box."

"Great. Then we'll all come round to your place." Some bright spark commented.

So they did.

I went home and threw some potatoes in the oven and got some meat out of the freezer. Having gone home to collect their various bits and pieces my 'guests' arrived at five. We had a great time and they left at about ten.

Just before going to Mfuwe, Ziggy had reminded me that our household insurance was about to fall due for renewal and asked me to calculate how much value we wanted to place on everything, in view of the impending rise in prices here.

Trying to figure out the value of anything in Zambia at that point in time was a joke. In October the Zambian government had, in its wisdom, decided upon a new system when it came to allocating foreign exchange. No-one could buy forex without a government-issued permit. And as Zambia didn't have much of it they decided to put it up for auction to the highest bidder.

The Bank of Zambia would announce how much forex was available that week and companies or whoever had a permit to buy were asked to say how much they wanted and then bid for it. Bidding was based on the US dollar. The forex was then sold, with the bulk going to the highest bidder, *at whatever the highest bid was.*

Before this started, one US dollar was valued at three kwacha. The first auction saw the dollar costing K5. The second week it went up to K6.2 and the third week it was touching K7. It slowly continued in an upward trend.

What this meant was that, bearing in mind that virtually everything you bought in Zambia had to be imported from somewhere, the price of everything went up. And up, and up. In the first week the cost of fuel had doubled, which obviously affected deliveries of everything, so trying to work out the value of things for insurance purposes was a nightmare.

I eventually estimated a value of K101,190 on our possessions which meant paying a premium of K1,092.47. Thank goodness the company was paying!

Ziggy had told me where the insurers were. I needed to get a pro forma invoice from them and take it to the company accountant to get a cheque, which I then had to take back to the insurance company's offices before the old policy expired at midnight on Monday. Simple, you would think.

On the same day Brad had been invited to a birthday party at 3:00 so, as I wanted to go and sort out the insurance, I said I'd drop him off a bit early so that I could get on with my business. We left our house at 2:30 and headed off in the general direction of his party. He had been there before so I thought he knew where they lived. Unfortunately it was a while ago and he couldn't remember. The only address we had was 57 Avondale, Avondale being a suburb, so I thought that it must be a plot number, but when I came to look I found that there are lots of street names with street numbers, not plot numbers, and that they were several number 57s. All Brad could remember for sure was that we had to go along a dirt road at some point to get to this house. So we travelled down every bloody dirt and non-dirt road we could find in the area, asking at all No. 57 gates if they were having a party, as you do. After loads of negative replies and strange looks I eventually gave up.

After three-quarters of an hour of searching, we arrived back home at almost 4 o'clock, where I had decided I needed to calm down before going off to sort out the insurance.

I stormed into the house calling the parents of the unfortunate child whose birthday it was all the names under the sun for not putting a map on the back of the invitation, and shouted at Brad to phone them immediately and tell them he was *not* going to their bloody party.

"But ask them where the hell they live." I demanded.

As he looked up their number Vicki came up and mentioned that she accidentally pulled the handle off my bedroom door while I'd been out, and that the other end had fallen off on the other side so we couldn't open it. I now screamed and ranted about that.

Then Brad announced that he couldn't find out where Zoe lived because our phone had been cut off. I'm sure you can imagine my reaction!

After I came down off the ceiling and the kids came out of hiding from behind the furniture, I eventually tore off in the direction of the insurance company.

First of all I went to the wrong building. I got redirected and eventually found the right office . A guy there confirmed that the premium was K1,092.47 so armed with a pro forma invoice I headed to Ziggy's office to get a cheque. Ziggy had told me who to see and what to say, so I did. But the guy concerned, Mr. Ngwera, wasn't sure that he should do as I said so he asked his superior, Mr. Nkomo, if it was okay but he didn't know either. I insisted that the company *did* pay our insurance premium as part of Ziggy's contract, but Mr. Nkomo said that, as he hadn't seen Mr. Patras's contract, he didn't know if that was true.

Now that peed me off big time because I wouldn't lie about such a thing, for goodness sakes.

Anyway, they announced, there was no one there at the moment to sign the cheque but they'd check it out with Mr. Martin when he returned. It so happened that I had seen Brian Martin arrive as I was entering their offices so off we went in search of him. His immediate reaction on being asked was, "Of course the company pays for Mr. Patras's insurance, give me the cheque and I'll sign it."

I turned and glared at the irritating little pleb with an expression of 'Told you so!'.

The only trouble was that all the cheques had to have two signatories and Brian was the only one there at the time. However he said that some of the others were due in the office within 10 minutes so to hang around and get it signed. By now it was 4:40 and the insurance office closed at 5:00 so I was getting quite anxious.

The pleb suggested that if I was in such a hurry perhaps I should drive over to the other offices to get it signed there. I said that wouldn't be much good if they were already on their way here, but perhaps he could phone the offices to see if they'd left yet. In the meantime I would go and get the car filled up from the company petrol pump.

It was just my bloody luck that it turned out to be the pleb who had to operate the pump and as I waited for him to come outside, who should drive in but Ziggy's immediate boss, Barry Major, who was, of course, a signatory. I went straight over to him and asked if he would sign the cheque for me urgently and he said, "No problem". Just then the pleb returned with the pump key so I asked him to give me the cheque, but he'd left it inside.

Instead of telling me where it was he handed the key to another guy who was hanging around, told him to fill up my tank then went off to his office. I followed.

Inside he took the cheque off his desk and instead of giving it to me he walked across the office to another signatory who'd just come in and asked *him* to sign it. Of course, this guy knew nothing about it and started scanning the cheque authority to find out what it was all about. I mean, K1092.47 is a lot of money and he wasn't going to put his signature to it until he knew exactly what it was all about. But by this time I had had ENOUGH!

"Look, if you don't mind I haven't got time to hang around while you decide whether or not you want to sign it. Just give it to me and I'll take it to Mr Major who already knows all about it." At which I whisked it out from under his nose and dashed off in the general direction of Barry who signed it immediately.

With the cheque in my hand I raced back to the car and was just about to drive off when the little man who'd operated the pump jumped in front of the car. Fortunately I stopped in time and he asked me to open my tank cover for him as he'd left the petrol cap off.

It was 4:52 as I drove out the gate into Cha Cha Cha Road and headed off in the direction of Independence Avenue. Only then did I see the traffic jam. Someone had broken down on the bridge at the beginning of Independence Avenue and there was total chaos.

I arrived at Premium House at 5:02 to witness people pouring out of the building faster than rainwater from a downspout after a cloud burst.

So I thought, "Stuff it!", turned the car around and headed off to the LGC for a drink to calm me down. The kids were still at home but I just couldn't be bothered to fetch them for the sake of half an hour, and anyway I knew they'd be behaving themselves under Benton's care as they wouldn't *dare* do anything naughty in the light of the temper I had been in when I left home.

Sure enough, when I arrived home at six they were all sitting quietly in the lounge watching a video.

Thankfully we weren't burgled during the night, so first thing on Tuesday morning I drove to Premium House to hand over that damned cheque.

WHEN I'D CALLED AT THE CLUB ON MONDAY WE WERE INVITED TO A PARTY at Kevin Flanagan's place on Tuesday evening to say 'goodbye' to a visitor of his who was flying out the next day. We went along to that and it was all very pleasant.

Wednesday was darts night at LGC so Benton babysat for me. He was always happy to do that as it meant he got to sit in the house and watch our television, as well as getting paid for it.

Thursday, being Independence Day, there was a big gathering at the club where a large braai had been set up for use by anyone. The kids were in their element as many of their friends were there and at the end of the day we all left very happy as I had made friends with a lot of people I'd barely met before.

Friday was flight day, and we were off to Mfuwe to join Ziggy.

As always, we thoroughly enjoyed ourselves, Ziggy having had the most amazing time on his own. He was so impressed he actually wrote a letter to my dad, which I shall quote verbatim here:

 My first week's holiday was supposed to be a walking safari where a crowd of people, together with a trail leader and an armed guard walk out of one bush camp, stopping for rest, drinks and food, and walk throughout the day to another camp, game viewing on the way. I booked my trip with Norman Carr's safaris, thinking that I do deserve the best. On the flight from Lusaka to Mfuwe I was reading Zambia Airways in-flight magazine and they had an article by Norman Carr about, would you believe, walking safaris. Norman you must understand, is about 70 years old and one of the 'old school'. When he was quoted in this magazine as

saying that you see less game and at a further distance when walking, as opposed to driving, but that you do get away from the 'infernal internal combustion engine' it took the wind out of my sails a bit. I had assumed that because you were on foot you'd get closer to the game and see more of it. Not so, it seemed!

So we arrived at Kakuli Camp out in the bush, seven of us, together with five who were already in residence, made up a full camp. The camp consisted of one major round open-sided hut where you spent your spare hours. The 'bedrooms' were bamboo poled, straw thatched, mud floored and quite basic. A breeze blew through the sides keeping you cool and filling the whole hut with dust - in your bed, clothes, etc.

To keep drinks cold they had a sack nailed to a tree with all the bottles in it and one of the boys threw water over it which, when it evaporated, was supposed to keep the bottles reasonably cool. Not very cool, but it's all you're gonna get so enjoy it! The toilets were grass walled huts, enclosing a hole in the ground, a bit smelly but functional. No baths but a shower (yes, another grass walled hut) using river water from an old oil drum. The whole camp was situated by the side of the Luangwa river. You couldn't swim in it because of big crocs and even bigger hippos. All the camp water came from that river. Of course, they boiled it first but it still looked and tasted muddy, it didn't matter whether you had tea or coffee, it all tasted muddy. BUT, I wasn't expecting five star accommodation, so no disappointments there.

At about 4:30 one of the trail leaders said that we'd be going out for an evening walk. It got dark at 6:00 and you couldn't stay out after that. During the walk, and they walked to the pace of the slowest walker, we saw at a distance, lion, giraffe, antelope (various), zebra etc.

Back at camp we had an excellent meal followed by a few drinks then everyone buggered off to bed. I had a whisky nightcap and then buggered off myself. During the night hippos were grunting and lions were being noisy, all very disconcerting.

The following day no-one said anything about walking to another camp and I felt a bit peeved having built myself up to it, but good company, good surroundings and plenty to see offset that. On Sunday we ran out of beer. Tragedy. Only lukewarm Coke, Fanta or whisky was left. Now I WAS getting peeved. Game or no game, company or no company, we all have our limits.

So I hitched a lift with a guard who was going to Mfuwe Lodge and had a few beers there. Then I saw the camp supply truck was loading up to restock our camp so all was well when we returned. We then went on a night drive.

These trail leaders must have six pairs of eyes each, they don't miss a thing. As well as the vehicle headlights (Land Cruiser) they also have a powerful hand-held spotlight. They pan that across the plains and scrub hoping to pick out the eyes of the game in the dark. We saw quite a lot of game: hippo grazing, impala and puku and zebra, but then the driver put his foot down.

The cruiser shot forward and next we were belting down a plain. Minutes later the spotlight picked out a lioness – she was pacing forward purposefully with head held low and some sixty metres behind her was the male. They were coming towards us so we turned around and now they were moving alongside us, ignoring us, the headlights, spotlight, diesel engine and all.

The lioness was about ten metres away from us, still moving alongside, when in the headlights we picked up impala. She had seen them before we did and had broken into a slow trot. The male, who by now was a bit closer, followed.

She broke into a run and then went full pelt - straight into the pack of impala. As one of them turned she was straight in, on top and broke its neck, a clean kill. And this was taking place right in front of us!

We drove up really close and were about eight metres

away, she was bathed in the headlights and the spotlight, totally unconcerned, still hanging onto the neck of the dead impala. Almost immediately the lion, who was left behind slightly, ran up, bowled the lioness over and took the kill. She seemed to shrug her shoulders, knowing that it's his supper, and started off toward the pack of impala again.

Within three minutes we had a repeat performance. Once she had selected her target she was off like a rocket and the impala had no chance.

Two quick, clean kills in the space of five minutes right before our eyes. It left me absolutely breathless. The lioness started to carry/drag her kill off through the scrub so we went back to the lion. He had taken his kill into the bush too so we found the lioness again and she'd started eating. After four or five minutes of watching her rip a fresh impala apart we went back to camp.

Needless to say that dispelled any doubts about the safari I might have had. Back at the camp we had another excellent meal and after a few nightcaps I hit the sack – before 10:00! Though hardly surprising as you're up and out at 05:30.

The rest of the week had a lot of memorables, all of which made my stay very enjoyable. Relaxation (the object of the exercise) came easily and any work problems were forgotten. The final accolade came from the trail leader who asked if I would come and work for them for four weeks next summer. Flattery - or bulldust?

Anyway sometime soon I'll do it again, money and Ann permitting.

*PS From Ann. When Ziggy had related tales of his experiences to me I was **so** envious. Maybe he will go on a walking safari again, but if he does I'll be with him!*

12

A WEEKEND WITH BIG BOY

We had a bit of excitement in Lusaka when Princess Anne arrived in the country for an unofficial five-day visit. We were told she would be arriving at 5:30 one Tuesday evening so a crowd at the club decided that, being a keen horse-woman, we should gather outside the Showgrounds wall and cheer her as she was driven past on her way to wherever she was going; we assumed the President's Palace. Even on an unofficial visit we couldn't see her getting away without a courtesy call to the Pres.

We all got togged up in red white and blue, and a friend at the British High Commission had supplied us with some Union flags. Someone else made some red white and blue streamers out of crepe paper which were draped around the horses. It's the biggest wonder it didn't scare the living daylights out of them.

Margaret Fenton kindly lent me a horse which I sat on with Vicki, and also a pony for Leon and Brad to share. As you might imagine they were *so* excited.

We all lined up by the roadside, or at least tried to. There were about sixteen horses as well as several people on foot and as we had to wait quite a while, the horses soon got fed up of standing still and kept wandering off.

There were quite a lot of local people waiting at various bus stops on the other side of the road and I'm sure they wondered what the hell was going on. It looked like quite a few of them let the buses pass them by just so they could wait and see what we were all there for.

Anyway Her Royal Highness eventually came along, and having been preceded by several wailing police cars and motor-bikes we were able to get ourselves into good order before her car drove past. As her limo drew near it slowed right down as she passed us, and she gave us all a wave and a smiling show of appreciation for our turn-out.

Of course everyone was dead chuffed, especially as some sour grapes inside the club had predicted that the car would just whizz past showing no interest in us at all. Being a glass-half-full sort of person, I'd taken the stance that we should be prepared for the best, which is what we got. We hadn't had so much excitement since the monkey fell off the donkey (or whatever the saying is)!

On the subject of cavalcades...

It always paid to keep a book in the car in Zambia as you never knew when you would be held up.

No, I don't mean with guns and stuff, although there was always a possibility of that, except you wouldn't be inclined to read a book under those circumstances. I mean held up by delays, mostly due to formal occasions.

Rule number 1: You simply weren't allowed to travel on the same road as the President. Before he even left his palace (or wherever he was leaving from) the roads President Kaunda was scheduled to take would be cleared of all traffic. Armed police or military would be posted at each junction he would pass in order to stop the traffic, not just from driving on that road but sometimes even crossing over it in order to take another route. If your location was at a point far from his start-up you could be in for a very long wait. Personally I reckoned they started closing the roads off before he'd even put his shoes on!

Even after our dear President and his entourage, surrounded by a multitude of motorcycle outriders and cars (no tanks though) had passed, the junction officer would still wait for a minute or two before allowing you access onto that road, presumably in case you felt inclined to chase after him.

As mentioned earlier, our house was located in an area off the Great East Road, and the Great East Road led to the airport. So if the President was on his way to or from the airport for whatever reason, you would just switch off your engine and sit back with a good book. Or if you were on your way out, simply turn around, go home and enjoy a coffee or two before trying again!

Picking the kids up from school could also be quite a hit-and-miss affair. You see, Lake Road School was located on the road which led to the cemetery. Here enters Rule 2. It was considered the height of disrespect if you crossed over that road while a funeral procession was making its way to the grave. And Heaven forbid if you should inadvertently drive onto the road and find yourself *in the middle* of a funeral procession, oh my word! And this wasn't as difficult as you might think.

Many of the mourners could be transported in the rear of bakkies or trucks, and you could easily mistake a slow-moving vehicle for an unlucky workforce who had drawn the short straw and been given a truck which was experiencing propulsion problems, only to find that it was, in fact, part of a cortège.

I suspect the comment about the 'workforce' will make absolutely no sense at all if you haven't read my first book. Perhaps I should mention that it was common practice for the workforce - or any quantities of people for that matter - to be transported from A to B in the open back of a truck or bakkie, Depending on the vehicle, they could be standing up or sitting on the floor/sides/cab roof of the vehicle as it crawled or sped along. Completely disregarding any concerns for safety, those passengers were invariably quite cheerful about their mode of carriage. You'll find an illustration of such a situation on my website.

Many, many trucks in Zambia had a tendency to travel with their front wheels in one lane, and the back wheels in another!

Yes, driving in Zambia could be an entertaining experience.

I STILL HAD THE USE OF BIG BOY AT THE RANCH FOR A COUPLE MORE WEEKS before Heather and David's lads came home from boarding school. One of the weekends promised to be pretty busy for me.

There was a jumping practice session on the Saturday, then on Sunday an organised breakfast ride. This was when a whole bunch of folk would go out for a ride together starting at about 7:30, and when they returned two or three hours later, some kind soul feeds them all breakfast. On this occasion one of the members who lived fairly close to the showgrounds offered for the breakfast to be held at his house, the only trouble was, he apparently wasn't much of a chef. I'm not sure how this happened but Ziggy managed to 'volunteer' to cook the breakfasts there.

What made this weekend more action-packed for me was that if I wanted to participate in all this I first had to get Big Boy to the showgrounds.

I drove to Heather and David's place early on Friday morning so that I could ride Big Boy the seven miles into town before the December heat kicked in. When I'd ridden him around the farm I had become quite familiar with the location of which gates led off their land onto less travelled dirt roads, so when I set off I had a pretty fair idea of which directions to take.

As we ambled down one unfamiliar track I came across a small compound of maybe 15-20 shacks.

A compound is an informal housing settlement. These are common on the outskirts of urban areas. While there are large compounds with small brick-built homes, the smaller compounds were usually occupied by the poorest of the poor Zambians, and their homes consisted of very roughly-built shacks. These are usually quite small by necessity because many of them did not have load-bearing walls to carry a proper roof. In most cases a roof will comprise several pieces of battered hoarding or corrugated iron fastened together, protected from lifting in the wind by old tyres placed on the top. There is little or no running water, electricity or sewage system in these informal compounds.

On the edge of this particular compound there stood a boy of about 11-12 years.

"Hello, how are you?"

"I am good, madam," he said.

"I wonder if you can help me," I asked.

"Me, madam?"

"Yes. Can you tell me, am I on the right track to get to Kaunda Square?"

"Yes, madam. I will show you the best way. Follow me on your horse."

"Thank you. What is your name?"

"Mulilo, madam. Mulilo Ngoni." He said standing proudly to attention.

I duly followed Mulilo Ngoni on my horse.

A stray mzungu madam on a horse around your home territory,

whilst not unknown, was not something that Zambian children encountered frequently.

"Why are you going to Kaunda Square madam?"

"I'm not actually going *there*," I explained, "but I know I need to pass by there on my journey."

"Where is your journey going to end?"

"Oh, just at the Lusaka Showgrounds Mulilo."

"There are many horses there, madam. I have never ridden a horse, but I am not afraid of them." With this statement he drew himself up to full height.

"But you must be careful around horses Mulilo, some like to kick and they can hurt you."

At this he moved away very slightly.

Within five minutes there were scores of children following behind us, all shouting "horsey", "horsey", "horsey" non-stop at the tops of their voices.

After passing beside Kaunda Square we eventually reached the main road where I thanked Mulilo for his help and continued along the wide grass verge which ran beside the Great East Road. The mass of kids continued to follow me.

It's the biggest wonder we didn't cause a traffic pile-up because all the passing drivers were looking goggle-eyed at this unusual sight of a mounted Pied Piper of Lusaka.

But the spectacle was soon brought to a halt when one of the kids decided to throw a stone at the horse shouting, "Run, run". Fortunately, instead of hitting Big Boy, the stone hit my leg.

I swung around in the saddle and shouted about the stupidity of the idiot who had thrown the stone, which could have caused one of the nearest kids to get kicked.

The reaction was unbelievable. As one, they turned and ran. I can only liken this sight to a cartoon drawing of pellets being sprayed out of a shotgun.

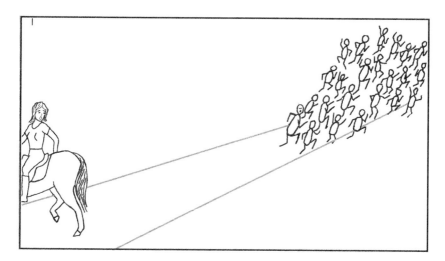

Way back down the road they stopped and turned, staring after me as I rode off into the sunset.

Well not sunset exactly, as it was only 9:00 in the morning, but you get my drift.

From then on I continued my ride in wonderful silence, apart from the occasional encouraging toots of passing vehicles. You certainly could not afford to ride a nervous horse around there.

Arriving at the showgrounds I gave Big Boy some carrot treats I had in my pocket, then handed him over to a groom for a cooling hose-down before being released into a paddock for the rest of the day.

I relaxed in the clubhouse until I could scrounge a lift to collect my car from the ranch.

The jumping practice on the Saturday went very well. On Sunday there were sixteen of us on the breakfast ride and we had a fabulous time.

Whilst I was riding, Ziggy had been slaving over several braais cooking up breakfast, which consisted of braai-ed bacon and sausages, as well as tomatoes, beans, mushrooms, hash browns, fried eggs and toast.

Apart from all of us on the ride, by the time husbands/wives/kids had joined us Ziggy finished up selling over 30 breakfasts; the participants drank the poor sod whose house it was out of beer, and the (questionably) vast sum of K20 was raised to boost LGC funds.

Still, it was fun.

On Monday morning I went along to the stables to collect Big Boy to ride him back to the farm, only to find that despite having been told on Sunday not to, the bloody groom had taken him out of the stable and put him in the cross-country paddock with dozens of other horses, and Big Boy didn't like to be caught! After a considerable time, Mathias and several other grooms managed to herd him back to the stable block. I was just about to shout at the groom for bringing the wrong horse when I recognised the shape of Big Boy's face. That was the only thing about him which was recognisable!

He must have found the cross-country water jump, which was by now just a huge puddle of mud, and swam in it. He was absolutely covered from the tip of his tail to the end of his nose in brown sludge. It was as if a giant had picked him up by the tips of his ears then dipped him into a vast tank of brown paint, it was so evenly dispersed. Thankfully it must have happened quite recently as it hadn't yet had time to fully dry on him. Even so, the time it would take for Mathias to hose him down to his normal white grey colour and dry him off sufficiently to be tacked up, would mean I'd be riding him in the full heat of the midday sun. Not good for either of us.

I eventually set off at quarter past three and, sod my luck, half an hour into the ride it started to rain. Fortunately I had taken the precaution of strapping a recently-acquired army cape to the saddle.

I had quite a struggle trying to put it on, and as soon as Big Boy caught sight of it flapping about behind him he got all jittery. Naturally the more he tried to move away from it the more it flapped. What a bloody performance. Luckily the rain turned out to be a relatively short shower so I was soon able to take it off.

This action also scared the crap out of him, and the more he jumped around the more difficulty I had trying to fold it up. It was an absolute scream.

I eventually managed to get it into a shape that I could sit on, securing pokey-out bits under the stirrup straps to prevent it sliding off the saddle.

Even without the encouragement of flying fabric behind him, Big Boy, realising that he was on his way home, proceeded at quite a cracking pace and we completed the journey in just under two hours.

Of course you will have realised that the garment I was sitting on was wet from the rain, so by the time we arrived at the McCleery homestead my pants looked like I'd peed myself! Oh, how they laughed!

Ah, yes. The joys of horse riding.

13

ENTER THE DRAGON!

I tried to restrict my riding at the McCleerys to when it wouldn't impact on the rest of the family, so would go in the mornings after the kids were settled at school. Sometimes Heather would join me, riding Rumtum, and show me different trails and accesses around the property. It was lovely riding country.

If she had other plans for her morning I would tootle off by myself, holding intellectual conversations with Big Boy, who always agreed with me. You could tell because he nodded as he walked along.

While this was going on I was still keeping my ear to the ground for a horse to buy.

Many people in the horse community were well established in Zambia and would not be leaving the country so rarely sold their horses, and horse breeders in Zambia were virtually non-existent. So like most other commodities they had to be imported. Most of the polo ponies in Zambia were thoroughbred horses usually bought from the Zimbabwe race tracks.

One evening when we were at the club David said he'd heard Otmar had recently brought in a couple of horses and might have one to sell.

The very next day I spoke to Otmar when he confirmed that he had recently bought a mare to use as a polo pony but, in his words, "She isn't suited to polo". I went to see her.

She was a lovely bay, standing at 15.2 hands high and her name was Dragon's Tail!

What? Are you serious? Who could give such a pretty horse a name like that? From the day she became my horse she would be known as Tilly.

That night I explained to Ziggy how our collective lives would be so enriched by the inclusion of a large animal and all the entrapments and associated 'fun', and that we must make this once-in-a-lifetime purchase at once. He didn't put up much of a fight and the deal was done the following day.

So I had a horse. Now I had to find a stable and a groom to look after her. All the members of the Gymkhana Club had grooms for their horse/s.

Someone mentioned to me that there was a woman who had several stables at LGC and did livery, which covered all basic requirements of stabling, bedding, feeding and grooming for a monthly fee, the only extras for me being veterinarian issues and shoeing. Luckily she had a stable going spare.

The other thing which was difficult to come by was the tack, possibly even more so than a horse, as it too had to be imported, so tack was rarely sold on by horse owners. At that time decent quality tack was only available to me from either South Africa or the UK. Knowing that I would likely be getting my own horse when I had recently been in the UK, I had gone along to a substantial stockist and set myself up with 'stuff'.

"I'm looking for a saddle."

"OK. What sort? Jumping, dressage, general purpose, horse or pony....."

"It's for a horse and I think I had better get a general purpose saddle." I said to the knowledgeable assistant.

"What size is your horse?" she asked.

"I don't know. I haven't got one yet."

"Excuse me? You're buying a saddle for a horse you don't have?"

"Yes, you see," I went on, "I live in Zambia," as if that explained everything.

She looked at me funny.

"I'm going to buy one when I get back in a couple of weeks, and I reckon it will probably be about 14.2 to 15.2 hands high. I don't want anything too big or I won't be able to get on it." I told her.

She gave me another funny look as if she thought I was a bit insane (as if!) but led me to a section of the store housing the general-purpose saddles.

"Any of these might be suitable then," she said, pointing to half a dozen saddles.

I chose one with a recessed pommel (the bit at the front) just in case I bought a horse which had high withers (the boney bit between the shoulder blades, which is also where the height of a horse is measured).

I bought the various components of a bridle, with an assortment of bits I might need depending on the horse I got, as well as grooming kit and other stuff. I was going to have fun fitting this lot into a suitcase!

In the event a crate of 'unaccompanied baggage' was utilised.

Actually, I think an explanation of unaccompanied baggage is called for, as I don't believe I mentioned this wondrous facility in either of my other books.

It was exactly as it sounded, having bags (suitcases or even cardboard boxes) which were checked in at the same time as you checked in for your flight, except you had special tickets for them to be put on a flight, most likely a different one to the one you were taking, hence 'unaccompanied'. This was a wonderful way of avoiding paying excess baggage on your cases, and all importantly, the unaccompanied baggage vouchers could be paid for in kwacha at the same time as you bought your air ticket, the only criteria being that you actually did have an air ticket. (Otherwise you could have posted the UBVs over to your family in the UK and have them send out cases of stuff any old time you liked).

Anyway, back to the horse…

It didn't take long for me to discover exactly why Tilly had been considered "unsuitable for polo". Obviously I don't know if you have ever watched a game of polo, but I am actually ashamed to say that even to this day I have not. However I do know it involves eight fellows on horses galloping up and down a field only 150 yards wide by 270 long. And it involves a lot of sudden stopping and turning. It was the stopping bit which Tilly had the problem with.

It would appear that she'd taken this racehorse background thing to heart, and once she got onto a piece of open ground she took this as an indication to tear away at a flat-out gallop. And she didn't want to stop until she'd won whatever race was in her head at the time.

One of the nice things about Tilly was that despite being a smallish horse she had a lovely long stride. I had ridden horses in my life which had short strides, and if you were out in a group you were forever having to trot to keep up with the rest. I did not find that fun. But the opposite applied to Tilly insofar as she could make her way to the front of a group with no effort whatsoever, which was not something I always wanted to do. This was chiefly because she really didn't like it if another horse got too close behind her as we went along in single file. It was not unknown for her to lash out with a rear hoof if she was crowded from behind.

Now that I had my own horse there was rarely a day when I didn't ride. Sometimes I would just ride around the racetrack with one or two of the other members, but doing that solo was about as interesting as watching your toenails grow. I much preferred to go for a wander into the bundu if I had time. Which was often.

As I mentioned earlier, our house wasn't far from LGC, nor was it far from the bundu.

Leaving the club I would mosey on out the gate and turn right up the Great East Road until there was a point in the traffic which allowed us to cross the four lanes. [The Great East Road was amazingly wide in comparison to other Lusaka routes at that time.] Just over a mile up the road we would turn left into Libala Road, then carry on until we reached Lukanga Road where our house sat on a corner. I would invariably call in for a coffee and Tilly would enjoy munching our grass as she was left to wander freely around the garden.

Back in the mid '80s there were only two or three roads of conventional housing north of us before we reached open ground. I loved riding out there. There were a few well-trodden paths which had been formed by years of people making their way to goodness only knows where. A scarcity of trees in the area meant there was very little birdlife. The only sounds came from Tilly's hooves on a path, the crackling of dried scrub underfoot where there was no path, or an unseen dog barking way off in the distance. I loved the tranquillity of those rides.

One day I was taking a previously untravelled open route and we were walking down a shallow dip towards a small ridge when I began to get a sinking feeling. Three more steps forward and Tilly was up to her knees in mud. I didn't dare dismount, not knowing how soft the ground would be to either side of her. The last thing we needed was for both of us to be stuck in mud.

"Okay Tilly, good girl," I said softly, trying not to engender a state of panic. "Let's go this way, shall we?" I said, slowly indicating with the reins that she should turn (towards home). Still sinking, she tried to shift her front legs, initially without success, but eventually managed to move a couple of steps to the right. I kept encouraging her quietly but her back legs were sinking in deeper. She strained and pushed forwards with her shoulders and with a sudden yank managed to free one of her back legs. Then she strained even harder before extracting the other leg and leapt forward in three bounds to get clear of the area. I was never so proud of that horse.

Once on terra firma I let her stand for as long as she wanted. As I looked back at where we had been, apart from slightly longer grass, there was really no indication that a marshy area lay there. As I was still feeling a little shaken by the experience myself, I decided to return to the stables.

To the north-east of our house there was an informal compound. We had to cross a stream on the edge of the settlement. I was amazed when Tilly walked into it without any hesitation after her previous harrowing experience. We often returned this way from our bundu-bashing trips and small children would watch with a mix of fascination and fear as Tilly picked her way through the rocks in the riverbed. While many Zambian children unfamiliar with horses were in the habit of throwing stones, these kids were not like that, but I cringed as I saw some of them playing in the horribly polluted water.

Back at the stables the groom immediately wanted to know what had happened. As I dismounted I could see why he was concerned. The mud on Tilly's back legs reached almost all the way up to belly height. That must have been quite a close call.

Looking back on it, I was amazed at how calm we had both remained during the episode

When I wasn't out enjoying the bundu there was plenty going on at LGC to enjoy with friends, especially at the weekends.

When there were no official events there would be workshops, usually for show jumping, most of them for beginner horses or riders. Rarely a month went by when there wasn't something official going on somewhere, so you needed all the practice you could get.

On top of this a regular crowd used to go for outrides beyond the confines of the showgrounds. These would normally range from two to eight participants. Beyond eight it got rather difficult to control.

Talking of 'difficult to control' leads me nicely into a little story of one outride:

One weekend some of us decided to ride to City Airport. From what I knew (very little) City Airport was restricted to light private aircraft, chiefly due to size at that time I suspect. I think our President used it occasionally too, for some military stuff.

The airfield was surrounded by a wide, deep donga. This was obviously a security measure. It was actually so deep that people on horses walking along it wouldn't be seen unless you were close to it. There were only a couple of areas where we could negotiate our way diagonally down and up the steep sides, but once there we could ride around the periphery of the airfield, at the end furthest from view, with relative impunity. Because it was reasonably well maintained and the grass was kept short it meant we could have a nice canter without having to worry about our horses stomping into hidden holes.

One of the problems with outrides, or even riding around our racetrack, was the hazard of termite holes. Termites would burrow into the ground, accessed by a hole sometimes no bigger than an egg cup, but underneath a huge cavity could be excavated. Generally you wouldn't know it was there until your horse, with some weight pressing down if you were cantering, stood on it and it caved in. Then you would have a horse with a broken leg, possibly the rider too! So for this reason we only cantered along stretches of ground which we knew to be clear.

Anyway, we asked around to see who wanted to go on this trek and about six of us did. Much to my dismay (or I think 'horror' would be a more appropriate word) one of them was a lady also named Anne, but with an 'e'. She was a very nice lady but despite being the eldest in the group, she was very 'forward going' as we would describe her if she were a horse. Full of energy and enthusiasm she would go tearing off on her horse at every opportunity.

The leader of our pack, I think it might have been Penny, stressed to her that we were only going to be cantering, NOT GALLOPING, at the airfield.

"No, no. I understand. That's okay." Anne had said.

So off we set. It was a lovely ride there. After carefully negotiating our way into the donga we climbed up its slope about midway down the airfield and peered over the edge to make sure there was no sign of military. All was clear.

We gathered together on the edge.

"Okay," said Penny "we'll set off in pairs at a trot then progress into a nice controlled canter down to the bottom of the airfield."

"Okay."

"Yes."

"Got it."

We set off. We hadn't done more than a couple of strides at a canter when suddenly…

"Yay! Wahhoo! Eeehaaaaa!" Anne yelled at the top of her voice, elbows flapping wildly, reins snaking up in the air and legs flailing by her horse's flanks like windmills. And she was gone.

So were the rest of us.

On hearing this commotion all the other horses must have thought it meant them too, and fairly leapt out of their sedate canter into a flat-out gallop. I was absolutely terrified.

Everyone was yelling at Anne, and at their mounts, trying to bring them under control. The theory is that they could be turned in a circle to compel a slowdown.

Once Tilly took off she remembered she was a racehorse and nothing was going to slow her down until she'd won the race. We passed Mad Anne as if she was out for a leisurely stroll. I dared not entertain the idea of trying to turn Tilly at the speed she was going as she'd likely somersault over sideways. The end of the airfield was rapidly approaching - complete with the very deep and wide donga. Even the best horse in the world would not be able to jump *that* gap.

Then Tilly seemed to realise she'd out-run all the competition and began to slow. Thankfully this was sufficient for me to steer her gradually off to the right, where we completed a large semi-circle slowing her further until we were eventually facing back the way we came. I think she must have sated her appetite for speed because she was then happy to canter sedately back to the others.

"Bloody hell Ann, I thought you were a gonner!"

"Jeez, missus, what was that?"

"I've never seen a horse go so fast."

"I didn't think you were going to stop. Weren't you scared?" One look at my white face and shaking hands answered that stupid question.

I won't repeat what I said to the Wild Woman of Lusaka.

THE NEXT HIGHLIGHT IN OUR CALENDAR WAS CHRISTMAS. I REALLY DIDN'T want my dad to spend it at home on his own, even though he would have had Doris for company. It would hardly be a 'Merry' Christmas just the two of them without my mum, but rather a harsh reminder of her absence. We bought my dad an air ticket so that he could come and join us amongst our crowd of friends. Doris wasn't so lucky as, now being in her 80s, travel insurance would be a problem, so we arranged for her to spend Christmas with her daughter Betty.

My dad was well occupied prior to his flight, shopping for the various gifts I asked him to bring out. It was wonderful to have him with us and he was soon embraced by the LGC community.

Even so, Christmas day looked like it could turn into a rather flat affair with just the six of us to share the day. However, a couple of days before this we were in the club and Clive Fenton asked us what we were doing on Christmas day. When I told him we had nothing planned he insisted that we should all join him and Margaret and, it transpired, about everyone else we knew, at their house on Christmas Day, which apparently had become a regular feature on the LGC calendar.

We had a fabulous time there with all our friends; eating, drinking and playing ludicrously rowdy games.

My dad's stay with us was limited to just a couple of weeks so we didn't have any excursions planned. Even so, the time flew by and we reluctantly waved him goodbye just a few days into New Year.

ANOTHER CHRISTMAS BONUS WAS THAT WE SOON HAD BIG BOY BACK ON lease as the McCleery lads weren't home for long. This time we kept him at the LGC stables, as Heather had agreed he would be suitable for the children. Fortunately, he also came in handy for me when, to my dismay, Tilly went lame. We weren't sure what caused it but she was out of action for ten days, so when I found there was an informal show going on I was delighted to be able to participate on Big Boy.

14

FIRST ATTEMPT AT CROSS-COUNTRY (IT WASN'T, BUT IT WAS)

Tuesday 28 Jan '86 - night-time

Dear Mev, Doris et al,

I was going to start off by saying that it seems ages since I wrote anyone a letter but that would be an understatement. It IS ages since I wrote a letter to anyone!

The weekend after you left us, Mev, Ziggy set off early to Kitwe on business, as planned. There was a two-phase event taking place at LGC so I went along armed with a coolbag full of beers, deck-chair, crossword book, raincoat, sunhat and a varied assortment of clothing. The reason for this is that I was expecting to get roped in as a jump judge for the day's cross-country event as Tilly was once again incapacitated. A couple of days previous we found her limping and eventually tracked this down to her having a thorn stuck in the frog (soft centre) of one of her hooves, and it had become infected, so I took her to Chris Oparaocha, the local vet, where she received an injection of antibiotics.

Knowing that all the competitors were due to walk the course at 09:30 I decided to get there at 08:00 so that I could take Tilly to the vet for her second antibiotic injection before all the fun started. The vet, it seemed, was running late, like he wasn't there yet. I figured I had plenty of time to nip home and collect the kids, who had still been eating their breakfasts when I left, and get back to try for the vet again.

Returning to the LGC I found that the vet had now arrived, and had about twenty other patients, judging by the number of cars parked outside. I went over to the stables and asked the groom to take Tilly along to the vet saying I'd join him there once the queue died down a bit.

While waiting for him to get his arse into gear I spotted a group of folk chatting over by Margaret Fenton's stables, so went and joined them. During the course of conversation Margaret very kindly offered to let me use one of her horses, Casanova, for the day's events. I had ridden him previously, not without some difficulty, and had also heard that he loved cross-country, in that he went round it at a flat-out gallop, so was a little reluctant to take up Margaret's offer.

Then one of my friends in the group, Robin Goreham – you remember him Mev, (no?) has a very strong Queen's English' accent and is Deputy Commissioner at the British High Commission - asked me if I'd like to ride his horse, who was named First Attempt. Apart from sounding very appropriate, since I'd never ridden him before, I recalled someone telling me the previous week that she had ridden him, and that he was quite a good jumper.

As Robin explained that he was unable to commit himself to the full day's events, I happily accepted his kind offer.

At this, one of the other ladies said "But you can't go riding in a competition like that, (I was wearing jeans) you must wear jodphurs." I knew she was pulling my leg as this wasn't an official show but I thought what the hell, I had time to nip home again and change as the groom had only just walked past, taking Tilly to the vet. So for the second time I dashed off home and was back inside eight minutes, suitably attired.

Fortunately, just as I arrived back the vet came out of his

surgery to give Tilly her penicillin jab. Except she wasn't having any of it. As soon as she saw him she must have remembered what had happened the day before. Every time the vet came near she pulled away, backwards. The vet told the groom to catch hold of one of her ears, a move which he said incapacitates a horse without fail. Tilly had obviously heard this one before too and reared up each time the groom stretched his arm up. By the time he had hold of an ear the bloody vet had disappeared inside the surgery to take a phone call. We both frantically shouted him that we had Tilly under control and he promptly abandoned the phone and dashed over to pump Tilly's shoulder full of penicillin. After expressing hasty thanks to the vet I left the groom to return the horse to the stable while I tore off in the direction of the cross-country course.

Mev, you might recall when you were here, I competed on Big Boy in a cross-country competition, in fact I'm sure you'll remember because I won first place, but there were only 22 fences. This time there were 30!

By the time I got to the course the other riders were already well into their walk-the-course, so I had to cut a few corners to join in. Then just as we reached the end I saw some late-comers starting off so decided I'd better join them to find out what fences I had missed at the beginning. By the time I finished walking round I hardly felt like doing it on a horse, but putting whichever was my best foot forward, I shuffled off to collect my mount.

First Attempt was a lovely-looking chestnut gelding, but as soon as I was on his back and began to walk I felt it might take more than a first attempt to get him over some of the fences. Compared to Tilly it was like riding a tortoise. Just trying to get him to trot around the practice arena left me knackered.

I eventually persuaded him over a couple of practice jumps and was pleasantly surprised to find that getting him to jump was easy once you managed to get him going. I felt we were as ready as we'd ever be for this party.

There were four classifications of entrants; child riders, newcomers, grade E and grade D. Although Firsty would normally be classified as E grade, Jenny Dodgson suggested that I should enter into the newcomers class seeing as I had never ridden him before. As she was an 'official' of the event I was happy to take her advice. As the classes took place in the order I mentioned above, I knew I would be starting fairly soon as there were very few child riders entered.

As I checked with Graham Wallace (who was the official Starter) that he had me on his list, to see when I would go in, the bell sounded for the next competitor to get onto the course. That was me!

In an absolute panic I shot off up the entrance chute to the course, passing a group of friends at about 40mph. As we approached the first fence I could hear a load of voices shouting at me from behind, saying what I hadn't the faintest idea. We were off.

One thing Robin kindly thought to mention to me as I was labouring my way around the practice arena was that "Firsty can be a bit difficult to get going away from home". Now he tells me, I'd thought.

So as we started our journey around the thirty fences, every time we were pointed towards 'home' he went faster, but as soon as I turn him in the opposite direction he slowed right down. I couldn't remember the last time I worked so bloody hard on a horse.

To give him his due, once we were well into the course it was quite easy to maintain a good steady pace.

As this was an unofficial event as far as the Zambia Horse Society was concerned, the club was trying out a new method of timing, part of which necessitated two horses being on the course at the same time. Once one was halfway round the course the next one started, then when the front horse had completed his round the next one went in. That worked fine unless you had a fast horse following a slow one, or followed a horse which had a few refusals along the way. Of course I had to cop for it, didn't I?

We were about halfway through a section of the course which I wasn't too sure about when I rounded a bend and suddenly there was another horse in front of me. What on earth do I do now, I thought, or words to that effect. I had a vague recollection of someone saying that if you came across another competitor during cross-country you should overtake, and that the offending party must allow you to do so.

The horse and rider were about twenty metres in front of me heading towards the biggest row of truck tyres you've ever seen, and the said horse didn't like the look of them at all and ducked out to the left. I hoped Firsty didn't think this was what he should do too. Fortunately he didn't and sailed over the tyres without so much as a blink.

Next I came to a fence which Heather was marshalling and as I approached she remarked how well we were doing, and that we were ahead on speed. I was so busy listening to her that I lost touch with what I was doing - like trying to ride a horse in a competition - and the bloody thing almost stopped at the next fence! Furious with myself I was determined that wasn't going to happen again, so I continued around the course with intense concentration.

One thing I should mention is that the course varies slightly at odd times, in that many fences consisted of two jumps side-by-side, one for use by competitors up to grade E, and the other one, higher or broader (or both), to be tackled by grade D or C riders. On approaching fence 28 I realised I was on the wrong side of a bush which separated two fences and was committed to the D Grade fence. Amazingly we sailed over it, though I really didn't feel like I could go on much longer,

We eventually popped over the final fence into the jumping arena, which signified the end of the cross-country course. A couple of people commented that we had completed it in a fast time.

It didn't feel like it to me! I had never felt so exhausted in my life. I was heaving for breath so much that I thought I was on the verge of a heart attack. After patting and hugging (mostly for support) my horse, he was led away by the groom to be given a well-deserved hosing down, while I repaired to the club bar to be hosed down on the inside with a cold beer.

Fortunately, having competed so early it meant we had a good long wait until we had to be up and running again for the show-jumping leg. As that wasn't starting until 2:30 I even had time for a tasty lunch of steak and chips with the kids in the clubhouse.

Perhaps I should mention that while I was out and about enjoying knocking myself out on a horse, my kids were not totally abandoned. There was always a responsible adult friend who was willing and available to 'keep an eye on them' for me. And they always found something fun to do with their friends at this wonderful place.

Again, I was one of the early entrants in the show jumping arena and amazingly had a clear round (little thanks to me, I almost missed a fence out). Very pleased with my temporary mount's performance I rode him back to his stable where he could enjoy a well-earned rest, a handful of carrots and a netful of hay.

I then collected Tilly from her stable and led her to a quiet corner of the collecting ring where she was able to munch on some juicy grass, and I could watch the remaining contestants in the arena nearby.

You could have knocked me down with a feather when one of the organisers came over to me and said that my first attempt at riding First Attempt had got us First Prize for the 2-phase Event, Newcomers Grade.

This was quite embarrassing. I had only entered two competitions since becoming a member of LGC and got first prize both times. As much as I liked it, it'd be one hell of a standard to maintain!

And as euphoric as all this made me feel, I was so yearning for the chance to put Tilly through her paces on something like this, regardless of what she achieved. It would mean **so** much more to actually do it on my own horse.

Talking of kids (well I was, half a dozen paragraphs back), they were now having official riding lessons.

When riding lessons were first discussed with them they had all immediately said that they didn't want to have lessons with Lorraine, as she terrified them. As they were still quite young I had to concede that such a fierce instructor might prove to be counter-productive in this regard. Another member I had befriended, Jenny Dodgson (or Jenny D as she was known, to differentiate from Jenny Fenton, aka Jen Fen), also gave lessons to children and we all agreed that she would be perfect for them. But one lesson a week wouldn't give them anywhere near as much riding as they liked, which was why I'd hired Big Boy.

In a short space of time they were all doing very well. Brad was keeping at or just above average standard; Leon was doing the best of the three at that point, with an incredibly good sense of balance; Vicki, although slightly behind Leon as far as accomplishment was concerned, was the keenest of the three, taking every opportunity she could to ride.

She was over the moon if the boys wanted to stay at home and play of an afternoon, because it meant she would be able to ride Big Boy and come out with me around the track. One weekend was a classic, as I explained in the letter to my dad.

15

HAPPY BIRTHDAY

Dear Mev and Doris,

A quick note as we have someone flying to UK tonight who will post this, though having said that, I sometimes wonder whether it's worth it as I gather some UK posted letters have taken longer to get to you than the Zambian post office variety.

It's Friday morning and I have masses yet to do ready for tomorrow, being Vicki and Leon's birthday party day. I haven't finished Vicki's party dress yet as my sewing machine broke down half way through making it yesterday. As soon as I've finished this letter I have to go to the repair shop to see if they've managed to fix it.

I've been quite busy at LGC, moving stables. I was paying a woman K180 p/m per horse for livery but she was hardly ever there checking up on her grooms, so they skived off a lot, so guess what? Muggins was doing most of the work! At that price I don't bloody think so! So I've now rented three stables (one for storing food/bedding) and have hired a groom (Kenias) who is working well, so far.

Then of course there's the new horse. As you know, Ziggy had said that we should get a pony of our own for the kids rather than just keep hiring Big Boy, who has to 'go home' when Simon and Jonathan are out from the UK during school holidays.

I found one who looks a lot like Nannette, the second pony I had as a kid, except she's a grey roan rather than a strawberry roan (if you know what that means). She's three-and-a-half years old. We weren't expecting to take her until May but apparently she's ready now and the owners have asked me to take her sooner.

The only trouble is they live on a farm about thirty miles away and the last sixteen of those consist of the worst dirt road I have ever had the misfortune to drive on, and that's saying a lot after all I've driven on over these last few years. It is essential to go there in a 4-wheel-drive vehicle to avoid ending up in a ditch or having the bottom knocked out of your car. I'm having trouble finding someone with horse transport who's willing to do the run.

On a totally different note, the kids are still doing very well at school. Brad has just joined the cub scouts. Having had his name on the waiting list for over a year, I hope he finds it was worth waiting for.

Well must dash now and fetch my sewing machine so I can finish Vicki's dress before she gets home from school.

 Well that was a waste of bloody time. The woman who was going to post your letter for me didn't come into the club before flying out, so it's been sitting on the mantelpiece.

It is now Sunday night. The party went very well yesterday, eventually. I woke at 04:00 with a terrible sore throat. I think there's a 'bug' going round at the moment as Brad was off school with it on Thursday. Anyway, I forced myself out of bed at 6:45 having spent the previous couple of hours sucking on throat lozenges, and immediately started to

make Leon's trousers for the party (I'd made his shirt the night before, after finishing Vicki's dress).

At 9:00 I had to break off sewing to take Kasongo, our gardener, down to LGC to help with a massive clear-up they were having in preparation for a forthcoming big event over Easter weekend. Then I brought my groom to our house to show him where we lived, so he could bring Big Boy along to ours later in the afternoon of the party. Then I did a bit of last minute shopping (and embarrassingly ran out of money!) before returning home to finish the sewing.

At about 11:00 I had a phone call from one of Vicki's friends asking if she could be dropped off early for the party, like straight away. While I really would have preferred not to have guests so early, she was normally a fairly quiet child so I agreed. Alas, when she was dropped off her father spotted me outside the kitchen door and came all the way down the drive. I thought 'he's just going to explain why he needs to drop his daughter off so early' but no. He got out of his car 'just to say hello', I now thought.

I politely (though hoping he wouldn't accept) asked him if he would like to come inside for a drink, and to my horror he said he would. THREE brandy and Cokes later, having noticed that we 'had sons' he calmly said he'd go home and fetch his only son and bring him to join the party! I didn't dare say we'd already got more than enough guests coming, in case he thought I was being a racist. Add to that the fact that during our conversations over the three brandies I had discovered he was a CABINET MINISTER, I figured I'd better let him get on with it.

With so much still to do, I made sure that I was taking a shower when he returned, to avoid a further three brandies' disruption. However I was not overly impressed when I walked into the lounge, to discover that he'd not only dropped off his son, but another daughter too! I later found out that this 'invite yourself along' approach was the Zambian way. I do wish someone had mentioned this custom to me before.

For ease I had decided to serve beefburgers, together with a few chips in paper cones, to the kids, but as numbers had increased somewhat I hadn't made enough so had to dive into the deep freezer and fish out some hotdogs, which was a fair alternative if it weren't for the fact that I didn't have any hotdog-shaped bread to serve them in. Fortunately I had recently added bread-making to my culinary skills and for good measure had taught Benton how to do it too, so I was able to get him to make some extra rolls. The plan was to have as much as possible part-cooked in advance so that the food would only need to be finished off on the hot braai.

What is it they say about 'the best laid plans...'? When Ziggy got around to cooking the burgers later in the afternoon he couldn't light the braai because the charcoal was damp from a downpour we'd had earlier in the week. This was despite my having got Kasongo to spread it out on the driveway in the full sun to dry it off two days ago. Ziggy repaired to the kitchen.

In the meantime Kenias had arrived on the dot of 3:00 with Big Boy. All the kids were thrilled to be able to ride him around the garden. Those who didn't know how to ride were led around by Kenias. Benton was enthralled by all of this so I asked him if he'd like a go. He apprehensively accepted the offer but loved it and after being led around had his photograph taken on the horse for posterity. Alas, I don't seem to have a copy.

Horse and groom eventually left just before five, but big black clouds were looming overhead so I lent him Ziggy's raincoat to be on the safe side. It was as well I did because five minutes later the heavens opened.

As is our normal procedure we had also invited several of our friends to come round for a drink and bite to eat; they arrived in dribs and drabs during late afternoon. Ziggy was reaching the tail-end of his stint in the kitchen when suddenly the power went off. Thank goodness it hadn't happened earlier or we'd have been well and truly stuffed with wet charcoal and *a now 'nonelectric' stove! The rest of the night was illuminated by paraffin lamps.*

In a moment of madness I had promised to give Vicki and Leon breakfast (of their choice) in bed on the morning of their actual birthday (Sunday) so was up bright and early, thankfully to restored power. The little darlings had, of course, chosen to have a full English, along with freshly squeezed orange juice.

Anyway I'm off. And I'll post this the conventional way now.

Love, Me xxxxx

As well as a sumptuous breakfast in bed, Vicki and Leon received another treat on their eighth birthday, although this one came as quite a surprise. Somehow, through his South Africa and transport connections, Ziggy had managed to buy them each a bike.

He had hidden the bikes in his office for the previous week and nipped out to fetch them while the kids were enjoying their breakfasts.

Once up and dressed they were told to wait patiently on the patio for a few moments. They were absolutely thrilled to bits when their dad appeared from around the corner of the house, pushing two gleaming BMX bicycles.

Although (being the end of March) it seemed like an awfully long way off, Ziggy decided it was time he organised his end-of-contract leave. In September it would be two years since he started working for Mutende. He spoke to Mr Siame who agreed to the dates Ziggy suggested.

My dad had recently been on holiday to Menorca with his brother and sister-in-law, Bernard and Rita, and said what a lovely time they'd had. It was suggested that we join them on a holiday there during our next visit home. We agreed that was a splendid idea and plans were put in place. Bernard would organise it all and just tell us how much money to hand over.

We would depart Zambia on 8th August and spend three weeks in Burton before going on a two-week holiday with Mev and Bernard and Rita to Menorca. Our return flight to Lusaka was booked for 22nd September.

ONE DAY VICKI ASKED IF SHE COULD USE THE TYPEWRITER TO WRITE TO Nannan. She didn't do too bad for a beginner, though I set the caps lock on the machine so she wouldn't have to remember how to capitalise at the start of her sentences.

DEAR NANNAN
THIS IS VICKI TYPING
WEHAVE GOT A NEW PONY HER NAME IS PANNASTRA
WE GOT HERON SUNDAY THE XX 13TH APRIL.
I HOPE YOU HAVE SETTLED AT THE HOSPITAL, AND
IHOPE YOUR LEG IS NOT TOO PAINFUL.
THANK YOU FOR THE BIRTHDAY CARD. BIG BOY THEX
HORSEXX CAME TO OUR BIRTHDAY PARTY SO THAT WE
COULD HAVE A RIDE. WE HAD SWIMMING RACES TOO.
SORRY I HAVE TO STOPP WRITING THIS LETTER I HAVE
TO STOP SO THAT LEON CAN LAY THE TABLE.
X IT IS NOW A FTER LUNCH SO I CAN WRITE SOME MORE.
WE HAD FISH WITH TOMATO AND CHIPS. DADDY CAME
HOME LATE SO HE ATE HIS LUNCH AT 3'o'CLOCK.
NOW I AM GOING TO TELL YOU A POEM.
POEM
ROSES ARE RED
VIOLETS ARE BLUE
SUGAR IS SWEET
AND SO ARE YOU
GOOD BY SEE YOU WHEN I XX COME FORMY HOLIDAYS
MENY KISSES
X FROM VICKI
X X X X X X X X X X X X X

WHICH REMINDS ME THAT I DIDN'T TELL YOU ABOUT MY GRANDMOTHER'S mishap. Apparently she was reaching the foot of the stairs at home one day when she felt a sudden snap. Her leg fractured.

We knew, from a situation many years ago, that she suffered with osteoporosis so this was always a possibility. After a few weeks in hospital she was allowed home, but it was realised that home could no longer be in our Saxon Street house with my dad, as she would be unable to tackle the stairs.

Apart from the kitchen there was only one large living room downstairs. There was no way that this could accommodate Doris's bed. The problem was discussed at some length and the decision made that Doris would go and live with her eldest daughter Betty, who had a ground-floor flat in the nearby village of Barton under Needwood and happened to have a spare bedroom. I don't think Betty was too keen on this plan, as she had had her grumpy mother-in-law living with her for almost all her married years and now, in her sixties, was enjoying her 'freedom'. Unfortunately there didn't seem to be an acceptable alternative.

16

A TRIP TO KALULUSHI

"You've got *what* in your front garden?"

"Seventeen trucks. Seventeen red and white Sisu, five-ton tipper trucks to be precise."

"What? Why?"

"Storage."

"Alright, stop messing me around now. Why on earth would you be storing seventeen damn great dump trucks in your garden? And you must have one helluva big garden!"

"We do. Let me tell you all about it."

I was talking to my friend Karin in Kitwe. Karin had not been to Lusaka since we moved there almost two years previous so she had no idea what our Lusaka residence looked like.

One project which my husband Ziggy had worked on involved fifty-five Sisu trucks.

Mutende Investments, the company he worked for, were the agents for Sisu in Zambia. FINIDA, the Finish aid project to Zambia, had very generously donated sufficient Sisu trucks to provide one for each district in the country.

After being shipped into Zambia, each truck had to be given the 'once-over' before being issued to its designated district. While waiting for this to take place the trucks needed to be parked up somewhere and you need quite a lot of space to park up fifty-five of them. While Mutende had various companies scattered around, there wasn't sufficient room within their boundaries to accommodate all the vehicles.

Having lived in Zambia for over five years at this point, we were all fully aware that you can't just leave vehicles parked up on any old piece of land near to your office. The chances were that even if they were still there the next day, they would be minus all the wheels, the batteries and probably the bulbs from the headlights too.

After every available company space had been filled with Sisu trucks, Ziggy was still left with seventeen of the buggers. And so it was that he came up with this brilliant idea of temporarily storing them in the most secure place he knew of. Our garden.

During the course of a week our garden sprouted seventeen bright, shiny, white and red, five-ton Sisu hydraulic tipper trucks and still had room for a pony. (Sorry, if that means nothing to you, it's a quip from a UK comedy series called *Keeping Up Appearances*.)

Just some of the trucks, along with Tilly, myself and Vicki, with Coke, Sally and Bass.

Suffice it to say that as garden contents go, it was different. Of course the kids thought it was great fun and Brad, in his inimitable style, said to his school pals, "Hey, you'll never guess what we've got in our garden!"

Of course they couldn't, and didn't believe him when he told them. It was only after he'd had a couple of pals round to play that the next day at school, "He wasn't kidding. He does have a load of brand new trucks in his garden. We counted seventeen!"

During this time if ever I couldn't find the kids, a wander around the garden would invariably find them inside one of the Sisus, 'driving' it somewhere. Thankfully we didn't hold the keys!

Unfortunately this didn't go down too well with our landlord, from whom we couldn't possibly hide the fleet of Sisus in view of the fact that he lived next door with only a three-foot wall separating our properties. Apparently the day after their arrival he sent a somewhat strongly-worded letter to Ziggy complaining about the trucks being parked there, and about a horse being allowed to graze in the garden too. Ziggy hadn't told me about the letter at the time, and I only found out about it a few days later when I overheard a telephone conversation he was having with our landlord after he'd had chance to cool down a bit.

Another large thing to be found in our garden was a bullfrog. At night time it made a horrendous racket which I reckon could have been heard from over a mile away. One day I went to see what was making all the noise, and located it at the bottom of the garden beneath our water tower. It was enormous - the bullfrog not the water tank, although that was pretty big too, high up on its frame.

As I neared the creature it clearly wasn't keen on company, and puffed itself up until it was almost the size of a football. I decided against getting too close and have since discovered why the dogs had not taken much interest in it. Apart from looking pretty menacing I later learnt that these bullfrogs are carnivorous and actually have nasty sharp pointy teeth which can inflict quite a nip!

THE TIME ARRIVED WHEN THE HORSE STUFF TURNED SERIOUS. SHOW TIME. Various national events were held throughout the year in the Zambian regions.

Big planning went into these events, especially for the ones taking us to other regions. Arrangements had to be made for transporting horses and grooms, as well as accommodation. And of course there were all the preparations, equipment and provisions for our own camping to be organised.

The first to hit the calendar was the Kalulushi Horse Trials on the Copperbelt. This was a three-phase event consisting of dressage, cross-country and show jumping.

The crowd from Lusaka were taking fifteen horses in total, so early on the Thursday morning we loaded them all into the back of a bloody great articulated truck, complete with all their grooms, and sent them on their way. Ziggy had managed to borrow a vehicle and trailer from work so we were able to pack all our camping gear, clothes and riding gear into the trailer, together with camping and riding gear belonging to Heather and to Jen Fen. We had been having some lovely weather of late - nice and sunny and warm - so were looking forward to our camping session.

We set off at about 11:30 but only arrived in Kalulushi at 5:00, so had quite a rush to set up camp before it got dark at 6:15. There were almost a dozen families camping so there was a pretty good atmosphere about the place, until we realised that the Kalulushi organisers had omitted to organise any catering for us for the Thursday night.

We had been told that all meals would be laid on during the weekend so I'd made no provision for food other than for tea and coffee and breakfast, and what I'd prepared for the journey up. Luckily I'd over-catered for the journey so we were able to get by on the remains of that.

Back on Wednesday someone at the club had commented that he was a little worried that his tent might not be waterproof, and received a response that it really didn't matter as the rainy season was obviously over now. Thus was planted the kiss of death.

We woke on Friday morning to find that it had been raining in the night and there was a bloody great puddle filling a hollow just inside the doorway of our tent. Judging from the sky, that wasn't all we were going to get either.

The camp site was on very slightly sloping ground, so armed with a sharp knife, stainless steel serving spoon and spatula I'd managed to scrounge, I spent a goodly part of the morning digging a channel about four inches wide by two inches deep outside the back and sides of our tent in order to direct any future watercourse around our tent instead of through it.

Then Friday afternoon was dressage time.

I am not a fan of dressage. This is probably due to the fact that I never really understood half the commands I was supposed to be giving my horse to make it do stuff correctly, so it was pretty hit and miss whether we did things right or not.

Dressage takes place within a rectangular arena. Now, as far as I'm concerned, this is where the problem starts. You see I could never remember where all the letters were.

"Letters? I thought you were supposed to ride a horse, not write letters in dressage." I hear you say. For the benefit of non-horsey readers I shall try to explain, with a little help from Google, a bit about dressage:

It would appear that there are actually two sizes of arena, the smaller one which is used for the dressage phase of eventing, and the standard one which is used for pure dressage (and major eventing competitions). Back then I didn't realise there were different sizes, but obviously we were using the smaller one.

Now these arenas have letters posted at strategic points around the rectangle and you have to do different things starting and finishing at different letters. Easy peasy, you'd think, as the letters are quite straight forward, being A-B-C-D-E-F-G-H-K-M-X.

First of all you might ask, "where are I, J and L?" Well *I* and *L* are only used in the standard, bigger arena, but for some reason *J* got missed out completely. Now I actually feel a bit miffed about that as my surname before I got married began with a *J*. I mean, if I'd gone around without my *J* I would have been Ohnson, which sounds distinctly Scandinavian, not from Burton on Trent at all. Imagine how confusing that would be for all my mates. But I digress.

Glancing up at those letters you might wonder why I should have such a problem with remembering them. Well here's the rub. Whatever idiot invented the dressage arena mixed them all up! They're all over the bloody place, for goodness sakes. I mean, just take a look at this.

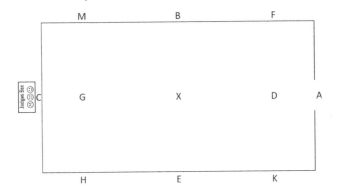

The powers that be very kindly allow letters to be placed around the outside, but you can hardly have stumpy G, X and D in the middle of the arena, your horse would trip over them.

As if I didn't have enough trouble trying to remember where all the letters were (you can hardly look around for them as you need to maintain a stiff, forward-facing posture) you had to criss-cross all over the place doing different stuff. It went something like this:

1	A X	Enter in medium walk. Halt, salute. Proceed in medium walk.
2	C HXF Between H&X	Track left. On the diagonal. Transition to working trot
3	A AK	Circle right 20m diameter in working trot. Working trot
4	Between K&H H	Transition to medium walk. Medium walk.
5	C	Halt 3-5 seconds. Proceed in medium walk.
6	MXK Between M&X	On the diagonal. Transition to working trot.
7	A AF	Circle left 20m diameter. Working trot.
8	Between F&B BMC	Transition to medium walk. Medium walk.

And so it goes on and on.

One of the things which had taken place at the LGC a few weeks prior to the Kalulushi Show was the official dressage tests which would affect one's ranking for the forthcoming season.

I had joined in a few dressage lessons during the preceding weeks so was persuaded by some of my 'friends' to give it a go. As Tilly had just gone lame I had to do it on Big Boy. Thank goodness I did because despite his rather sturdy physique that boy knew a helluva lot more about dressage than I did.

Dressage is taken very seriously by that fraternity and everything must be 'just so'. The horse had to be 'very well turned out' having been groomed until the coat shone, hooves polished and, in the case of the mane, plaiting was compulsory.

My attire too had to be appropriate, with polished boots, jodhpurs, dark jacket, white shirt with a white cravat and of course riding hat, underneath which long hair was normally constrained inside a snood (droopy hairnet to the uninitiated).

You may have noticed by now that I don't tend to take anything very seriously, so I determined to adhere strictly to the rules, and so plaited my hair too. But I didn't plait it into two long lush plaits pinned tidily together like normal people would. My hair wasn't really *that* long, nor could it remotely be described as being 'lush', as it was in fact fine and straggly. So rather like Big Boy's mane, I put it into several plaits. Seven small wispy ones to be precise. Poking out from under my hat, they looked wonderfully ridiculous.

As I approached the dressage arena I passed my friends and gave my plaits a flick to make sure they were sitting nicely outside my collar. My pals were rendered either rigidly speechless or fell about, helplessly doubled over with laughter.

Big Boy and I walked in and, as was required, duly stopped at X and gave the required courtesy nod to the judges before proceeding with the exercise. As we walked past the judge's table for the first time, out of the corner of my eye I caught sight of one of the judges whom I knew, and could see she had her hand in front of her mouth desperately trying not to laugh.

You could have knocked me down with a feather when at the end of this, out of sixteen competitors, we came fourth. I was chuffed to bits, as was Heather (her horse!) and all the girls who had encouraged me to enter. What was even more amazing was that I didn't get disqualified for insubordination.

But back to Kalulushi, I didn't have time for all that plaiting nonsense for myself this time. I needed all my concentration to get Tilly to do as she should. We failed abysmally, coming 24th out of 27 competitors. In hindsight maybe if I *had* plaited my hair it would have distracted the judges from our dreadful performance.

To be fair, this was Tilly's first dressage test and I thought it was quite an accomplishment that given her 'forward-going' nature we managed to complete it without her galloping out of the arena.

Saturday was the bit I was most looking forward to, being cross-country. It reminded me greatly of my young days when I used to join the local hunt on my pony, except in the case of cross-country you actually knew what and where the fences and ditches were going to be that you would jump over.

Tilly appeared to be in her element and completed the course beautifully. After combining the points from the dressage and the cross-country we were now lying 6th out of the 27 competitors in our grade! This was no mean feat for her first performance. Unfortunately it is a pity the performance of the rider wasn't up to the same standard because when the jump judges returned from their remote positions on the course it was announced that we had taken one of the fences from the wrong direction and so were disqualified!

What a twit. I couldn't imagine how on earth I had done that but didn't question its validity. At least now I knew that my horse was more than capable, even if her rider wasn't!

On the Sunday morning the organisers actually still allowed us to do the show jumping although we were classified 'non-competitive'. Even after having one pole down we would have finished in sixth place in E Grade at the Kalulushi Horse Trials, had we not been disqualified.

Some of the competitors packed up and travelled back to Lusaka as soon as the show jumping was over, as they had kids flying back to boarding school in the UK on the next flight. That left about seven families to still have fun.

The food that had been provided by the event organisers had turned out to be bloody expensive so after my moat-digging on Saturday I had nipped quickly into Kitwe (a few miles away) and shopped for meat, veggies and bread as well as borrowing a braai and some charcoal from our friend Nandy.

For Sunday night's supper I had bought a huge bag of pork chops and some large potatoes for baking. The braai was lit and some of the guys built a fire in the middle of the camp, around which we all sat in our picnic chairs as the meat and veg were cooking.

We were about to plate up the food when it began to spit with rain, so decided to take no chances and took refuge, with our food, inside the biggest tent. We were just getting settled when the heavens opened. There were eleven of us *plus kids* in Dave and Bev's tent, which was about the same size as ours but without the sleeping compartments, and their floor was dry. We'd had some rain on Saturday night and the living area of our tent, not having a groundsheet, was a bit soggy underfoot to put it mildly. Fortunately our sleeping compartments had a stitched-in groundsheet so had stayed dry.

Not long after we'd finished eating it was time for the kids to go to bed. We settled them down then returned to our friend's tent with the rest of the gang for a drinking, chatting and laughing session.

Most of the crew sat around on their chairs but I chose to sit cross-legged on the edge of Bev and Dave's mattress putting me closer to the ground, which turned out to be quite fortuitous because it was from that close proximity that, after about an hour, I noticed the water. It was slowly seeping through the groundsheet.

We were all aware that the water was not coming in through the roof, so it must have been coming up from the ground. I decided to check on the kids. Thank goodness I did!

As I sloshed into our tent it was obvious all was not well. The entire living area was now under water. I unzipped the kids' sleeping compartment to find them sleeping soundly on their lilos which bobbed gently like ducks on a pond, caused by the water under the groundsheet. As I stepped into the cubicle I could feel the water sloshing underfoot, which created hollows as I stepped between the lilos. A change of venue was clearly called for, so I tried to wake the kids.

This was easier said than done as by now they had been in bed for over an hour, and as I moved around the lilos rocked soporifically on the liquid floor, enhancing their sleep.

I eventually managed to wake Brad and through his haze told him to stand up and pick up his sleeping bag and pillow. Then I woke Leon, telling him what to do, and finally Vicki who was sleeping furthest from the doorway. By the time I'd helped her out of her sleeping bag and turned around, Brad had laid back down on top of his and gone back to sleep. I had to start over.

I eventually got all the kids lined up just inside the tent doorway, ankle deep in water, clutching their bedding. I hollered and hollered, shouting to Ziggy to run ahead of us and open the door to the clubhouse. Luckily we had asked the organisers to leave it unlocked in case of any emergency. This was definitely an emergency!

Ziggy finally shifted his arse and sprang into action, soon shouting that all was opened up and on the count of one, two, three, "GO" we raced through the deluge into the dry building.

We pushed armchairs together for beds. Thankfully I'd had a single towel draped over a line inside the tent, and got the kids dry (from running through the rain) before settling them back in their sleeping bags, although without a pillow for Vicki. Some water must have started seeping inside the sleeping compartment and her pillow, drooping over the end of her 'bed', had absorbed it. Half its length was sopping wet.

Ziggy and I then went back to our tent to retrieve our mattress and bedding, only to find that water had already entered our cubicle and we could forget about using the mattress. Fortunately our pillows and duvet had not yet been vandalised by the weather so we returned to the clubhouse with those, and after pushing together several coffee tables and laying armchair cushions on top, we had a more than adequate bed for the night.

Having got ourselves sorted we headed back to our friends to find out how they were getting on. Dave and Bev had to abandon their mattress as it was, by now, quite sodden. Thankfully their kids were much better off as they were sleeping on camp beds, so were well off the ground. Bev and Dave ended up sleeping in their van.

We suggested to a few of the others in "iffy" tents that they might join us in the clubhouse but they declined though, sadly and damply, regretted it in the morning.

All our suitcases, shoes, clothes and camping equipment had been sitting on the floor inside the tent during the night and *everything* was saturated. As usual Ziggy did a runner early in the morning with the excuse that he needed to return the braai box and remaining charcoal to Nandy before we could reload our vehicle for the homeward journey. Ever the typical male seeing an old friend, he was gone for over two hours. By the time he got back I had emptied the tent; got rid of all the damaged breakfast food; deflated the lilos; hauled the extremely heavy, soaked mattress into the bottom of the trailer where it kept company with the wet dismantled tent. I then wrung out the soaked clothes and placed them back in the damp suitcases. The only dry clothes we had were the ones we had slept in, so that remained our attire for the day.

In the midst of all that I'd had to nip along to the stables to dress Tilly up. Most of the horses got padded up for road trips to protect their knees, hocks and tails before the artic full of horses commenced its return journey to Lusaka. I had made suitable attire for Tilly, in our stable colour (yellow) for such occasions.

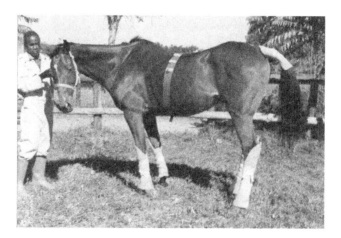

As we eventually set off for home in convoy with some of our mates I reckoned, all things considered, it had been a fabulous weekend.

17

PROGRESSING WITH MAZABUKA AND KITWE

Next on the list of events was Mazabuka. If my memory serves me correctly this was called Bernapen because it was organised by Bernie and Penny Evans, and was a very popular event with the horsey fraternity.

For this the horses were loaded into as assortment of trucks which had been begged, borrowed or hired for the occasion. Six trucks drove the 70 miles down to Mazabuka from Lusaka, carrying 35 horses, accompanied by their grooms.

Many more were travelling from other areas of Zambia to participate in the event.

Yet again we were camping and at least this time we knew we wouldn't be in for any rain, as we were now well into the dry season of Zambia's weather cycle.

It was held at the Mazabuka Polo Club which has quite expansive grounds.

A sizable area was set aside for campers and we took most of our regular gear.

From what I'd been told by my pals who were regular Bernapen participants, we were in for a fun time. They weren't wrong. What stayed with me about this horsey experience that made it so different from other events, was the race.

They had set up a race track, complete with some small hurdles, around the perimeter of the grounds. Tilly was going to race again!

Except it wasn't actually a race as you know races, alongside other horses. It was a timed event of one lap of the circuit for each horse.

I wasn't sure if I was excited or terrified at the prospect of actually being on Tilly's back and encouraging her to go as fast as she could.

When the time came, we had already completed the cross-country course where Tilly had thoroughly enjoyed herself, and I actually went over all the right fences, in the right order, from the right direction this time. We were ready to race.

From a standing start in front of the small grandstand we shot off for about thirty yards before jumping over the first hurdle, then it was a long run before the next one. The course was a rounded rectangular shape and as we approached the first corner which arced to the left we encountered another obstacle.

Just past this corner, to the right, was the exit to the grounds, and Tilly began to head towards that. It took all my strength and persuasion to return her to the track, but that done she then took off like a rocket. I leaned as flat as I could onto her neck and kept calling "Go, go, go Tilly, go!"

My next fear was that she was so intense in her gallop that she wouldn't see the hurdles. As we approached the next one I shouted to her "Look, Tilly, look!" as she was a few strides away from the fence and yelled "Jump!" at the top of my voice as we reached it. It worked. She cleared the hurdles and hurtled on around the course. The race finished where we had started, in front of the grandstand, and I was astounded to hear everyone cheering wildly as we galloped past.

At the end of our race I can say this was the first time Tilly immediately listened to me when I started to slow her down. She'd given it her all and must have been knackered.

After a relaxing walk back to the stables, I left her with the groom giving her a nice hosing down, then went to join my friends on the stand to watch the rest of the racers.

"I've never seen anything like it," said Heather, quite breathless just talking about it. "You flew around that course. I'm telling you, all I could see was a flat horse. For all the world it looked like her feet never touched the ground."

And I was so thrilled when, at the end of the session, I was told that Tilly had come 6th out of 72 participating horses! We might have come in the top three if we hadn't had the hindrance of that attempted deviation at the beginning of the race.

Alas, when it came to the show-jumping event Tilly became so hyped up when she arrived in the show arena (no doubt anticipating another race) that I battled to control her, and we had several fences down, which dropped us heavily down the points list.

While this horsey stuff had been going on Ziggy and the kids had been having a great time with their various pals and we all agreed that it had been a wonderful weekend.

THE EVENT OF THE YEAR BACK AT OUR OLD STOMPING GROUND KITWE, WAS the Copperbelt Mining, Agricultural and Commercial Show which is held each year in June. The main horse event in the schedule was the Merchant's Derby, a highly esteemed event attracting riders and horses from Zaire, Zimbabwe, and Botswana, as well as from all over Zambia itself.

That actual Derby was, of course, way beyond the capabilities of me and my horse but there were several lower grade events in which we would be able to compete.

I proceeded to get myself well and truly organised. I asked Benton if he would like the opportunity of a free little holiday to visit his family in Kitwe by coming with us. I just asked that he be at the campsite for an hour in the morning to clear up breakfast dishes and generally tidy up, as I would be busy with Tilly. Naturally he jumped at the chance (if you'll pardon the pun). We arranged for his wife Catrina to feed our dogs whilst we were away.

Then a minor disaster struck. Four days before we were due to leave for Kitwe Tilly went lame. I had no idea how this happened, maybe she twisted something when she was running in from the paddock at feed time. No-one knew. I was devastated. There was little point in us going camping at the event if I couldn't participate.

Luckily the bush drums were soon beating out the word and the next day I had a phone call from my friend Robin.

"I hear you're without a horse. That's a bit of a sod," he said.

"Yes. There's no way Tilly will be fit enough to participate by the weekend. I'm gutted."

"Well," he continued, "I had been hoping to go to Kitwe myself, you may have noticed I've been doing some training with First Attempt lately. But we suddenly have some VIPs arriving at the weekend so I have to be here. How would you like to take Firsty instead?"

"Really? Are you serious?" I was flabbergasted.

"Yes, absolutely. It would be a shame for him to miss it after all the hard work I've put him through, and you've already proven you can ride him just as well as me."

What a marvellous man!

"Thank you very much indeed, Robin. I would be thrilled and highly honoured to ride your horse for you."

So that was settled. I would take the lovely chestnut gelding First Attempt up to Kitwe and, as I was used to working with him and plans were already in place for him travelling, Kenias would come as attending groom, and Robin's groom would look after Tilly in his absence.

The kids were really excited about this trip as they knew they would get to meet up with most of their Kitwe friends. I was looking forward to that opportunity too. Well, not to meet up with the kids' friends, but with my own. Not that there was anything wrong with the kids' friends you understand. *Shut up Ann!*

It transpired that Kitwe's premier annual event was to be honoured this year with a visit from His Excellency President Kenneth Kaunda. On opening day the Zambia military marching band was in attendance in full regalia giving a relatively impressive rendition of the Zambia national anthem and various other military band tunes, as the President stood in the 'royal' box to be appropriately paraded past.

The afternoon progressed with an assortment of displays and traditional dances being performed in the main arena. There being no horsey events we took the opportunity to enjoy the spectacles from the bar-lounge beside one of the main stands. It was all very jolly.

After a couple of hours of various performances the President took his leave of the showgrounds, but not before going on a short informal walkabout to mingle with the peasants. There was great excitement as he and his entourage (mostly bodyguards) paused at the entrance to the social area in which we sat, where the President shook hands with various members of the public who happened to be standing by the doorway. As the Pres walked away to climb into his waiting limo Brad came racing up to us, excited fit to burst.

"Mummy, mummy, mummy, I just shook hands with the President!" he shouted. Why was I not surprised?

But then I looked down at the first child to depart my loins to see the dirtiest, scruffiest little urchin you could *ever* imagine, smiling broadly up at me. Goodness knows where he'd been or what he'd been doing (I didn't want to know) before this memorable encounter took place, but I would imagine that after seeing what he'd just shaken the hand of, his Excellency the President felt the need to make his way swiftly to his nearest washroom!

I won't try to fob you off with excuses, but I reckon our Kitwe cavorting must have been quite a boozy session because I can't recall that much more about it.

I do know that First Attempt and I came home with three or four rosettes, two of them being bright red, 1st Place ones, because I still have them. One event I remember is the Handy Hunter competition.

In this particular case it consisted of jumping various fences or obstacles (rows of tyres, oil drums) and doing an assortment of weird stuff, including:

> riding the horse over a tarpaulin laid on the ground;
> walking between two posts with balloons attached to them (that can be trickier than you think, I can tell you);
> taking a jug of water off a table, riding to another, and pouring the water into a bucket;
> opening, passing through and then closing a latched gate.

All this was done without getting off the horse and was 'against the clock'.

And we came first! You can't imagine how chuffed I was about that.

THERE WAS NOW QUITE A LULL BETWEEN SHOWS AND ONE WEEKEND A small gang of us went out for a long hack one Sunday morning stopping along the way, as was our normal wont, at a local shebeen for some liquid refreshment. Whilst enjoying our cold beers (that's all they ever had, but at least they were cold) some idiot (it was either Pat Lee or myself) suggested that our jolly crowd should go out on a progressive ride at some time.

For those of you who don't know, a 'progressive ride' is, you get on your horse and progress from one person's house to another, taking refreshments in each one. In this particular case we got a bit carried away (not just by the horses) and decided to make a meal of it. It would be a progressive lunch.

Discussions were held and plans were laid for the following Sunday.

Seven of us gathered at the stables. As well as Pat and myself there were Penny Nain, Liz Weinand, Robin Goreham, actually riding his horse himself for a change, and Anne and Graham Wallace. Graham didn't have a horse of his own, but Bev couldn't make it so she kindly lent him her horse Luxor to ride.

We began very well with a punctual start at 10:00. Riding out past the Polo Club we headed first for Robin's house where we would enjoy morning coffee (suitably laced) and biscuits. From his place we rode on to Penny's house for starters. There we were treated to a delicious pâté with toast and a glass of white wine. Having climbed back onto our nags we then had to ride to Pat's residence for the main meal.

However, some considerable debate first took place as to the route we should take. The trouble was, the easiest and most direct route would be to go straight down Independence Avenue, which would take us past the Presidential Palace.

In view of the fact that they had done something he didn't like, or hadn't done something that he would like, His Excellency President Kenneth Kaunda had announced a State of Emergency against South Africa only two days earlier. We figured that it might not be too prudent for seven 'whities' (even though none of us were South Africans) to go riding past his front gates on a Sunday, despite the fact that we had Robin in our midst, who was Deputy Commissioner at the British High Commission. So we judiciously went the back way.

In hindsight we realised it might have been better taking our chances against the Zambian military.

Going 'the back way' introduced us to about half a million Zambian children from a nearby informal settlement, who followed us shouting, "Horse kangoma, horse kangoma", which translated to 'horse go faster' at about 120 decibels. We suffered this for almost half an hour until we left their comfort zone, but even so continued to be pestered by about twenty kids until Anne, who was bringing up the rear, shouted, "I've had enough of these bloody piccanins running up my horse's arse!"

When I asked her about it she said that the kids had actually reached the point of running up behind and grabbing hold of her horse's tail. Knowing Tilly wouldn't stand for any nonsense someone suggested I take up the rear position, but I decided against it or there could have been seriously unpleasant consequences.

Oh, I don't think I told you about the black dog incident, did I?

I was returning home after one of my solo bundu-bashing rides one day. I had our ridgeback dog Bass with me at the time, so made a point of not going through the informal settlement for fear of provoking a dog fight. I was riding down a road about five minutes from our house where most of the properties were like ours, positioned inside large fenced or walled gardens.

Knowing he was near home Bass was trotting about 25 yards ahead of us and Tilly was maintaining her normal long-striding walk when out of nowhere a black mongrel came tearing up behind us, its legs going sixteen to the dozen as it scrabbled across the tarmac, teeth bared and growling viciously. It was stupid enough to race straight up to Tilly and try to bite her.

Without even breaking her stride she lashed out with one of her back legs and kicked it smack in the teeth. This was a fat, Labrador-sized dog, yet the impact of Tilly's kick sent it somersaulting three times over before it eventually came to a 'lie-still' on the edge of the road whining and howling. Obviously I stopped and was wondering what to do about it when Bass came running back to see what all the noise was about. As he approached the black dog, it leapt up and ran off, disappearing around a corner to goodness knows where, as by the time I reached the corner it was nowhere in sight. I didn't think it would bother any more horses, poor thing.

So I'm sure you can understand, I wasn't going to risk a Tilly encounter with children, no matter how pesky they could be.

But to continue with my story…

We eventually made it to Pat's house, minus the entourage. We had arranged for Ziggy to fetch two grooms from the stables who had put together a bootful of buckets containing the horses' lunchtime feed, which they duly distributed. While the horses munched, so did we. Pat had made a rather scrumptious Lasagne which was served with a lovely crisp salad and crusty bread. And more glasses of white wine.

By the time we made it back to where the horses were already tacked-up and ready to head off to our final destination, we were rolling pretty good. A nice steady walk saw *The Progressors* arrive safely at our Lukanga Road residence for the pudding course of the luncheon.

On the Saturday I had made a fruit flan, an apple pie and a lemon melingwe tat (or lemon meringue pie if you haven't read *Into Africa with 3 kids, 13 crates and a husband*) as well as procuring the makings of Irish and French coffee.

With a gardenful of semi-tacked horses, kids in the pool and dogs behaving amazingly well, more supporters (spouses/kids) of *The Progressors* arrived until we had quite a party going. I was in the middle of handing out slices of the flan when a couple of latecomers arrived. Unfortunately our guard was clearly not paying proper attention, and failed to close the huge metal gates timeously, as per the strict instructions I had given to him.

Before you could say, "Grab that horse!" Tilly, who'd been grazing nearby, trotted outside the gate. Seeing her movement Luxor decided he didn't want to be left behind, and trotted after her. Of course, that was all it took for Tilly to think this was a challenge and immediately took off down the road with Luxor racing close behind her.

Screaming for the nearest rider to come with me I yelled at the latecomer to rapidly reverse out and 'follow that horse'. Sadly they couldn't do exactly that, as having taken the trip back to the stables many times before, Tilly knew the shortcut which was through some open ground. I chased after the horses while the car took the longer road route. We reached the Great East Road at about the same time, where I jumped into the car for further pursuit.

At a speed which would definitely have got us arrested we tore along the Great East Road just in time to see the two horses gallop across the four lanes, heading for the showgrounds entrance.

By the time we got inside the grounds, both horses were standing in their respective stables, heads high, snorting heavily from their carefree escapade.

Thankfully they were none the worse for their adventure which is more than could be said for me, and others in the car, who were left a jabbering bag of nerves from the experience. It was deemed a miracle that the traffic had been so light on the roads and no accident was caused.

With the naughty nags now safely fastened inside their stables and left under the care of a couple of handy grooms, we motored back to my place where the progressive party continued until it was time for the other horses to be ridden home, in a more sedate manner, before it got dark.

All things considered, everyone agreed it had been an enjoyably successful day.

Of course, the biggest event as far as the gymkhana club crowd were concerned was Lusaka's annual August Agricultural Show.

Every building in the Showgrounds was now a hive of activity promoting merchandise; from turkeys to tractors, pigs to ploughs and cockerels to corn bins, and Lusaka's residents came out in force to view them.

On the equestrian front, events ranged from lead-rein pony classes to the ultimate Lusaka Derby. Leon drew the winning ticket to ride Pannastra in the former event; neither pony nor rider were accomplished enough as yet to compete in anything more challenging. Despite having given my groom adequate notice, Kenias had not prepared Pannastra as he should have when I checked up on him a short while before the event. I hastily plaited the pony's mane while he oiled her hooves. She was then quickly tacked up and Leon mounted ready for his first official show.

Unfortunately the time taken seeing to those issues had used up all the time I had allowed for horse and rider to 'warm up' in the collecting ring. We were last to enter the show arena as the final call for all entrants was made during our arrival.

All participants were led in a large circle around the judges, who stood in the centre of the arena. After a couple of circuits we lined up along one side of the arena as each horse/rider/leader was called into the centre and asked to walk then trot in a circle before being called to the judges for a short chat.

It came to our turn and we were fine until it came to the trot part, because Pannastra decided that she didn't want to do that, and demonstrated her dissent by rearing up, several times! Leon clung bravely on. We eventually achieved a short trot, which culminated in a defiant buck from our young mare.

And while the judges were not impressed with the pony's behaviour, Leon was commended for managing to remain seated during this rodeo show. Then we were admonished when a judge noticed Pannastra's bridle was stained with old chewed food. I was horrified that, contrary to my instructions, the groom had *not* thoroughly cleaned the tack. All told I think we came away with minus points.

On a brighter note, I entered Tilly in every show-jumping event she qualified for. I must confess I hadn't realised that the fences would be so high. As we walked the course I found some of the poles we were going to have to clear were level with my boobs, and as wide as my horse was long!

I wondered if I was asking a little too much of my relatively novice mare (not to mention *my* abilities) but at the end of the weekend we proudly strode out of that big arena with three rosettes. Albeit they were only two fifth places and a fourth, but considering she'd never been asked to jump until I bought her less than a year ago, I was chuffed to bits with our successes.

18

END OF LIFE AS WE KNOW IT

And so we reached the end of Ziggy's current two-year contract with Mutende, which of course culminated in our extended trip to the UK. I made arrangements for someone to supervise my groom's care of the horses, as well as making sure everything was organised for Benton to look after the house and dogs in our absence. I wasn't taking much notice of what Ziggy was up to.

On the appointed date we flew out to the UK and spent an enjoyable couple of weeks in Burton on Trent. Next came our holiday in Menorca. I had been on holiday to the Balearic isle of Mallorca many times in my younger years but not to Menorca, the second largest of these Spanish, Mediterranean islands.

My dad's brother Bernard had organised accommodation comprising a couple of two-bedroom bungalow-style apartments. There was a lovely pool area, and other amenities like cafés and bars were close to hand.

One afternoon towards the end of our stay we were lazing by the pool when Ziggy said, "I think it's time we spoke to your dad about looking after the kids when we go back."

I looked at him.

"What *are* you talking about?"

"Well, when we go back to Zambia to pack up our stuff it would be silly to take the kids with us."

Despite the heat of the Spanish sun I suddenly went cold.

"Ziggy! What the hell are you talking about, 'packing up our stuff'?"

"I've decided not to renew my contract with Mutende. I've mentioned to you several times over the past few weeks, there are very few projects to keep me occupied."

I wracked my brain to think when he'd said anything.

"I remember you saying something once, but I didn't think you were serious. I certainly don't remember the 'several times' bit!"

"Well it's not my fault you weren't listening. But that's beside the point. We need to sell stuff and pack up what you want to bring back, and we can do without having to entertain the kids during the process. Besides, it will take time to get my tax clearance issued once our stuff is packed and ready to be shipped out, so we'll need to stay with friends or something. We couldn't expect them to accommodate *five* of us."

I sat back speechless. I was in shock. I simply could not take in what I had just heard.

LEAVE my beloved Zambia? Leave all my friends? What about Tilly? What about the dogs? How could he *do* this to me?

My mind was now in a whirl.

"Can't you get a job with another company in Lusaka?" I asked. "Surely there must be *somewhere* you could work?"

"Oh, I've looked around and made enquiries here and there, but nothing much is going on. There's certainly nothing going on in heavy engineering, which is one of the few fields in which they still employ expats."

"But to be honest I've had enough of having to work with people who don't know, or care, about what they're doing. Who are employed simply because they belong to the right church or are relatives of the right people. I try to teach them where I can but they just don't seem to want to listen. I've had enough of the incompetence and indifference. I want out. So it's back to the UK for us."

I was absolutely devastated.

For what remained of our holiday I walked around in a daze, unable to get my head around this bombshell.

My dad was, I believe, quietly happy about this turn of events and more than willing to look after the kids for a few weeks. He was still living in our house in Burton, although by now, of course, he was on his own, Doris having gone to live with Betty.

But even with Doris no longer there, it was going to be a tight squeeze when we returned, as our house only had three bedrooms. It meant all the kids would have to share one room, Ziggy and I would need the other double room previously occupied by my dad, who would be demoted to the remaining tiny single bedroom. It certainly wasn't the most enthralling prospect.

When we arrived back in Burton from our Spanish holiday we were dismayed to hear that Doris was in hospital. Betty explained to me that one day she had been sitting in her living room and Doris had been walking along the passageway, returning from the kitchen, when she heard a *crack* and a cry from Doris. Another leg bone had snapped. She was taken to the main Burton hospital. We went to see her there and I had the opportunity to speak to the ward sister who said she didn't think Doris would be walking again, and would probably have to live in a nursing home from now on. Not surprisingly Doris had not taken this news at all well, and apparently kept most of the other patients in the nearby (and not-so-nearby) beds awake at night as, being an insomniac, she lay crying and wailing. And if they sedated her for the benefit of the majority it wasn't much better, as she snored like a barnyard full of pigs.

It was heart-wrenching to see her so sad, though she did cheer up a little at hearing that her 'babies' would be close by now, and she'd be able to see them more often.

When we broke the news to the kids that they were not going back to Lusaka they were initially excited, as they were enjoying their holiday in England. But when they realised this would be the end of their horse-riding days, and that they wouldn't see their friends again, and especially the dogs, there was a more despondent reaction and we were not without tears.

They wrote letters to their friends for us to take back, promising to keep in touch and see them again if they ever got the chance.

One thing they were quite happy about was their return to Edgehill School. From their short experience there the previous year they knew they were in for an easy time, having been far more advanced in their maths and English than their classmates. Some of the other subjects were going to be quite different to what they'd studied in Zambia, especially geography and suchlike, though they didn't seem to be at all concerned about such issues.

Being, by now, the very beginning of September, the school office was already accessible so I was able to register them quite easily, especially as the school already had all their details and the secretary actually remembered Brad. Again, why was I not surprised?

And so it was that we left the kids in my dad's care and took our final journey back to Zambia.

THE NEWS DID NOT GO DOWN AT ALL WELL WITH OUR FRIENDS AT THE gymkhana club.

"What do you mean, you're leaving?"

"That's terrible news, I can't allow it!"

"You *can't* leave us!"

"What are we going to do without you?"

But after they got over the initial shock other questions flowed.

"Can I buy your braai box?"

"I'd love your sausage-making mincer machine."

"Would you sell me your pressure cooker?"

So we did a tour of the house and decided what we wanted to take back to England and what we were prepared to sell. Without a doubt, three of the things going back to England were the kids' bikes, heaven forbid that we should sell those!

And while almost all the furniture in the house belonged to the landlord, a couple of very special items had to accompany us. These were two very large coffee tables made out of mukwa, a wood common to Zambia and the south-central area of Africa, which Ziggy had the carpentry shop make for us at his first job in Kitwe. They had also made the two wall units which housed our books and ornaments, but these were far too large to consider taking back to the UK, whether it be from a transportation point of view or where on earth they would fit in our Burton home. When announced for sale these were instantly snapped up by our good friends Lorraine and Rob Chalcraft.

The first move before any of the household items left our premises, or even before the swift African drums beat the message out, was to tell Benton that we were leaving and that he would need new employers. I offered to try and find him a job locally but he said now that we were leaving he and his family would return to live and work in Kitwe.

He was given references as well as the required redundancy bonus for his five years of service. His bonus would actually have been a lot higher were it not for a change in him since we had moved to Lusaka. It was as if he had decided that he didn't need be quite so diligent now that we were committed to his services in this city. It only showed through occasionally, but there were a couple of incidents which did not sit well with us.

Not long after we arrived in Lusaka, Ziggy arranged for Benton to have driving lessons and take his test. Later, when I was on my second trip to the UK, Ziggy was going somewhere for the day with one of his colleagues, and they went in the other guy's car. When he returned home that evening he went to put something into his car ready for the next morning and noticed a dent and a scrape in one of the rear passenger doors that most certainly had not been there before. He called Benton.

"What happened here?" he asked.

"I'm so sorry boss," Benton had responded, "but we needed some food for the dinner so I took your car to the shopping centre. When I came out of the shop this mark was there. I don't know what happened to it."

"Okay Benton, these things happen," Ziggy said, and left it at that. Benton returned to his kia.

Vicki had been standing in the kitchen when this conversation took place and had heard Benton's explanation. When her dad went back inside she said to him, "I saw what happened, daddy."

"Why, did you go with him to the shops?"

"No, it happened here. Benton drove it into that," she said, pointing to the post supporting the washing line.

Ziggy went over to the post and looked. Sure enough there was Skyline-coloured paint on the metal pole. He then looked at the car door, got into the car and reversed it close to the post. The marks lined up perfectly with the paint on the post.

"Benton!" he called.

Benton reappeared and walked over to where Ziggy now stood. Pointing to the post and the damage in the car door, Ziggy looked at him quizzically.

Benton hung his head, uttered "Sorry, bwana" then turned and walked very sheepishly back to his kia. It wasn't the damage to the car that we had a problem with so much as the blatant lying about how it happened.

The other incident had occurred after we returned from our horse-event trip to Kitwe. Benton had spent an hour each morning clearing up after breakfast and tidying up our campsite but the rest of the day was his.

On the other hand Kenias, my groom, had a much heavier than normal workload during the Kitwe trip. On our return to Lusaka I gave Kenias a well-deserved bonus for all his hard work.

Three days later Benton accosted me in the kitchen.

"Madam, where is my bonus?"

"What?"

"Where is my bonus?"

"Bonus for what, Benton?" I asked.

"For going with you to Kitwe,"

"Why on earth should you get a bonus for going to Kitwe, Benton?"

"Kenias got a bonus for going, so I should get one too!" he answered, with an insolent look on his face, the likes of which I'd not seen on him before.

"Benton, Kenias had to work very hard and put in extra hours during that trip to Kitwe. He travelled the whole journey in the back of the truck with the horses and other grooms. He deserved a bonus. You accepted the opportunity to come up to Kitwe where you had virtually all day to do as you pleased with your family and friends, which most certainly does not warrant a bonus."

Benton was not happy. From the look on his face I thought he was going to argue, but he must have read the look on mine and decided against it.

After that his general demeanour was never quite the same.

WHILE THE FATE OF THE VARIOUS HOUSEHOLD ITEMS WAS BEING TOSSED around I had to sort out the animals.

Sadly there was no way we could take any of the dogs back to England with us. Air-freighting would have been exorbitant, sea shipment would have been too stressful for them, and either way the necessity of a six-month quarantine confinement at the other end was simply unthinkable. We needed to find new homes for them.

The homing of Bass I knew would be a doddle. Friends of the couple we got him from had always wanted him, and jumped at the chance to finally have their wish come true.

I advertised Coke for sale in the Times of Zambia. He was highly pedigreed and having never been neutered could sire some lovely puppies. I knew we would soon find him a home. In my advertisement I made a point of saying that he wasn't suitable for a home with small children. His naughty habit of trying to steal food out of the hands of kids might turn ugly if it happened to a small child. A lovely Dutch couple with young teenagers were delighted to take him.

You may wonder at my actually selling him, rather than giving him away. It was a security issue. If someone had to pay good money for a dog they had to be certain it was the right dog for them, so would deter chancers or anyone who might mistreat him.

As we worried over who would be prepared to take Sally we were saved the concern when one of our friends at the club said he would be happy to have her, as she could join the family of dogs at their farm.

Then we only had the horses to worry about. Pannastra's placement was very straight-forward because as soon as Nilla, who I'd bought her from, heard we were leaving she offered to buy her back. Similarly the word was already out that Tilly was available.

Before I had chance to advertise her for sale my friend Ruth said she'd be interested in trying her out. I was quite surprised by this because Ruth already had an Arab mare and a Hanoverian. Ruth and her husband Rolph, a Swiss couple, had already offered Ziggy and I accommodation for the time when we had to vacate our home until we were actually cleared to depart. I would be delighted if Ruth decided to take Tilly. We agreed for Ruth to 'try her out' one afternoon in one of the schooling paddocks.

I don't think I've mentioned this before, but Tilly was in the habit of tripping a lot when walking or even sometimes when trotting. I swear she did it on purpose because all she really wanted to do was gallop!

Having been a regular member of the weekend outrides and followed us along the various trails as well as chatting as we rode, I assumed Ruth had noticed Tilly's bad habit. Unfortunately it seemed that she had not picked up on the extent of it.

As Ruth walked around the paddock Tilly did one of her customary trips, but instead of checking the horse's fall, as I would have done, Ruth followed the horse's downward trend, leaning on Tilly's neck, which sent Tilly stumbling to her knees. Ruth continued over her shoulder and finished up on the ground. Thankfully Ruth was unhurt, other than her pride, and decided that perhaps she and Tilly would not make a good match.

I wish I could have said the same in the 'unhurt' stakes for Tilly.

The unexpected forward weight and twist on her forequarters as Ruth tumbled resulted in Tilly suffering a strained shoulder. As she limped back to the stable it became clear that there was no way I would be able to sell her now, as no-one would be able to try her out while she was lame.

As the days to our departure neared, the worry of my unsold mare was lifted considerably when Heather offered to take Tilly to their ranch for convalescence, saying she would be happy to sell her for me once she was 'up and running'. What wonderful friends I had.

Once our goods were packed, collected and ready for departure to the UK, Ziggy was ready to file his final tax papers. We just had to wait for the issue of the Tax Clearance Certificate before he could finalise our financial situation. (The TCC verified that all income tax had been paid up to the time of departure from the country. Neither he, his possessions, nor his money would be allowed to leave the country without that.)

But we didn't just sit around on our arses waiting, we had plans.

19

SOBEK

I have never been brilliant with water. I was forced by my grandmother to go for swimming lessons when I was about eight years old. A man named Mr Potts who lived a few doors down from our shop used to give private swimming lessons at the Burton Public Swimming Baths on a Saturday morning.

I was very skinny as a child and used to get goose-bumps the moment I divested my clothes in favour of a swimsuit. This was especially the case at Burton Baths, which to me seemed a cavernous place built of cold bricks lined with cold tiles. It always stank of chemicals and was incredibly noisy. I think most of the noise came from children screaming from not wanting to be there for swimming lessons.

As a result of the noise, Mr Potts used to bellow out instructions like a sergeant major,

"Kick! Kick! Kick with your legs. No, both of them at the same time! Like a frog." This as he towed me along as I clung like a leech to a small square of polystyrene attached to a long rope. I went through months of this torture before I was eventually forced to abandon the white float and attempt to swim with my arms too. It is amazing that I am here to tell the tale as, with not an ounce of fat to assist floatation, I invariably sank.

By the time swimming lessons became compulsory at school, at the age of 11, I could just about swim a width of the main pool at Burton Baths without drowning, but that didn't stop me from trying to get out of swimming with school every week, because I still got the goose-bumps.

I have always had trouble holding my breath under water. And I hate getting water in my eyes. So jumping into water has always involved holding my nose, screwing my eyes closed and shutting my mouth tight. There are those who would say that I should do the latter more often. But that is not the subject under discussion here.

Learning to dive seriously challenged one of those precautions insofar as I needed both arms outstretched when diving, and I couldn't hold onto my nose. So when standing on the edge of whatever diving platform I was on (usually solid poolside) I would take in a great gulp of air then shut my eyes and mouth before leaping into the depths. As soon as my face hit the water, if not before, I would snort the gulped air out of my nose in the hope of keeping water from rushing into it. For this reason I always tried to shallow-dive so that I didn't run out of snort before resurfacing. The instant I did resurface I had to stop and wipe the water from my eyes before continuing to swim.

Unfortunately if my diving platform were higher than the average poolside - say diving off a small jetty when on holiday - my shallow dive could result in a painful belly-flop instead. The shock of that would invariably cause me to shout out, thus ingesting vast quantities of undoubtedly very unhealthy sea water.

I was into my late teens before I would go swimming by choice, and then it had to be in the height of summer with water the temperature of a warm bath, and definitely not at the old Burton Public Swimming Baths.

Why, you might wonder, is she telling me all this now? It is because I want you to fully appreciate the magnitude of my horror when Ziggy suggested that we go white water rafting down the Zambezi River, at Victoria Falls.

You may or may not, dependent on if you have read *More Into*

Africa with 3 Kids, Some Dogs and a Husband, be aware that I had visited Victoria Falls with my grandmother Doris in 1982, so I had seen how much water came hurtling over those cliffs into the canyon. It was a lot. And Ziggy wanted me to get into a raft and be tossed around in ferocious rapids at the bottom of that lot. The man was completely out of his mind, of course.

Unfortunately the alternative was for me to hang around Lusaka worrying myself sick as to whether he was now a drowned, bloated, blob in a boat, or being chewed up by a crocodile. I was assured the latter wasn't an option as crocs don't inhabit the white water areas of the river, and the former was highly unlikely as he once swam for his county when he was a young teenager at school.

"Anyway," I was told "it's not dangerous. They use big rafts with an expert doing the steering and stuff, and you wear a life jacket. It's the opportunity of a lifetime. You don't want to miss that, do you?"

Well since I'd already been charged by elephants, almost leapt on by a lion and zapped by a zillion mosquitos, what else was there to do with my sense of adventure?

So it was that we flew down to Livingstone to spend a day getting exceedingly wet.

Our adventure was organised by the Sobek Group, who I believe were the only ones running rafting trips at the falls at that time. We were instructed to report for a briefing in the grounds of the Mosi o Tunya hotel where we were staying. As we waited for latecomers I heard a familiar call and turned to find Heather walking towards us. We had no idea the McCleerys were visiting Livingstone, and I soon wished they weren't.

Heather went to great lengths to tell me about a friend who nearly drowned the previous year when she was tipped out of the raft at one of the rapids. Never one given to understatement, Hev persisted in telling me how dangerous she thought it was, and said she wouldn't do it if they paid her a million dollars! As you might imagine, this did not instil me with a lot of confidence.

Wishing us a 'lovely fun day' my witch-friend then disappeared in the direction of the hotel's restaurant to enjoy a hearty breakfast.

With all interested parties now present and correct our Sobek leaders handed out life jackets and helmets to all participants and proceeded with their briefing, where we were given some indication of what to expect of these rapids.

We would start at the foot of the falls. That was a comfort at least. All the water which cascades over the length of the falls comes together in a wide chasm at the eastern end of the cliff, to resume its format as the Zambezi River, carving its way through the canyon via a series of rapids, We were to commence our adventure at the 'Boiling Pot' and then pour ourselves over nine out of the ten rapids, culminating with 'The Gnashing Jaws of Death'. This sounded all very inviting, or NOT.

Each raft, which could hold up to eight passengers, was inflated and attached to an aluminium frame which included a central wooden plank on which sat the oarsman, the expert man in charge of sending the raft in the right direction.

We were instructed on how to help direct this vessel through the more hectic rapids with our weight on his calls of 'high side left' and 'high side right'. The scariest was when we might be confronted by a huge wave which had the capacity to flip the entire vessel front-over-back. A cry of 'punch front' would come from our leader, then we all had to punch our bodies onto the front of the raft to push it through the wave instead of allowing it to ride up the wave and cause the flip-over.

The bigger/heavier crew members would be positioned at the front of the raft with the lighties and/or ladies hanging on grimly in the rear to balance it out.

In the event of anyone falling out, a 'man overboard' shout could come from anyone who saw it, when our oarsman would bring the raft round after safely completing the rapid, and every man (or woman) would man (or woman) the sides ready to grab and secure the floating deserter.

Finally we were told that in the event of the raft tipping over and someone being trapped under the raft, just to hang onto it inside the air pocket which would be trapped underneath and they would 'soon be rescued'.

I think it was at this point in the 'elf and safety' briefing that all blood had drained down to my feet, as I was told I had turned very pale.

Of course, before all this fun could be enjoyed we first had to get to the rafts by climbing over 350 feet down the side of the gorge to river level.

"Okay, everybody, let's go!" called the Sobek leader, and led the way to the point where we could begin our descent into the unknown.

I looked down at the gorge. "Are you seriously expecting me to climb down that lot?"

"Yes. Get a move on!" My husband was not sympathetic to my concerns.

Before I was to become the subject of death by drowning, I was being forced to climb down a treacherous slope. There was something which passed for a path at the beginning, but further down it seemed to just fade away. From then on it was a hit-and-miss, do-it-yourself, find-your-own-way arrangement through the rocks.

There were huge boulders as big as bull elephants surrounded by big rocks the size of rhinoceri (my word). These, in turn, were interspersed with medium baboon-sized rocks which were combined with smaller rocks like dassies. And if that lot didn't send me hurtling to my death I could slide down on my arse on the odd patch of scree, which would be about the size of kudu droppings. It was a typical African gorge access.

I was never good with rocks.

When I was a kid I used to love going with my parents on a Sunday to a beauty spot known as Dovedale, in Derbyshire, but there was always a long queue of frustrated people behind me as I slowly made my way over the stepping stones crossing the River Dove. I was terrified of slipping on a wet stone and finishing up in the sparkling cold waters of the shallow river.

Put me on a horse and I have perfect balance, but ask me to go rock hopping and I'll be on my backside, likely with broken bones, in no time at all.

Clambering down this gorge was rock-hopping on a whole different level. Or not. It seemed that no matter which rock I chose to stand on it most certainly was not level. My arms flailed about like droopy windmills as I tried to keep my balance. I carefully tested each rock before I gave it my weight and slithered down holding onto anything remotely holdable. It was going to take a long time to reach the bottom at this rate.

Fortunately those who had already accomplished this feat were finding the next stage of the adventure quite a slow process too, so my presence had not been missed.

By the way, dassie is the local name for a rock hyrax, which is like a cross between a large guinea pig and an elephant.

As I caught up with the group at the foot of the gorge I then had to walk several yards along a narrow ledge that a house cat would baulk at taking (well, *I* thought it was narrow) to reach the outcrop of rock from which we were alighting down into the rafts. As I inched my way along the ledge, *trying not to notice the sheer six-foot drop into the fast flowing river*, the bulkiness of my life jacket kept bumping on the rockface we were up against, making my balance even more precarious.

The natural consequence of all this is that I was a bag of nerves before we'd even started on the rafting bit.

There were five rafts in total, most holding six passengers, which we had been told was generally the ideal number for the journey. Ours was the last to board, and as we cast off from the flat launch rock our captain rowed as fast as he could upstream towards the falls to join the rest of the party who had been rowing round in circles fighting the river's current waiting for us. I felt sorry for the guy who'd been the first to launch as he must be knackered from the effort of fighting the flow before we began the journey downriver.

The International Scale of River Difficulty has six grades of difficulty in white water rafting. They range from *simple* to *very dangerous* and *potential death or serious injuries*. The grade of a rapid could also change according to the level of water at various times of year.

Like I said, we were going to be encountering ten rapids down the Zambesi. The most ferocious rapid was number nine named 'Commercial Suicide', and had to be portaged around. No-one was allowed to do this rapid as it carries a Grade 6 rating. We were, however, going to tackle two Grade 5s, which luckily I had not heard them say when they mentioned it at the onset, otherwise I'm sure I would have chickened out of the whole deal.

The Boiling Pot is where it all starts. It is like a series of watery speed-bumps before the river takes a sharp ninety-degree turn. Our leader back-paddled upstream as we waited to take our turn as the party set off down the Pot.

I sat in the rear half of the raft and clung to the rope which ran around the top of the inflatable as if my life depended on it. Even above the noise of the falls and the water swirling around us, I could hear the whoops and cheers of the guys in the preceding boats, clearly thoroughly enjoying their first wavy 'hit'. As the boat in front of us mounted the final wave of the Pot we saw one of its passengers gracefully somersault out of the raft into the river.

I held on even tighter! But I too was soon hooting with delight along with the rest, as we buffeted against the roll of waves which started our adventure down the Zambezi.

By the time we turned the corner the 'man overboard' had been retrieved. It was the oldest member of the party, a lady in her early sixties, and as she was hauled back into the raft she was laughing fit to burst. I'm not sure I would have found it *that* funny had it happened to me!

We soon encountered our first rapid, the Wall, which gave us a good idea of what we were in for. After this was the appropriately named one, the Bridge, which tumbled beneath the road/rail bridge linking Zambia to Zimbabwe. But the rest had been given the weirdest names.

At number three we had Morning Glory then there was the Stairway to Heaven; the Devil's Toilet Bowl; Gulliver's Travels; the Midnight Diner; Commercial Suicide and culminating, for us, in the Gnashing Jaws of Death!

We continued our merry way down the river, admiring the magnificent formation of the gorge when the water was quiet, and crashing through heaving waves and hurtling round enormous boulders when it wasn't.

Exciting. Scary. Exhilarating. Breathtaking. Stimulating. Majestic.

Wondrous. Heart-stopping. Sensational. I could blast you with so many words but they would barely touch the surface of this experience.

This raft is smaller, but similarly controlled to the one we'd been on.

Halfway through the trip we beached our rafts onto an atypical sandy patch and took a break for a light lunch. The rafts were equipped with watertight containers into which were placed enough food and drink for our party to enjoy during our break. They also stored our small personal bags containing things like wallet, camera (unless you had a waterproof one - highly unlikely in those days) and other small items.

Once suitably refreshed I was now actually looking forward to getting back on the river. I have to confess that the exhilaration of what I was experiencing far over-rode my previous apprehension. Even the first Grade 5 rapid we encountered hadn't put me off.

But that was until we met the next one. It was a biggy. I must admit I was crapping myself at the thought of doing this. After instructions from our leader as to what course we were going to take down it (boulders and sinks had to be avoided), we set off.

It was wild and fast and long and very, very scary. About two-thirds of the way through the rapid the raft smacked down particularly ferociously and to my absolute horror as I wiped water from my eyes there lay our leader, flat on his back, oars waving uselessly up in the sky. Looking quickly to the front, from my position kneeling at the back I was able to see that after the next drop we would come up against a huge wave. The big guys in the front were in the middle of spray and wouldn't have noticed this.

"Punch Front! Punch Front! PUNCH FRONT!" I screamed at the top of my voice as we were about to hit the wave.

Thankfully they heard me and did as they were bid and we crashed through the wave, otherwise we would have been up it, and flipped into the drink without a doubt. To say it took me a while to regain my composure after this would be somewhat of an understatement! Luckily for me, given my now rather shaky condition, we were in for a relatively smooth ride from then on.

We eventually reached the penultimate one, Commercial Suicide, where the raft was portaged. We all got out and the raft was held aloft as we clambered over 100 yards of rocks. All crew are supposed to help carry the raft but my arms weren't long enough to reach as high as the others, so I was able to give more attention to my rock-balancing act. As we stopped to admire rapid number nine we could see why this was banned from use. It was ferocious. The Sobek legend had it that a large colourful block of polystyrene was once thrown into the rapid and was never seen again!

The final rapid on our itinerary was a pleasure to enjoy, and at the end of the run it appeared customary for all crazy participants to take the opportunity for a swim in the river. It's not like any of us had to worry about getting wet as we were already soaked through to the skin. After all the excitement and adrenalin my previous aversion to swimming was well forgotten, and it seemed the perfect way to end the adventure.

But it turned out that, for me, the worst was yet to come.

It was a matter I had given no thought to until it was staring me in the face. The climb out of the gorge!

This was to be accomplished, unaided, after several hours of rafting, in October temperatures - one of the hottest months of the year in Zambia!

The height from water level to the top of the gorge was almost six hundred feet! Put in perspective, that is about the height of a 60-storey building! Can you imagine walking up the stairs of a 60-storey building? Can you imagine doing that walk without actual steps or a handrail?

Other than a few rocks and boulders around the base, the climb was up scrubby, vague paths or simply over patchy wild grass. There was nothing to hold on to and the gradient was so steep that with no sense of balance I dare not stand upright. I climbed virtually all the way out of that gorge on 'all fours'.

As I sweated and cursed my way up that slope, men employed from the local villages whizzed past carrying aluminium poles and oars on their shoulders, as well as the storage gear and huge bundles of collapsed, folded raft on their heads. And they did this with the ease of someone out for a brisk walk on a Sunday morning.

It took me half an hour to reach the top, by which time my knees were knackered, my pulse was pounding and my temper was in tatters.

Why had no-one installed a cable car? OK, maybe that was expecting a bit much, but they could have at least anchored a rope onto spikes which one could use to haul oneself up, or just hang onto for a bloody rest on the way up!

I gather that facilities have improved a bit over the past decades.

This video gives you a bit of an idea of what it was like, except in our case, none of us had paddles, just one central oarsman. https://www.youtube.com/watch?v=Yz7FjWlA6U4

We stayed one more night at the Mosi o Tunya Hotel where we had time the next morning to admire Victoria Falls from the top. It really is the most amazing spectacle, though what you can actually see is highly dependent on the time of year/volume of water flowing over that 350' drop. Luckily by October the flow was low, so the masking mist which fills the air during high water was not a problem for us. I would have loved to have seen it from even higher, by taking a chopper flight over the area, but alas by then time (and funds) were against us, as we flew back to Lusaka that afternoon.

ONE OF ZIGGY'S COLLEAGUES MET US AT THE AIRPORT WITH THE COMPANY car so we then had to drop him back at the office. I waited in the car while Ziggy went inside to touch base with the guys there for ten minutes.

As we drove back to the LGC Ziggy was amazingly quiet, then he cleared his throat.

"I'm afraid I've got a bit of bad news," he said.

I waited.

"There was a telex waiting for me in the office. It said they'd tried to telephone us but the phone just rang and rang."

"Who tried to phone?" I asked.

"Your dad, and I'm sorry to have to tell you this, but Doris died a few days ago."

I was stunned into silence. My grandmother, the one who had brought me up, was gone.

"Apparently she passed away peacefully in her sleep, in the hospital."

After several minutes I was able to speak.

"I know this is must sound a terrible thing to say, but it's perhaps for the best. She was incredibly unhappy about having to go into a nursing home. I know Doris, and no matter how good a place it might have been, she would have absolutely hated it."

I telephoned my dad that night. The funeral was set to happen in three days' time, There was no way I could make it home to attend. In those days there were only three flights out of Lusaka to London per week and the next available one, in the unlikely event that I could get on it, was on the eve of the funeral. With a ten-hour flight to London, then onward to East Midlands, by the time I'd have reached Burton the funeral would be over.

Anyway, it was probably as well I wasn't able to be involved with the funeral. Many, many years previously Doris had made me promise to carry out her special funeral plans when she died.

"I want my coffin and a load of booze to be put in the boot of a chara[1], which can take me and all my friends to the cemetery. Two charas if there's a lot of people. And first they must go for a drive in the countryside and stop somewhere along the way to have a knees-up."

Could you just picture it?

Two charas parked in a layby with the boots open, one operating as a mobile bar while the other displayed a large coffin, as a bunch of half-pissed people stood around, laughing, singing and dancing to the loud music emitting from one of the charas.

The mind boggles.

If I had tried to honour that promise I really didn't think it would have gone down well with the funeral parlour loading a coffin into the boot of a bus, or at the cemetery when it was delivered by a couple of busloads of drunks, although I'm sure quite a few of the friends and family would have thought it was a blast!

Yes, it was perhaps as well I was confined to Zambia at the time.

But I was very sad that I wouldn't be there to say goodbye. Instead, on the day, I went for a ride in the bundu, and at the time of the funeral said my weepy goodbyes to Doris from the back of my horse. She would have appreciated that.

---

1. **charabanc** noun / also chara, UK. a large old-fashioned bus, especially one used by groups of people for visiting places of interest.

20

WALKING SAFARI

Returning to Lusaka after our aquatic adventure we soon had to prepare for our next experience. Recalling the time Ziggy had been on the walking safari the previous year, he said that despite some drawbacks he'd had a wonderful time, and suggested we take a couple of days to do one together before we left Zambia for good.

I let him make all the arrangements.

Packing for the event was a doddle because clothes were down to basics. We knew there was little need for anything other than shorts, t-shirts, socks, walking shoes and underwear once we were on location. And hats. Photography would be limited to our SLR Olympus camera and mningi rolls of film; taking our video gear was not an option due to the sheer weight of the equipment which would need to be carried, and probable lack of charging facilities.

We took an uneventful flight to the now very familiar Mfuwe airport where we were greeted by a game ranger driving the customary three-tiered Land Rover. It took us about two hours to reach the bush camp, which was some distance past Mfuwe Lodge where we previously stayed in comparative luxury.

For the life of me I cannot recall the name of the bush camp place we went to, but it was a semi-permanent base consisting of four wood and thatch sleeping huts for guests, two either side of a large thatched rondavel which served as a lounge/bar and dining area. There was also, of course, staff accommodation, storeroom and a kitchen. Power for cooking and chilling facilities came from a generator, lighting was supplemented with paraffin lamps and communication with distant humans was limited to short-wave radio contact.

The sleeping huts were designed solely for that purpose. They were big enough to contain two single beds (with mosquito nets over, of course) placed either side of a central bedside table, plus there was a plain chair and a low bench onto which to place one's baggage. The walls were windowless though there was a small window in the door, which was secured by a very basic lift-and-drop latch.

The ablutions were something else.

Basic cleansing consisted of a table positioned outside one's hut on which was placed a large enamel bowl and jug of water, bar of soap and a towel. There was also a small quantity of boiled water for teeth-cleaning. (There was no such luxury as bottled water for sale back then.)

Guests were provided with two toilets situated on opposite sides of the outer 'boundary' of the totally unfenced camp. Each was a wattle-built construction about three feet by four feet in size, in which a bottomless metal drum was placed over a long-drop hole about five feet deep. Luxury came in the form of a plastic toilet seat perched precariously on the drum rim, and a toilet roll dangling on a piece of string from a protruding stalk of wattle. There was, of course, no flushing facility.

One did not linger long in there.

And before entering it was good policy to stand well back and whack the wattle walls with a stick to 'flush out' any unwanted visitors, such as rats or snakes or elephants.

(Just kidding about the elephants!)

This toilet design was quite good exercise for getting one's bodily functions into a strict routine, as I didn't dare go in there after dark.

For a thorough cleanse you could take advantage of the amazing shower facility.

This consisted of a three-sided wattle stall, the fourth side being completely open and facing the river. You didn't have to worry too much about peeping toms as no-one in their right mind would want to stand beside the crocodile-infested river for voyeur purposes. The base was made of wooden slats which would also benefit from being wacked by a large stick before entry to expel any wildlife lurking underneath.

The plumbing comprised a hosepipe, one end of which was fixed into a water butt, whilst the other end had a watering-can head attached to it. This was held in place above head height by string and crossed sticks. The temperature of the water for showering was dependent upon the time of day, i.e. the earlier in the day you took a shower the cooler the water was likely to be. Solar heating at its most basic soon increased the water temperature during the day.

As you can see, Ziggy spared no expense in providing top-notch accommodation for his beloved wife of twelve years.

We enjoyed these wonderful facilities along with a few guests - two other couples and a single Italian chap. During our forays into the bush we were led by a game ranger armed with a long walking stick (as opposed to a walking-stick). Oh I don't mean the stick walked, but that it was a stick of wood about five feet long hewn from a local tree, as opposed to a short one with a bent top used by old men in the street. Got it? For ease of identification we'll call him Jason (the ranger not the old man in the street) because I can't really remember his name after all this time.

Alongside Jason was a Zambian ranger (who we'll call John) who kindly carried a backpack containing a few pouches of boiled water. We were also accompanied by an official Zambian park warden who came armed with a rifle. It was comforting to know that we had protection against hungry lions, packs of wild dogs, charging warthogs, or whatever else came our way.

One thing Ziggy had mentioned was that for safety reasons when out 'viewing' you had to keep quite a distance from most of the game. Consequently our first two-hour stroll was quite bland. We only saw a few buck and zebra in the distance and some small monkeys chattering in the trees. But the walk was very pleasant, so peaceful with only birdsong and the swish of the dry grass beneath our feet.

Back at the camp we were well fed and at night we sat in the boma and listened to the rangers' tales of some of their more unusual experiences. Before turning in for the night we were advised that it was unwise to wander out of our huts once camp was closed for the night as 'animals wander through occasionally'.

The next day we were up bright and early and went off in a different direction. Alas again we didn't see much of any interest, certainly when compared to what we had seen when we'd been out on game drives on previous visits to South Luangwa. As we returned to camp the ranger said that his colleague would go out in the Land Rover that night to see where the game were settling in readiness for a more interesting walk the next day. I was listening to him as we walked along a track worn by various animals on the move when a sudden movement caught my eye: I simultaneously screamed and leapt into the air as if I had a rocket up my rectum and just caught sight of the snake beneath me before it slithered off into the long grass. I have no idea what sort of snake it was, neither did anyone else who'd managed to see it. I was shaking like a leaf for a few minutes and after that I kept my eyes firmly fixed to the ground ahead in case it had any family lurking around.

When we reached camp we all headed to the boma for a drink. After we were all seated enjoying cool beers a ranger who had stayed in camp told us that there had been a spitting cobra resting on the drinks shelf behind the bar. I quickly looked around to make sure it wasn't now anywhere near me.

"Oh don't worry," he said "I killed it and threw it outside." He didn't say *how* he'd killed it but that it had been necessary. So long as it was gone it was fine by me.

We chatted amongst ourselves for some time before I decided to brave the wattle WC. I almost didn't need to go that far. As I walked out of the boma, unexpectedly lying outside to the left of the open doorway was the dead, but none-too-small, spitting cobra. This time I nearly shat myself as the scream escaped my lips. Of course, the sickos back in the boma thought this was hilarious.

Every time I went out that doorway from then on, even though I knew it was there, I still jumped when I saw it.

If I never saw anything else, I had certainly had my fill of snakes at that place because later in the afternoon one of the other guests, the Italian gentleman who was quite an expert on snakes, came across a small one, fortunately of the harmless variety, in his hut. It was trying to eat a frog. Unfortunately for the snake, but luckily for the frog, it had made its assault on the wrong end and was trying to swallow the frog back-feet-first. This left the frog's front legs free to wave around at right angles to its body, stopping the snake from swallowing it. We watched it, totally fascinated, for nigh on ten minutes before the snake finally accepted defeat and spat it out. The frog quickly hopped away to safety.

At night we again sat around the boma listening to yet more scintillating tales of life in the African bush, occasionally joining in with some tales of our own experiences. One of the things mentioned in response to an experience I'd had at Mfuwe Lodge was that they often awoke in the morning to find spoor (footprints) of lion which had strolled through the camp at night. That just reinforced my determination never to go to the loo once it was dark. At about ten o'clock we all headed off to bed, ready for an early start the next day.

Goodness knows what time it was, but in the middle of the night I was suddenly awakened by the most horrendous noise. It sounded like someone had tipped a dumpster-load of empty beer cans outside our hut and was stomping on them. What the hell?

I jumped out of bed, well, as much as one can jump out of a bed which is shrouded in mosquito netting, and made my way to the door. I crept over to the hinged side of the door so that if it were suddenly opened by something I would be hidden behind it. The door stayed put. I then slowly moved my head until I could see through the small window.

Not three yards away stood the biggest bloody elephant I had ever seen (well I was standing on the ground instead of sitting atop a Land Rover). This jumbo was stretching its body until its front feet were lifted, and was reaching up into the tree which stood beside our hut. With its trunk it tugged on something high out of my range of sight which it then placed in its mouth and began crunching. *That* was the noise I had heard. I watched, fascinated for several minutes, at the same time somewhat worried that if it needed to scratch an itch and chose our hut instead of the tree, the entire thing would come tumbling down around us.

Only the buzzing of mosquitoes around me forced me back into the relative safety (from mozzies, not elephants) of my bed. Of course Ziggy slept through all this.

I told the rangers about it next morning, but they had already seen the spoor and debris left on the floor from his visit.

"Oh, sorry. We forgot to tell you about the Winterthorn tree being one the elephants' favourites. The just love eating the pods", they said matter-of-factly.

Over an early light breakfast we were told our plan for the morning. The ranger had found a pride of lions tucking into their night's kill, a young buffalo, 'within reasonable walking distance' of camp, which we were going to see. We were very excited (and more than a little apprehensive, I can tell you).

After walking a mile or so we came across a huge herd of buffalo.

Before we go any further I think I'd better explain a few things to those not so familiar with the wilds of Africa.

In regard to game there are the Big Five (originating from hunting I'd assume). This consists of Elephant, Rhinoceros, Cape Buffalo, Lion and Leopard. If you get to see all the Big Five while on a game viewing trip you can consider yourself extremely lucky.

Whilst you might think that buffalo are nothing more than a large cow or bull they are, strangely enough, considered to be extremely dangerous. I quote:

"The reason early trophy hunters included the African buffalo, as one of the big five is that they were considered to be one of the most dangerous species to hunt.

When hunted by humans, buffalo have a reputation for circling back on their pursuers and counter attacking.

The danger lies with older males who usually live away from the herd. Their "attack is the best defense" strategy can make them very dangerous."

If you would like to read more, here's a good site: http://www. africa-wildlife-detective.com/african-buffalo.html]

Now we were about to walk through the middle of a bloody great herd of them.

There must have been about a hundred animals off to our left, with a gap roughly half a mile wide before reaching the bulk of the herd, which must have numbered up to three, even four hundred beasts.

We had to cross about four hundred yards of ground to pass between the two sections of the herd.

I was not happy about this arrangement but there was no alternative - I certainly wasn't going to risk walking back to camp alone, even if I'd been allowed to.

Of course we succeeded with this stroll through the park without any incident and carried on in search of our pride of lions. We walked pretty much parallel to a dry river bed for about another mile or more; Jason was in the lead along with the park warden and his trusty rifle, followed by the rest of us with John bringing up the rear.

The pace was quite casual and the going easy as most of the grass in this area had obviously been worn flat by the passing or grazing of various game over the months. We were walking through a sparsely-wooded area and conversation was kept to a minimum as we all enjoyed our peaceful surroundings, so it came over loud and clear when the lead ranger suddenly said, "What was that?"

We all stopped and tried to see what he was looking at. About 50 yards ahead of us we saw a boulder in the longer grass. It moved. Towards us!

"Buffalo!" called the ranger.

Everyone scattered!

I ran to the nearest tree, which would have given me about as much protection from a charging buffalo as a mouse hiding from a cat behind a matchstick.

Next thing a shot rang out. It was loud.

"Did you get it?"

"I think so."

"You *THINK* so?" cried Jason.

The park warden looked worried. "Let us see," he said.

"Everybody take cover." Shouted the ranger.

I decided to abandon my tree and instead ran the few yards to the edge of the river bank. There was a narrow ledge a few feet down before dropping another six feet to the river bed. I figured if I got on that ledge and crouched down, even if the buffalo decided to race in my direction and leap into the dry river, it would sail over my head.

I took up my position and peeked over the top. The two men were walking towards where the 'boulder' had been. Before they reached the spot someone shouted, "There it is!"

It was trotting away about 70 yards to the right of us.

Now the park warden stood and took aim. BOOM! Another shot rang out.

As we watched we could actually see a puff of dust rise up from the buffalo's flank before he galloped away, out of sight.

The ranger and warden returned to where we were, calling us all together. I must admit that being aware of the buffalo's reputation I was somewhat reluctant to leave my place of safety.

Once we were gathered, the lead ranger enlarged upon our situation - as if we needed much enlargement, until...

He explained that the warden had managed to hit the buffalo with both shots, but obviously not in the right place to down it. There was no point in trying to track it to finish it off as,

a) It could run a lot faster than we could, and

b) The park warden didn't have any more ammunition.

WHAT????

We could not believe our ears.

He was only armed with *two* bullets, for Pete's sake?

We were told that the government restricted the amount of ammunition which wardens were allowed to carry, and that limit was two bullets per day!

We had set out on foot in the wilds of Africa in search of LIONS and he'd only come armed with two bloody bullets? Given the nature of lions, we might have stood a chance, as they would most likely run away at hearing a shot. Or especially two. But a buffalo - never mind a twice-wounded buffalo - is not likely to be so forgiving.

"So what now?" we asked.

"We have to get back to camp as quickly as possible so that I can get on to headquarters and arrange for more ammo to be collected. Then we can try and track him and put him down before he does any damage, or suffers too much." The ranger looked distressed.

HE was distressed?

So now we had to turn around and walk two miles or more back to the camp, with a pride of lions somewhere behind us, a herd of hundreds of buffalo to walk through the middle of, and a wounded, probably very angry buffalo charging around God knows where in between.

I have been frightened many times during my life in Africa, but I have never been so terrified as I was that morning. My knees were shaking like crazy and my legs felt so weak I could barely put one foot in front of the other, never mind propel myself forwards at a brisk walk.

That was the longest walk of my life. And during it my imagination was in overdrive. Picture this:

We are walking between the two herds of buffalo when the large male, who is carrying two bullets, losing blood and feeling a bit miffed, comes charging into the back of the rear herd in search of the bastard who shot him. The herd are somewhat startled by this and in panic, immediately stampede in our general direction. Result: instead of being gored to death by the angry bull's enormous horns, we are trampled flat by hundreds of his teammates.

OR

The pride of lions, having been rudely awakened from their post-supper slumbers by two very loud bangs decide to check out what the hell's going on. Ah, within minutes they smell blood.

Perhaps the buffalo they had been feasting on the night before was only a baby one, and they now felt a little peckish: "Ah, what else is this we smell? Humans? Frightened humans at that! Let's check this out chaps."

So the pride breaks into a slow trot following the scent of their next meal. And lo and behold, there they are, stumbling their way through the grass as they head towards the gap between two herds of buffalo. And they are so busy watching the movement of the large beasties that they don't even notice that they are just about to be pounced upon from behind. What easy pickings for the lions.

I can tell you I was almost sick with relief when we arrived safely at the camp. After taking instructions from Jason on the way back we hastened to our cabin and quickly gathered up our possessions. We were to head straight off in the Land Rover to Mfuwe Lodge. There the park warden would find a suitably-qualified colleague to help track down the wounded animal.

Before returning to the camp with two wardens *and extra ammo*, Jason organised for Mfuwe Lodge to provide transport to take us onward to the airport.

What a whirlwind end it was to our few days on safari. Alas, we never did hear how they got on with tracking the buffalo, but hoped it was humanely dispatched.

ONE OF THE THINGS (AMONGST SO MANY) WHICH I KNEW I WAS GOING TO miss in England was the wonderful flavour and low price of Zambia's fillet steaks. Having several spare hours to hand during our last two days in Lusaka I decided to make good use of it. I went along to my regular supplier and bought three huge beef fillets. In the kitchen of our friends Ruth and Rolf, I seared the meat all round before wrapping the whole fillets in foil and putting them in the deep freezer.

I figured that in the couple of hours between them being taken out of Ruth's freezer and being in my suitcase in the incredibly cold temperature of the hold up in the jet stream, they would not thaw out. We could then wean ourselves off this luxury slowly once back in Burton on Trent.

The day of our final departure from Zambia arrived. I spent most of it in tears as I passed through the hugs of the many friends I had made in Lusaka.

I know I've mentioned this before, but there is something different about the friendships you make with fellow expats, which will always be special. Having said that, several of my friends at the gymkhana club were actually born in Africa, so weren't exactly expats, but they were special nonetheless.

Quite a crowd gathered at Lusaka airport to say their final farewells "and to make bloody sure you get on that plane" some wit said.

So once again I was crying on an aircraft, albeit for a less traumatic reason this time.

21

BACK TO BLIGHTY

Our journey back to England was a little eventful. We were flying via Italy and Germany and amazingly the aircraft was not full, so Ziggy was able to move to a better seat to watch the film while I utilised our two rear seats to have a little sleep. After all the alcohol I'd consumed at our farewell-at-the-airport-party it didn't take me long to nod off. When we landed at Rome most of the passengers disembarked, leaving even more space for a good stretch-out and continuation of my night's sleep. Or so I thought. First we had to get off the ground.

A short while beyond our estimated time of departure the pilot announced that our take off was delayed due to adverse weather conditions in Frankfurt, as the airport was completely enveloped in freezing fog and no planes were able to land. Shortly after this announcement the coffee trolley came round.

Half an hour later Captain Grundy announced, "Ladies and gentlemen, I am sorry to report that the fog is still in place in Frankfurt so we will now be serving breakfast."

After that was all consumed and cleared away he came on yet again. In an effort to appease his irritated and bored passengers a film was going to be shown. Alas it was one which didn't interest me so I entertained myself with crosswords, and the various music and comedy channels available through the headphones.

As the film ended a cheery captain spoke to us once more saying he was about to commence his pre-flight checks as a gentle breeze was now starting to clear Frankfurt airport.

On our arrival in Frankfurt it came as no surprise to find we had missed our connecting flight to London Heathrow and, of course, all outgoing airlines were battling to now accommodate the sudden surge of passengers who had missed earlier flights. When we eventually arrived in London we discovered one of our suitcases had not. And it had to be the one containing all the frozen fillet steak! We then had to report the missing luggage. We advised the clerk that that particular suitcase contained 3 litres of whisky and 400 cigarettes, though accidentally forgot to mention the fillet steak. An hour later we were able to secure a flight to our final destination of East Midlands Airport.

When we had eventually knocked on the door at our Burton house at quarter to ten on the night of our arrival we were given a great welcome by the kids and my dad. It felt like we'd been away from them much longer than the three weeks it was.

The following day we had a call from British Midlands Airways to say they were sending our suitcase to us in a taxi and needed our address. Five minutes later there was another call to say, "Sorry, but unfortunately the fillet steak which was in the suitcase has been confiscated by customs." We'd much rather have had them take the cigarettes and whisky!

My dad and the kids had been getting along nicely in our absence, and he reported that they had been relatively well behaved, apart from one minor incident.

While they were at school my dad told us about it. Apparently he had trouble with Brad and Leon arguing, though he couldn't even remember what it was about. But they'd had a row resulting in Leon being sent to his room, where he sulked for the remainder of the afternoon.

The following morning, after the kids had gone to school, Mev found a folded note on the dining table, bearing the words "To Grandad" on the outside. Inside was written:

"I don't like living here with you any more so when I get my bike I'm leaving home. Signed Leon James Patras"

Happily by the time his bike arrived from Zambia some weeks later he had changed his mind although, even to this day, if he gets a bit miffed with someone, he gets asked, "So are you leaving when you get your bike, Leon?"

Now I know this book is supposed to be about our lives in Africa, but it would be pretty daft to leave a total void of what we got up to in the UK because, let's be honest, the lunacy of the Patras lives does not alter just because we're back in the country of our birth, so I'll continue rambling on about 'the bit in the middle'.

Before the bikes had arrived with everything else, we'd been occupying our time doing a different unpack. In order to find room at the house for all the stuff due to arrive, we had to go through all the boxes we'd left behind when we first moved to Zambia. A fine tooth comb was required to see what we could throw out from that lot. Then we went through my dad's stuff too, lots of which he didn't use and he reckoned never would.

Unlike Zambia where everything had a high second-hand value, the UK did not. The local charities fared very nicely from our donations of discards.

Then it got boring as we waited for the excitement of unpacking our Zambia crates. The miserable British weather did nothing to lift one's spirits and the most excitement we got was when Ziggy, Mev and I fought over who was going to wash the dishes.

Eventually, on Wednesday 26th November, at 2:05pm to be precise, our crates arrived. After unloading the back of a small truck dedicated entirely to our stuff, our count-up revealed that we had the right number of boxes, except they weren't all ours. We found a large packing crate which was bound for Amsterdam with someone else's name on it, and one of our crates was missing. That issue was eventually rectified, but in the meantime we found other problems when we began unpacking the boxes.

The first thing we realised was missing was our dartboard, which had been the last thing packed into one of the boxes. As we came to use stuff over the following weeks, other things came to light as having been nicked, like scarves, clothes and even cosmetic items, of all things.

That was the one thing which I would *not* miss about Zambia, the amount of theft and need for constant vigil and security.

When I had been packing our stuff in Lusaka I was horrified and deeply disappointed to find that several items of jewellery were missing. Nothing vastly expensive: some small gold ankle chains and bracelets which had been all the rage a year or so earlier, as well as a couple of dress rings. There was absolutely no doubt that these items could only have been stolen by either Benton or his wife. I suspected the latter, as she had occasionally helped in the house when Benton was off sick or at special church meetings, and of course when we were horsing around in Kitwe. But whomsoever, the fact remained that I had trusted them completely, and had tried to help them in so many ways over the years Benton had worked for us.

One thing I *was* already missing greatly was horse riding. It got to the point where I wouldn't watch westerns on the television, nor horse racing, because that reminded me so much of Tilly. Even when we went to our local pubs I had to avoid looking at their calendars which, having been supplied by the local bookies, sported pictures of racehorses and instantly got me thinking about what I was missing. I know, it was ridiculous!

But I wasn't the only one missing the riding. Christmas was rapidly approaching and to get an idea of what they would like in the way of presents, we asked the kids to write letters to Santa. I knew they had now reached the stage where they knew Santa was fictitious but to keep up the spirit of Christmas they still went along with my ruse. This says it all:

"Dear Santa

*All I want for Christmas is a Sledge, some Snow and a Pony. If you
think I deserve anything else I'll leave the choice up to you.
Love Leon"*

He showed me the letter before putting it in the 'Santa envelope'
and I explained to him that I was afraid he had no chance of getting a
pony as apart from the fact that we weren't in a position to keep one at
the moment, Santa would never get it down the chimney! But he did
get his sledge and, eventually, some snow. And what fun that led to.

It was a cold January day when it started. Within an hour of the
first snowfall Leon was out in the garden with a trowel trying to collect
enough snow to build a snowman. He could barely raise enough to
make even a small snowball and eventually gave up until the morrow.

The next day we had another sprinkling of snow where he
progressed to trying to scrape it off the greenhouse roof, resulting in
enough to make a big snowball.

On the third day we awoke to a Siberian blizzard when the
snowman was temporarily forgotten as this was clearly the stuff
sledging was made for. Leon of course had his very own one-man
sledge, a pre-formed plastic oblongish disc with raised edges at the
front and back and handles at the side. The previous day I had the
foresight to buy a similar but larger sledge which could accommodate
both Vicki and Brad. To ensure fair play (and safety) I decided to
accompany them on their first wild sledging adventure.

Well it wasn't too far out in the wilds, as we'd heard a good place
for sledding was along the slopes surrounding the local
comprehensive school located at the top of our street. These were
about 30 foot high with a slope of about 40 degrees which was just
enough for them to get a bit of speed up. We found a nice spot for
our enjoyment and I stood at the top of the slope as chief pusher-
offer.

You may be wondering now how a sun worshiper like me was
coping, standing out in these arctic conditions. Easy: I had donned
thermal vest and leggings, a t-shirt, two jumpers, jeans tucked into two
pairs of socks, riding boots and the whole lot topped with a sheepskin
coat and mittens, a woolly scarf and hat. I could have stayed out there

all day! Well I could have if I hadn't got snow up my sleeves and down my back.

You see, the kids looked like they were having a fantastic time and I decided I should join in. The bigger sled being the subject of considerable demand I decided to try my luck on Leon's little sledge. So, perched at the top of the slope I carefully lowered my well-padded butt into the form of the seat, which filled up over half the available space. I then had to bring my knees up under my armpits in order to fit my feet under the front rim of the sledge. This necessitated me grabbing my ankles with diagonally opposite hands and pulling with all my strength.

Now completely wedged in the sledge I was preparing to push myself off when one of the kids beat me to it. Of course, with my weight on top of it, it didn't take long for the sledge to gain momentum. Just as I was beginning to enjoy myself the bloody thing started to veer off to the left, straight into the path of an advancing 14- · year-old who was pulling a massive metal-framed sled back up the slope.

I immediately screamed at him to get out of the way, but instead the bloody idiot started to veer off to his left, making our potential point of impact even closer. Just before collision time he leapt into the air while I threw myself off to the right to avoid colliding with his sled, and proceeded to roll, arse over tit, down the rest of the slope and beyond. The sledge came to rest somewhere further along.

As I picked myself up and tried to remove the snow from up my sleeves and out of my pockets I looked up to see all the kids - and not just *my* kids - in fits of hysterics over my 'downfall'!

Despite what you may expect I did have another go, several in fact, though I then used the larger sledge.

The next day brought more snow and considerable drifting so we had to pick a different site. The kids took great delight in trying to wade through the drifts, though I had to put my foot down at one point with Vicki when she disappeared up to her armpits. Meanwhile the intrepid Leon found an ideal slope where he could ramp off some of the ridges in grand style.

Not yet out earning our daily bread, Ziggy had deigned to come with us this time and was responsible for most of the runs being increased in speed and length by some fifty percent as a result of an almighty shove at the onset. And of course, not to be outdone by these kids, I had to have a go at the ramp too, didn't I?

As the bigger sledge was being utilised some way off I decided to use the smaller one again. You'd think I'd learn, wouldn't you? But no, I crammed my body into the small disc once again and made a point of holding onto the side handles so as not to get caught out by the sled falling away from me as I soared off the ramp. So, having ensured that absolutely nothing or nobody was going to get in my way this time, off I went.

With the master shover sending me off, I hurtled downhill and hit the ramp at a slight angle, so instead of soaring through the air then gliding on across the snow, the airborne sledge with me still on it began tilting to one side. I leaned back to try and break the impact and nearly broke my bloody back! I'd forgotten about the raised ledge at the back of the sledge, and as it hit the ground, with my almost horizontal form, my backbone carried the full weight of the rest of me as I slammed onto the ledge.

I fell off the side of the sledge expecting to find myself paralysed, but eventually managed to roll over, completely winded and with a terrible pain in my back. After crawling along on all fours for some yards I managed to stand up and stagger back up the slope.

I limped home and haven't been on a sledge since. Not that I haven't been invited. In fact the very next day, as I was still hobbling around in a permanent stoop, Leon asked me if I was going sledging with them again. I told him, in no uncertain terms!

When we had a second bout of snow a few weeks later I stuck to making snowmen.

22

SETTLING BACK IN

We had settled well into our English house, where my dad had been living for the previous two years, but found ourselves much more crowded than we'd been used to for the past six years. My poor dad was really cramped up in his bedroom which barely managed to accommodate a single bed and a small wardrobe. Hardly what he had been used to most of his life.

Another issue made things a bit awkward first thing in the morning too. Invariably my dad was the first up, and by the time the rest of us surfaced he had been long settled with his newspaper and cups of tea. Opening the door to our combined lounge/dining room was like rounding a sharp bend in a country road and being confronted by a pea-souper fog. My dad enjoyed a smoke, and plenty of them. We would walk in wafting our hands in front of our faces in an attempt to clear the haze.

We eventually lessened these problems by buying a caravan which we parked well inside our drive, on the edge of the rear garden. That gave my dad a much more spacious bedroom as well as the freedom to smoke uncriticised. Once we were all moving around after breakfast he would join us in the house, where doors being opened and closed on a continuous basis dissipated most of the smoke he created.

Considering that we had three generations living together we managed remarkably well.

It came as no surprise that the kids soon settled into life in England. They renewed old and made new friends at school, which was a five-minute walk away, and had a whale of a time when winter presented them with snow, although the novelty of winter soon wore off after that was gone and their playtime was frequently limited to indoor activities, a situation alien to them. Their friends' addiction to television also came as quite a surprise.

One small incident will always remain with me. Vicki had a friend, Trixie, and all the kids were playing a board game when the girl chimed up, "Ain't you gonna switch the telly on? It starts in five minutes."

"What does?" asked Vicki

"EastEnders!" said Trixie.

"What's that?" asked Leon, shaking the dice.

"Ain't you 'eard of it?"

"Nope."

"EastEnders, it's on telly every Tuesday and Thursday."

Leon and Vicki looked at each other as if she were talking Greek.

"It's my mum's favourite. *Everybody* watches EastEnders." persisted Trixie.

"Well *we* don't. So if *you* want to watch it you'd better go home. Whose turn is it?" said Brad with finality.

ONE OF THE THINGS WHICH WE DID LIKE TO WATCH ON TELEVISION WAS ICE skating. As a result, in a rare moment of madness, I suggested to the kids that we go ice skating one day. Silly me.

There was no such thing as an ice rink in Burton, but I had heard of one somewhere in the vicinity of Solihull which was where our pals Jane and Robin lived. I figured that they'd be able to find the rink much easier than me, so arranged to meet at their flat and Jane would come with us.

We found the place without problem and queued for fifteen minutes to get inside, then a further twenty minutes to get skates.

Of course I had opened my big mouth early in this proposition and said that I too would give it a go. When you've said something like that to a bunch of under tens they don't forget it, so I couldn't back out.

I warned the kids that ice skating was nowhere near as simple as roller skating, at which they were already well accomplished, and that they mustn't go dashing off in wild abandon as I didn't want to see any broken legs.

As soon as Brad had laced up his skates he stood up and, closely followed by Leon and Vicki, strolled over to the rink entrance, saying he couldn't understand what all the fuss was about. And off they skated.

Finally strapped into my skates I stood up, wobbled around a bit without even moving my feet, and promptly sat back down again.

"How come my kids don't have rubbery ankles like I have?"

Clinging desperately to Jane's arm I slowly walked over to the ice. She, very sensibly, had elected to 'be in charge of the coats and things'.

Once I was on the ice it was unbelievable. I thought I just needed that familiar feeling of smoothness under my feet to recall my past abilities. Only after I pushed myself away from the barrier into the mainstream of skaters, did I remember that I actually had no abilities in the past when it came to ice skating, unless you counted the ability to make an absolute prat of yourself.

I dared not move. Hordes of kids and a few accomplished adults came whizzing past me. I wanted to turn and try to make the half-dozen shuffles it would take to return to the gateway through which I'd entered, but there was a very strict code of travel in one direction only, anticlockwise.

There was a short lull in the traffic so I plucked up the courage to at least try and make it to the barrier. Easier said than done, as I seemed to be travelling one slide forward to two slides back.

I lunged forward, and as I stretched to grab hold of the perimeter board I looked up to see Jane doubled over in raucous agony. She was having a fit of hysterics in the stalls, and when I saw her I started to laugh and then daren't move at all. It wasn't helped by Jane who, coming up for air, shouted that I'd better not wet myself or the warm pee might melt the ice, then I'd be in big trouble with the officials.

How I made those last couple of feet to the edge I do not know.

I vowed never to go ice skating ever again. But one good thing did come out of it. It was the most I'd laughed since leaving Zambia, which cheered me up no end.

ON THE WORK FRONT ZIGGY STILL DIDN'T HAVE A JOB. HE'D APPLIED FOR A few posts, and had even been offered a couple of positions, but when he'd looked into them further found they weren't exactly what he wanted so turned them down. But he hadn't appreciated how tight the job situation was, and as we were approaching the end of February realised he perhaps should not have been so hasty in his decisions.

While he continued to look I figured I'd better see if there was some office work I could do in the meantime and registered myself with a couple of employment agencies. I was offered my first 4-day temporary position with an out-of-town company, starting the following Tuesday. I spent most days copying statistics from computer sheets onto large sheets of paper, using a pencil. Then totting up the columns using a calculator - I had to make sure they balanced before overwriting it all in pen. I have never been so bored at a job in my life!

This was in an office full of seven other women who worked telephone sales, and when they weren't yakking to their customers they were prattling amongst themselves. By lunchtime on the second day I had completed all the work it normally took the regular employee all week to carry out, so they were looking for things to keep me occupied. They found something - a serious backlog of filing. Even as a secretary the one job I had detested was filing, now I was stuck doing it for over two days.

When I got home on Thursday, Ziggy told me I'd had a call from another agency. I quickly phoned them and they offered me work for the following two weeks at Allied Breweries in our town. I'm sure you can imagine my joy when, back at the boring office on Friday, I was able to decline their request for me to work the following week.

It was while I was working at Allied that Ziggy got in touch with an old boss of his. Well he wasn't actually *old*, but Ziggy worked with him *of old*, as they say, and asked him if he knew of any jobs going. Alan told him, "Get your arse over to Immingham straight away," as the company he worked for was crying out for people with Ziggy's skills.

He was offered a permanent post straight away, but he first wanted to find out a bit more about the company and the working conditions at the location, so they agreed to accept him on a contractor basis for the time being.

It was great to finally have a regular income, but we were now back in exactly the same position we'd been in before we went to live in Zambia, with Ziggy going off to work on a Monday (or Sunday night depending on transport) and only returning home on Friday night. Not my idea of a happy way of life!

During this time we didn't have our own car. Fortunately I had the use of my dad's, within reason. One week when the kids were on half-term holiday I decided to take advantage of Ziggy's location in Immingham on the coast and on the Monday take the kids to the 'seaside'. Setting off early it only took us two hours to drive there in my dad's car. We dropped Ziggy at his site and were on the Cleethorpes sea front before 8:00, but what to do now?

The first question Brad asked was, "So Mummy, can we go for a swim in the sea?"

"Er, yes."

"But Mummy, where *is* the sea?" asked Vicki.

"It's out."

"Out where?" asked Leon.

"Out there." I responded, pointing to the horizon.

"Well, all I can see is sand," said Vicki, squinting into the distance.

If you're a Brit, you won't be surprised by this if you've ever been to an English seaside, but for those who haven't…

When the tide is out the sea is so far away you'd be lucky if you could see it, so goodness only knows how far you'd have to paddle before it was deep enough to be able to swim in it! That aside, it really wasn't a day for swimming outdoors anyway. While not exactly cold, it wasn't warm either. It was a sort of overcast 'none' day.

After a short stroll along the empty promenade we eventually came across the local swimming baths, to find they didn't open until 9:00. To kill time I found a sea-front café that was open, only to discover that my financial status was limited to 90p in my purse. So I had a coffee and the kids made do with some pop we had in the car. But now we had to wait around until 9:30 when the banks opened so that I could get some cash (we weren't yet equipped with ATM cards). We eventually arrived back at the leisure centre for the kids to have their swim.

It was a very pleasant facility. There was a water chute and a wave machine, both being quite a novelty for our kids in those days. I was almost tempted to get changed and join them in their fun. Almost. At 11:30 we were kicked out as our session had come to an end. We wandered back along the 'front' to see what alternative excitement awaited us. There we found a small roller coaster, a mini big wheel, an average looking helter skelter and one of those roundabouts which has chairs dangling on chains and goes round at about fifty miles an hour and makes all the participants feel like barfing. Of course, the kids went on everything.

After hamburger and chips for lunch at a seafront establishment, and the compulsory purchase of sticks of rock and bags of candy floss to take home, I decided that in the lack of anything else of interest there, it was time we made our way back to Burton.

When we had dropped Ziggy at work he had suggested that we try an alternative route home.

"Go through Lincoln and Newark, it's dual carriageway most of the way and a lot less boring than the motorway," he said.

Ten miles outside Cleethorpes I got stuck behind a load of lorries for the next thirty miles, after which a stretch of dual-carriageway allowed me to overtake. At the next roundabout I took a wrong turn and by the time I got back on the right road all the lorries were in front of me again. After an hour and a half I was crawling along in a traffic jam in the middle of Newark. Once I exited that town I actually managed to bypass Nottingham quite nicely and things were going well until I realised that instead of heading south-west towards Burton I was heading north-west towards Derby, where I *really* didn't want to go.

Now that mistake had taken me along a route which was littered with roadworks and temporary traffic lights, so I didn't want to retrace *those* steps. I decided to cut through a residential area to get to where (hopefully) I should be going.

Have you ever had one of those moments where you've thought *I really shouldn't have done that*? Of course you have. Listen to me, you'd think I was the only person who continues to do very stupid things. What? Okay, so I am.

I found myself behind a car which seemed to be doing the same short-cut thing as me - until he turned into his driveway. I drove on, in what I hoped was the right direction.

By this time the kids were really fed up, having long since tired of their game of 'let's see how many red/blue/green cars (one colour each) we can count', and Brad was complaining of not feeling so good.

As I drove along the Yew Tree Avenues and Buttercup Ways I heard the familiar, dreaded sound of retching. I glanced sideways to see Brad had thrown up his burger and chips all down the front of his jacket and was continuing, possibly to see if he could reach as far as his shoes. I was personally surprised to see so many onions - I hadn't realised they had put so many in the burger. I thought I could also see parts of the stick of rock I'd bought him to take home.

By now Vicki and Leon in the back seats were leaning forward to see what was happening. If they catch sight of that lot, I thought, it will probably set them off, and I'll cop for the lot down my back from Leon, who was sitting behind me.

"For God's sake, DON'T LOOK!" I screamed at them.

It was then I realised that we didn't have any tissues in the car, and the best I could find in the car's glove compartment was a couple of bar counter advertising cloths which had been used for wiping the windscreen. I waved these over Brad so that it might at least wipe his face and cover up the mess.

While all this was going on I was still driving around the bloody housing estate, trying to find the A38 dual carriageway that would take us home. Then I spotted a row of shops off to our left so I headed for them and pulled over. I handed Vicki and Leon some money and sent them off to the shops to buy tissues. Even that action was easier said than done, as my handbag sat on the floor by Brad's feet which, as I leaned over to reach it, brought me perilously close to the stinking mess which splattered his trousers.

Getting out of the car I went round to the passenger side and tried to extricate Brad from the front seat without spreading the diced carrots any further. I hadn't realised they put diced carrots in beef burgers! Anyway, this was a precarious operation having to first unfasten his seat belt, which entailed me leaning across him to find the catch. Brad couldn't possibly do it himself, having his hands full at the time, as it were.

I eventually got him out onto the pavement and proceeded to remove his clothes, leaving the poor lad standing in his pants and t-shirt. He even had to take off his shoes and socks which had unfortunately copped for a lot as he stood up. By this time Leon and Vicki had returned, only to announce that all the shops were closed.

Only then did I remember the swimming towels in the boot of the car. I used one to contain his stinking clothes and a second to try to remove what I could from his face, hands and arms (as he'd held his hands to his mouth the bloody stuff had run all down the inside of his sleeves as far as his elbows). Then I covered him up with the third.

By this time I was ashen. Trying desperately not to throw up myself, I gagged and heaved my way through trying to mop up the front seat and carpet.

I made sure that the other two kept well away from Brad as he was still reeking of regurgitated burger, onions, tomato ketchup and Cleethorpes rock. Eventually I was ready to re-seat him in the front, only to find that his seat belt too was still covered in slimy gunk. No way could I put that on him, it would be right under his nose and probably set him off again. Now, fresh out of towels, I was back into the swim bag and resorted to wiping the belt with damp swimming costumes.

"Oh, no, Mummy," cried Vicki, "I'll never wear that swimsuit again as long as I live!"

Back on the road it only took two more turns before I saw signs for the A38 and I soon found myself in familiar territory, from where we made a rapid drive home.

We arrived outside our door at 6:00, three hours after our departure, being half as long again as it had taken us to get to Cleethorpes in the morning.

My dad was horrified when he saw the state of affairs but, bless him, offered to clean up the car while I cleaned up Brad in the bath. A round-off to the day was in the garden, having to hose down all of Brad's clothes, as well as the swimming stuff, before putting them into the washing machine. There was no way I could risk catching sight of diced carrots swirling around in there.

Needless to say, certain items were not included on our menu for some considerable time.

23

SOOTY

Time shuffled along and, as Vicki and Leon's birthday approached in March, thoughts had to be directed towards presents. Leon was easy, he wanted to have piano lessons.

I thought this was an excellent idea barring one minor setback. I recalled from my own childhood when I too had piano lessons, that it was necessary to practice quite regularly between lessons. This could prove to be an issue for Leon, since we did not own a piano. Of course, when I mentioned this slight drawback to Leon he announced that it wouldn't be a problem at all as his friend Christian's dad conveniently had a Casio keyboard which he was willing to sell cheap (an unused Christmas gift, I suspected). Problem solved.

Lessons and keyboard were duly purchased.

Vicki wasn't so easy to choose for as she didn't have any particular interests at the time, but I knew exactly what to get for her. Something which had been missing from her and our lives for too long.

When they returned home from school on the day of their birthday they opened their other gifts before Leon unwrapped his *surprise* keyboard and opened an envelope containing his voucher for music lessons in town. Vicki was presented with a cardboard box.

"Open it carefully Vicki, it's very fragile." I said.

She approached the box, which I had placed on the coffee table, and reached for the lid before leaping back with a startled cry.

"Mummy, it made a noise!" She wailed.

"Don't be daft," I said, "how can a cardboard box make a noise? Go on, open it."

Standing well back she gingerly stretched out her arms to reach the lid and opened the first flap. Another slight thump came from the box, but this time she was more curious than afraid and inching forward with eyes wide as saucers she pulled back the flaps and peered inside.

"Oh, Mummy!" she yelled, and reaching into the box, pulled out a ball of black fluff. A ball of black fluff with four legs, a head and a tail. It was a puppy!

Earlier in the week I had paid a visit to the local RSPCA while the kids were at school. I fell in love with the black fluff ball on first sight. After a discussion with the lady in charge we thought it was likely to be a Labrador/retriever. He was totally black apart from a small white star on his chest. After going through all the formalities and paying the fees, I arranged to collect him just before school came out on the birthday.

What a superb dog he turned into. Vicki called him Sooty. When we first took him to the vet to continue his course of vaccinations, the vet thought he might be a Newfoundland cross. I had never heard of a Newfoundland before, but the vet was able to show us a picture of one on a chart he had. Given the size those beauties can reach I was thankful that the vet turned out to be wrong.

We had a large garden at the rear of our house. There was a good-sized lawn and a couple of apple trees, and then beyond some flowering shrubs and the garden shed our land stretched a goodly way back. Most of this area was given over to row upon row of vegetables which, with the help of a gardener once a week, was my dad's hobby. At the far end there were a couple more fruit trees and more grass. The whole place was surrounded by fence and hedge at least five feet high.

All this gave the kids and Sooty plenty of space to play in. The only trouble was, as he got older, Sooty became an escape artist when left on his own. He'd go wandering off around the neighbourhood, always returning home after a short while, but we just couldn't figure how he was getting out. One day our next-door-neighbour called to me; she said she saw him come sailing over the dividing hedge to land in her garden from where he had easy access to the street. I found this difficult to believe and suggested perhaps she'd been hitting the sherry bottle too much.

Then one morning I was alone at home and Sooty was sniffing around in the back garden. Before I could say *Grand National* he ran across the lawn and leapt over the five-foot hedge like a prize-winning racehorse.

It wasn't long before the inevitable happened. One day while out on his escapades he was hit by a car, though thankfully he was able to limp home. His leg was broken so off to the vet he went. Thank goodness he wasn't a horse! After setting it in a cast the vet suggested that, once it was mended and the cast removed, we should take Sooty back to be neutered, which he felt should curb his wanderlust. This we did but still took the precaution of locking the little rascal inside the house on the rare occasions when all of us went out without him.

Our suburb of Stapenhill was, well, still is unless something drastic has happened, on the east side of the River Trent and just a mile's walk from Burton's town centre. Back in the 'olden days' there were only two ways to cross the Trent for many miles. Vehicles (and pedestrians) were accommodated by the splendid 150-year-old Trent Bridge, its twenty nine brick-built arches supporting four lanes of the almost 500 yard-long structure.

Pedestrians also had the benefit of the Ferry Bridge and viaduct, which was closer to where we lived, and spanned the river as well as the surrounding floodplain known as The Washlands.

[Eventually a new road traffic bridge was built close to this. St Peter's Bridge was opened in 1985 and greatly eased the clogged Trent Bridge.]

The River Trent flowed along the Stapenhill side of The Washlands. Beside it lay Stapenhill Gardens, a lovely, colourful area beautifully maintained by the council.

We would often visit the Gardens with Sooty, where he would be let off leash by the water's edge and he'd jump in the river, happily swimming around for as long as I'd let him.

The walk into town was always very pleasant. The Ferry Bridge is close to the Gardens and spans the actual river before melding with the viaduct, which was supported a couple of yards above ground by metal columns.

Click here to see photos of this beautiful area: https://annpatrasauthor.com/2019/11/27/uk-photos/

One day we were walking along the viaduct heading home from town, there weren't many people around so Sooty was off the leash. As we approached the Ferry Bridge Sooty decided he was going to take a short cut and trotted down a ramp which led from the viaduct to the meadows below. From there he raced across the grass to the river, where he jumped in and swam happily across to the other side.

Knowing there had been no point trying to stop him, I ran along to the end of the bridge to meet up with him in the Gardens. The only trouble was he didn't land in the Gardens.

One solitary house sat between the bridge and the Gardens, which is where he came ashore - into someone's private garden.

As I stood shouting for him at the front gate, a lady appeared and came to open it. I was stopped mid-sentence in my profuse apologies for my dog's misdemeanour when she said, "Oh don't worry about it my dear, he isn't the first and I doubt very much he'll be the last dog to come ashore into the garden. He's a lovely boy." At which she ushered Sooty through the gate, with a friendly pat to his soppy rump.

24

A FLEETING EXPERIENCE

With Ziggy now working I was back into the groove of having to get up early to organise the kids' breakfasts before they went off to school, so one Saturday morning I was taking advantage of a nice lie-in when Vicki appeared at my bedside with the phone.

It was some strange woman from a company I had never heard of wanting to know if Ziggy was still interested in a job he'd applied for. I asked her how long ago he'd applied for the job. She said it was probably quite a long time ago as it had taken them ages to sift through all the applications but that if he was still interested, would he be able to attend an interview the following week? I said I'd do my best to contact him and get him to respond accordingly.

I was very surprised when I was able to reach Ziggy straight away on the site phone, and totally amazed when he actually remembered the job in question, and, yes, he was interested. It was the position of Contract Manager for a company in Fleetwood, Lancashire.

After scooting back and forth across the Pennines from Immingham on the east coast to Fleetwood on the west, *twice* for interviews, he was eventually offered the position. I was thrilled that he was now going to have a 'proper' job, though I wasn't too sure about the location.

I had heard of Fleetwood and knew roughly where it was. It lay just north of the famous English seaside resort of Blackpool. Bearing in mind that we planned to move, if necessary, to whatever area Ziggy found permanent work, I was not too enamoured by this. Not that I had anything against Fleetwood, after all I had never been to the place. But my last experience of Blackpool was memorable, for all the wrong reasons.

Back in the late 1960s my friends and I, like many of Burton's teenagers, would spend many nights at Burton's main (read virtually only) night spot, the 76 Club. One Friday night we were chatting between dances and agreed that we fancied doing something a bit more exciting that weekend. Some bright spark said, "Let's go to Blackpool!"

At the time I was the lucky one who had a car, an olive-green Triumph Herald. We could easily fit all five of us in that, so at about half past midnight we all piled in and I drove round to everyone's home for them to pick up whatever they would need for the trip and tell the parents what we were planning. By the time we'd got ourselves sorted we must have left Burton at about two o'clock in the morning.

We set off full of enthusiasm and merriment, singing as we went, but it wasn't long before things quietened down and my pals all slowly drifted off to sleep. I soon began to feel a bit drowsy myself, and was afraid that I might fall asleep at the wheel. I *think* that at the time I was driving through Stoke on Trent, so we'd hardly travelled very far at all, but being the only one with a driving licence left me no choice. I pulled into a large car park in the town centre to grab a bit of shut-eye. I got as comfortable as I could behind the steering wheel and dozed off.

I could only have been asleep for about ten minutes and almost jumped out of my skin when someone knocked heavily on the car window and shone a torch into the car. Or tried to.

My friends too were now wide awake from this sudden disturbance.

"Who the devil's that?"

"What do they want?"

"I don't know," I said, "but don't open your doors!"

With five 'hot chicks' crammed into a small space it was only natural that the windows would mist up in the cool early morning hours, so we couldn't see out any more than whoever was out there could see in. We sat there in silence, terrified.

Knock. Knock. Knock.

"Open up! Police!" came the voice.

Oh, for goodness sakes!

I wound my window down a fraction and peered through, just to be on the safe side, until I could verify his identity. It was the police all right.

I wound down the window and a torch was poked through followed by a head. The officer looked a tad surprised at seeing five teenage girls.

"What's going on here, then?" he asked.

I explained our situation to him and how I had got tired so pulled over for a snooze.

"That's all very well, but you can't sleep here in this car park. So let's have you on your way." He said abruptly.

I must admit I was pretty dumbfounded as I thought he should have been sympathetic and grateful that I had stopped driving rather than risk having an accident, but he obviously wasn't receptive to negotiation so I straightened myself up and drove off. We agreed that my pals would make sure there was always someone awake to talk to me during the rest of the 120+ mile drive.

We hit Blackpool sometime after six and the place was like a ghost town. This was hardly surprising as no-one in their right mind would be up and about at that time of day when they're on holiday.

We found a car park complete with public conveniences and parked fairly inconspicuously by some other vehicles. Sufficiently rested by now the others decided to go for a walk around, leaving me to stretch out on the back seat for a nice sleep.

They arrived back at the car before noon, coinciding perfectly with my awakening. Being silly teenagers we thought we'd go for a paddle in the sea, but we couldn't see it. The tide was out.

We reckoned that by the time we'd traipsed across the sand to dip our toes in the sea we'd be halfway to Ireland! So we gave up on going for a paddle and instead everyone agreed they were hungry, so we set off to find a bite to eat.

It would be almost sacrilegious to be at the 'seaside' and not have the traditional British fish and chips, so we found a stand which looked popular with other holidaymakers and got ourselves sorted with our preferred choice. Traditionally packed in greaseproof paper and then wrapped in newspaper, we took our lunch to eat sitting in deckchairs on the sands, and used our imaginations on what waves might look like.

The chips, and fish especially, were delicious, and I normally love the crispy batter it's coated in, but today it tasted different to what I was used to. I couldn't quite put my finger on it but there was a strange 'twang' to it.

Half an hour later I began to get pains in my chest. What the hell was going on?

I questioned my girlfriends but they said they all felt fine. I described to them what it felt like. Then Noreen said, "You know, I think you might have indigestion. It sounds very similar to what my Gran often gets, especially after a meal."

At our age, none of us had had the pleasure of experiencing indigestion. Until now. And I felt terrible.

I didn't feel in the least like strolling on damp sand or going on any fairground rides. I gave my buddies my blessing to go off on that jaunt, leaving me to suffer quietly sitting on the pier, waiting to see if the sea actually existed.

By the time my pals reappeared at about six o clock I was feeling pretty much back to normal, and asked what we were going to do next. On their meanderings around the town my mates said all the 'entertainment' they could find consisted of bingo stalls, penny arcades and ballroom dancing at the Tower, none of which was really our scene. They found nothing that came even close to our favourite venue.

Following some discussion we piled back into the car and drove home to Burton, finishing off our Saturday as it had started out, dancing in the 76 Club.

Anyway, where was I? Ah yes, the job in Fleetwood. I digressed a bit again there.

After Ziggy had been working in Fleetwood for a month or so and decided he liked it, I figured it was time to start looking at houses in the area.

Borrowing my dad's car I joined Ziggy one Tuesday.

I found that Fleetwood only had two sides to it, the east and the south. This was because the west side fell into the Irish Sea and the north was cut off by the River Wyre. I spent most of the day searching out estate agents, establishing what they had to offer and driving around getting the feel of the area.

One of my concerns was with schooling, and after chatting to agents I established some areas where I did *not* want to live. These had previously been served by four schools and now fell in a large catchment zone of one enormous school which had recently opened. I didn't like the sound of that.

With this in mind, on the second day I decided to check out the villages on the other side of the river Wyre. I got a bit of a shock when I found that the bridge was in fact a toll bridge, and felt a right idiot as I fumbled around in my bag for change as other motorists quickly hurled money into the kiosks virtually without stopping.

Ziggy had mentioned that he'd heard there was a ferry going across the river which he could possibly take to get to work, so once over the other side I made my way to the village where I was told it docked. Not only was it not a car ferry, but you might just manage to fit eight passengers on it so long as they weren't carrying heavy bags. I certainly wouldn't entertain the idea of crossing the mouth of the Wyre on *that* if there was even the slightest hint of a breeze!

I spent the day driving around, viewing one house from the inside, several from the outside, and failing to find many more. Just after five o'clock I decided to head back across the river. On reaching the bridge I was horrified to be faced by hundreds of cars lined up waiting to return home to their rural settings over the Wyre. It hadn't occurred to me what a bottleneck that bridge would be during rush-hour traffic. I couldn't possibly ask Ziggy to go through that twice a day, every working day of the year, so north of the Wyre was now off the menu.

So my first trip to Fleetwood proved very disappointing, but before leaving I looked in a local copy of the Yellow Pages for more estate agents' phone numbers.

Once back at home I phoned as many agents as I could, making arrangements to view before taking my next trip north. One property which I'd actually found privately advertised in the local newspaper, sounded very promising.

The blurb said that it had four bedrooms, large bathroom, lounge, sun-lounge, dining room, breakfast room and kitchen. Outside there were two drives and plenty of standing room for boat or caravan as well as assorted outbuildings. This sounded too good to be true but I decided to check it out anyway.

I should have realised what it would be like before I even set foot inside the place. As I stood waiting for my knock on the front door to be answered, I took in the shabby appearance of the paintwork (what there was left of it) and the very dubious-looking condition of the window frames.

If that weren't sufficient evidence, my first sight of the incredibly shabby-looking owner, Mr Butcher, should have told me everything. I stepped gingerly into the hall, as being an animal lover I didn't want to harm any of God's creatures which must surely have been living inside what passed vaguely for a carpet.

First of all I was led by a beaming Mr Butcher to view the living room which was a square, incredibly boring room with a hideously old-fashioned tiled fireplace housing a gas fire circa 1955, and dingy furniture. I tried to be polite about the room being 'a good size' but the words didn't sound too convincing.

From there we looked into what was the sun-lounge; an afterthought built onto one corner of the house and which was far from sunny, all the windows being concealed by several odd pairs of half-hung, dust-laden curtains. Even had I wanted to, I couldn't have gone inside for a better look as the floor was strewn with assorted items of decrepit furniture. He closed the door on that lot and then led the way upstairs.

As I followed him I wondered if each step was going to be my last as the stairs felt as if they were made of cardboard. I know that in even the best kept properties stairs tend to develop a creak after a few years, but these were well past that point.

The whole place, I decided, must have been riddled with dry rot and/or alive with woodworm, as everywhere I walked the floor felt sort of spongy - and it certainly wasn't due to any luxury-pile carpet!

As we entered the main bedroom Mr Butcher apologised for its untidy condition but explained that his wife had only recently returned from a camping trip, and the place was a bit of a mess. Jeez, she must have been away for several months and brought back all the garbage with her because 'a bit of a mess' was a bloody understatement. If I'd let my kids and ten of their friends have free rein in one room for six months I doubt they could have got it into as bad a state as that bedroom.

The fact that the threadbare carpet was one of those square ones which leave a two-foot gap between it and the walls was no issue, as you could barely see the 'gap' for junk anyway. Across what I think was the chimneybreast, was a very wide floor to ceiling cupboard, which was full of scrappy-looking books and papers, which you couldn't miss because the cupboard had no doors.

Mr Butcher must have seen the direction of my gaze as he went on to explain that the cupboard was 'a little untidy' because it contained stuff relating to the Girl Guides, a group of which his wife was Leader, which explained the camping trip. It was at this point that I spotted Mrs Butcher, who had been on the far side of the room, behind a chest of drawers, shifting stuff from one pile on the floor to another.

A thin woman of equally scrappy appearance to her husband and her house, managed a cursory "Hello," and continued with her rummaging. The thought of this woman being in charge of, and potentially being a role model to, a group of young girls made me cringe. The fact that she would also have provided food for them during a camping trip made me feel quite nauseous.

We next moved into what I assumed to be a storeroom, until it was pointed out that behind the two chests of drawers which divided the bedroom in half was a mattress on the floor, which was their youngest daughter's bed. I was surprised that she would be able to use it as it lay invisible beneath piles of sleeping bags.

Further down the corridor we came to the original bathroom. It was a huge room and contained the toilet and a hand-wash basin complete with home-made vanity unit; the centre-piece of the bathroom was an absolutely superb cast iron bath on ornate feet. That must have truly been a collectors' item, even with the brown stains under the taps.

Next we came to the third bedroom, or at least I think it was. Immediately inside the door was a double wardrobe, and you had to pass between that and the wall to get inside, only to be confronted by a large office desk. I was told there was a bed somewhere beyond that.

After reversing out of there we followed the twisting passage even further back to the fourth and final bedroom, which maintained the standard of the rest of the house. My only recollection of that room was that it contained a double divan bed base with two single mattresses piled one on top of the other. Shades of the old fairy tale, 'The Princess and the Pea'?

We made our way (carefully) back downstairs and into the dining room, though why so-called I'm not sure as it didn't contain a table. I made some comment about it being nice to see a 'real' fireplace, only to be told that they couldn't use it because the chimney was blocked. Why was I not surprised?

Making our way to the kitchen we passed through a structural appendage which turned out to be the breakfast room. It sort of resembled the sun-lounge which was on the other corner of this side of the house. Mr Butcher went to great lengths to describe a wooden bench which should have been fitted in place behind the table, but which they'd temporarily removed to make more chair space, and assured me it would be returned for my pleasure if I bought the house.

We then found the kitchen. A gas oven was nestling among an assortment of base cupboards. One of the cupboards had a drawer missing, looking like it must have been in a fight with the sink-unit door, and Mr Butcher advised that he was in the process of replacing the drawer. I figured it wasn't at the top of his 'to do list' as someone had already inserted a piece of three-ply wood between the drawer runners to carry a motley collection of kitchen utensils. After catching sight of a rather hideous and grubby six-foot kitchen cabinet, I didn't venture further into the kitchen for fear of disturbing anything, dead or alive.

You may be wondering by now why I continued with the charade of the potential purchaser. The trouble was Mr Butcher enthused so continuously about everything I had trouble fitting a word in. Apart from that, I think I had developed a morbid fascination with the place.

I think I was the only potential buyer who had come through his door and he was determined to hang onto me for as long as he could, but by now I was seriously beginning to itch.

He steered me towards the first of his storage rooms, which turned out to be the lower level of the fourth bedroom extension. He just managed to fit both of us inside the doorway, though it meant leaning on the door to keep it open to achieve this. The room, about 10' x 12' was - surprise, surprise - absolutely crammed full of junk.

There were tables, stools, bikes (3), lawn mowers (2), a cupboard, lamps, boxes, chairs, and on the farthest side of the room was the bench that belonged in the breakfast room. As he attempted to scale the mountain of junk to reach the bench I wailed that it was quite alright, I could see it from where I stood and it looked just fine.

Next we visited the first of his outside free-standing store rooms, a very dubious-looking structure which appeared to be made from asbestos, and he couldn't get the door open. Despite my insistence that it really didn't matter if I didn't see inside the shed, he continued to fight with it until he got the bloody thing open.

There, before me, lay the biggest collection of cups and saucers I had ever seen in my entire life.

"I'm in the sales trade, you see," he said proudly.

"Well of course you are dear," I thought, "You're hardly likely to be storing this lot for the Premier Inn, are you?"

But this was only the beginning. We moved on to the next shed, a wooden edifice, where he began fumbling with his keys. I tried yet again to tell him there was no need to go inside as I could see its size from outside, and look through the window, but by this time he had the padlock unfastened and the door was creaking open. A padlock? I wondered who in their right mind would want to steal a load of crockery, as I'd rightly assumed was in there, though this time there were plates and dishes as well. Rows and rows and rows of them. From floor to ceiling, from front to back, with a space down the centre barely wide enough to enable someone carrying a box of crockery to walk down.

In shallow cardboard boxes, wooden trays and metal baskets, there were simply hundreds and hundreds of rows upon rows of pots. And they were all covered in well-established layers of dust.

I really couldn't take much more, and unable to think of anything sensible to say I asked him how long it would take him to clear all this lot out if he did sell his house. He said about three days. Never in this wide world . . . weeks if he was lucky!

Finally (I dearly hoped), we headed for the garages. The first was a double garage, though it was double length-wise in that you could probably fit in two cars nose to tail, if they weren't too big. Well you couldn't actually, because the garage was full of gravy boats, soup tureens, vegetable dishes, plates, bowls and, yes, more cups and saucers.

Fitted with several rows of Dexion shelving (you know, that stuff like giant-sized Meccano) it was so crammed you couldn't actually see to the end of the garage.

The second garage was attached to the side of the first, though how it could be called a garage was completely beyond me as not three yards in front of the garage doors stood a bloody great pear tree, which any idiot could see had been there long before garages were even invented! I would defy the best driver in the world to get any vehicle more than two feet wide past the tree and into the garage.

The yard servicing these wondrous facilities had, at various stages in its existence, been paved with slabs, concreted, or stoned, and all were in various stages of disrepair. The garden areas, I was told, hadn't had much attention for twelve months. Nonsense! Twelve years more like.

But it was the crockery which had blown my mind the most, I just couldn't believe it. And what I could see of it, it was all such absolute CRAP stuff too!

Apparently he had a shop in Blackpool. Now that didn't surprise me one little bit. I remembered looking into some shops in Blackpool when I went there as a little kid with my grandmother. They seemed to be full of chintzy cups with flowers, petals and rosebuds creeping up the sides, with twirly twists around the rim, like you make on the edge of the pastry on a pie.

I promised myself that one day I would take a tour of the touristy shops of Blackpool to see if I could figure out which one belonged to Mr Butcher. Talking of whom, with the viewing of the stores complete, he asked me if I'd like to take another look inside the house, and perhaps join him and his wife for a cup of tea.

Not on your life! Or mine, to be more precise. The very thought of going back inside there made my skin crawl. As for drinking anything prepared in that kitchen... just writing about it is giving me the shudders.

I thanked him for his time, clambered over the weeds and debris of the garden rather than go back through the house, and shot back to the car.

I really needed to talk to Ziggy, so raced back to Fleetwood.

For almost three-quarters of an hour I had been rendered pretty much speechless in the house of horrors but now, as Ziggy and I sat in a bar with a beer apiece, it all came pouring out like someone had opened up floodgates. I rabbited on so much that Ziggy was almost at the end of his second pint before I even stopped for breath.

Then I couldn't wait to get to our room so I could take a shower, after first putting all the clothes I'd been wearing into a plastic bag, tightly sealed until I could get them into a washing machine.

You see, as I had ranted away to Ziggy I'd been getting twitches on my legs. Having had the misfortune of living in a house with a flea-ridden kitten for three weeks when I lived in Canada, I knew only too well what those twitches were. The worst of it is, I saw no signs whatsoever of any cats or dogs while I'd been in the House of Pots. URGH!

The following day I found a property I liked.

It was a detached house with some character and stood in a fair-sized garden. It was just within our budget. I took Ziggy to see it the next day. He wasn't as keen on it as me, but said since I'd be the one spending the most time in it, it was up to me. I duly put in an offer for the property subject to satisfactory results of a private survey and the sale of our house in Burton.

Once back home I immediately went along to a local estate agent and charged them with selling our home in Saxon Street. Within days of being put on the market we had a buyer for our house. Then the first bomb dropped. The survey of the property in Lancashire revealed that the house was riddled with damp and would cost a considerable amount to put right, so we withdrew our offer to purchase.

It was going to be a while before I could return with Ziggy to Fleetwood to resume my search for a house as the company he worked for sent him over to Ireland on a project for a few weeks.

On his return the second bomb dropped! When Ziggy mentioned to his boss that I'd been looking at properties in the area he asked us to hold back on the house-buying business as there was a chance Ziggy might be posted to a different location, depending on what he was eventually going to be put in charge of. Shades of short-term projects were creeping in again here.

In the event, a few weeks down the line Ziggy decided he no longer wanted to work for the company. It transpired that they were encouraging the operation of procedures which he knew to be substandard. Having enjoyed a good reputation in the construction field for many years, there was no way he was going to drop his standards for this two-bit company.

Then came bomb number three!

The fact that the estate agents had honoured their contract and found us firm buyers meant that we were still bound to pay their fairly substantial fees. We didn't have that sort of money going spare. We would have to continue with the sale of our house in order to be able to pay them off.

Then we would be homeless!

In the event, the potential buyers for our house couldn't wait around for us to make up our minds where we were going to live, and withdrew their offer to purchase. But one of the ladies at the estate agency said she and her husband had talked about it, and they would like to buy our house, when we were eventually ready. So at least the pressure was off.

25

SPACE

I'm guessing that you've realised by now that it was only a matter of time before I got myself 'involved' in something. Oh, nothing as dramatic as my absorption into the theatre club in Kitwe, nor the gymkhana club in Lusaka, this time it involved SPACE.

No, no, no, I wasn't donning a silver suit, bubble helmet and big heavy boots. SPACE stood for the Staffordshire Police Activity and Community Enterprise, a school holidays programme organised by our local constabulary. Conveniently based at our kids' Edgehill Primary School, they organised loads of special activities to keep the kids safely occupied during the long school summer holidays. For a mere £1 each, Brad, Vicki and Leon enrolled in the programme and got their membership cards.

Activities included a variety of sports-related stuff, trips to theme parks, treasure hunt, etc., all sorts of things. It certainly kept me off the streets - not that I was prone to walking the streets you understand! I would go along and help out where needed, like dish out lunches, be a 'responsible adult' on trips, - okay, okay, don't fall off your chair laughing - or just be around as a general dogsbody.

A fantastic project, geared towards the end of the SPACE programme though asked early on was, "Who you would most like to meet?", and SPACE would try to organise it. Of course, most of the children filled in their wish cards with the names of pop and film stars or sports personalities (especially footballers). I suggested to my kids that they chose someone who might realistically be able to spare time for a bunch of school kids, rather than the likes of Bryan Robson or Michael Jackson, but it wasn't easy for them.

Having spent most of their young lives in Africa and a minimal amount of time in front of a television set, my three were not fanatical about anyone or anything in particular. As Leon and Vicki drew a blank Brad eventually said, "You know, mummy, I'd rather like to meet David Bellamy."

For those of you not in the know, David Bellamy is a well-known British botanist and environmental campaigner who appeared regularly on television. But in Brad's field of knowledge, he was also the Patron of the Chongololo and Conservation Club of Zambia, of which Brad had been a proud member. When we lived in Kitwe, the club used to take kids out on field trips, like showing them habitats of various birds and local creatures, and the importance of conserving the different areas they inhabited. It may sound a bit heavy for such youngsters but, following in the footsteps of David Bellamy, those involved made everything sound *so* interesting.

Brad posted his wish card in the entry box, which would later be emptied by the organisers and a plan laid to get some unsuspecting celebrity to 'come to the party'.

Another one of the highlights at SPACE was a fabulous trip to Alton Towers. This was where I donned my 'responsible adult' hat. There were a couple of coachloads of kids and helpers transported to Alton. I had six kids under my care, being my three along with Phillip, Christian and Lyndsey. What an amazing time we had. Alton Towers wasn't anything near the size then as it is now, but for us it was a dream world. We queued, as one does, for all the favourite rides, and some lesser ones which were quicker to get on. Me being me, I enjoyed them as much as the kids did. The only thing I drew the line at was the Pirate Ship.

There was no way I was going on that! It wasn't so much that it was scary, but as a kid I'd never really got on too well with swings, as they tended to make me feel nauseous. As far as I was concerned the pirate ship was one bloody big swing, and I really didn't fancy throwing up my lunch from the top of it. I mean, it wouldn't really be fair on the poor kids located below me, would it?

In no time at all we found ourselves in the final week of the SPACE programme. Leon had been totally enthralled by it and was adamant that he wanted to be a policeman when he grew up, so that in his summer holiday he could be part of the SPACE programme.

On this final Monday the SPACE leaders announced that somebody's 'wish to meet' would be visiting the next day. They were bombarded by kids wanting to know who it was, but not a hint was given.

The next day all the kids arrived in their favourite gear ready to meet the special celebrity. After an agonising couple of hours distractedly playing various games we were called to the playground. Then we heard the sirens of one of the larger police cars, complemented by flashing blue lights, as it turned in to the playground and pulled up a few metres in front of the excited crowd.

A police officer got out of the car then went to open the door for the special passenger in the back. Exiting the vehicle, a large figure loomed before us and bellowed, "**Is there anyone here called Brad Patras?**"

You could have knocked me down with a feather, and Brad's face was an absolute picture. After a few moments of shocked silence his hand shot up as he called, "I'm Brad Patras! I'm Brad Patras!" with the biggest, fattest grin on his face I'd ever seen, in response to David Bellamy's call.

Everyone was ushered into the school hall where Brad and I were seated on the stage alongside the two leading SPACE organising officers, and David Bellamy gave a talk on nature and conservation, taking questions from his captivated audience. Brad said it was quite surreal meeting one of his heroes off the TV, and that he and the rest of the kids had loved meeting this larger-than-life character.

In stark contrast (for me) to the success of *that* event, was a show put on in the school hall on the final day. The highlight of the show was a hypnotist. You think you know what's coming, don't you? We shall see.

He asked for adult volunteers to participate and, of course, yours truly had to step forward, didn't she? I have always said that no-one would ever be able to hypnotise me as I am so strong willed, so was more than happy to participate.

After being assured that we wouldn't be put through anything *too* embarrassing, five of us were called up onto the stage and I positioned myself at the far left side in the hope that I wouldn't be singled out for anything special.

All seated on hardback chairs we were 'put under' by our esteemed hypnotist. I followed all his instructions, standing, sitting, dancing round the chair, pretending to drink a cup of tea. We were told we wouldn't be able to raise our arms when later asked to, so upon the said command I duly struggled in vain with extreme concentration on my face. Alas, I apparently put on such good act it backfired on me. The hypnotist called me over to help him with his next 'trick'.

"I am going to ask you to lay across three chairs, and when I remove the centre chair you will remain straight and supported only by the chairs under your shoulders and feet."

Holy crap, the hell I will! I was mortified! I was certainly no heavyweight in those days, but nor was I super strong! If he removed a chair from under my bum I would drop to the floor like an elephant on a tightrope!

I leaned closer to him and, doing my best ventriloquist impersonation, said through gritted, smiling teeth, whispered "I was only fretending!"

"What?" he similarly replied.

"I wasn't really hyfnotised. I was fretending to be."

"Shit! OK I'll ashk someone else. Go fack to your chair."

Although his gritted teeth had still been smiling, his eyes intimated that he was furious with me and especially, I think, because he had been hoodwinked himself into thinking I was 'under'.

Fortunately a slender young man who was also on stage was able to step into the breach with, to my amazement, a very successful result. As soon as the show was over I beat a hasty retreat before I could be accosted by the miffed mesmerist.

And so ended our excursion into SPACE, and what a great expedition it had been.

Hold on, hold on just a minute,

Oh sorry, this is Brad speaking and I have to interrupt here. My mother has missed out quite a lot of experiences from SPACE, including one which, in my recollections, fought with the David Bellamy experience for the most memorable.

We had so many great days out to various theme parks; army obstacle courses; forest exploration on bikes; hiking trips and raft building, you name it, but the highlight for me was the Stafford showgrounds extravaganza. They had everything fun; a motorbike formation and stunt display in the arena with parachutists landing on targets; abseiling; plenty of cool stalls and activities, but best of all was the BMX trial course! I couldn't wait to give that a try.

I watched everyone to go through the various options before queuing for the ultimate activity. Helmet on and stopwatch started, I scooted over a seesaw and a few ramps, through tyre obstacles and over a big table top, and got into the top five of the day. I was overjoyed! Even more so when, later that night, I sat in front of the TV with spaghetti hoops on toast, and the local news programme showed a piece on the day's event, complete with a filmed clip of me doing my run! I was so excited and sent a letter to the TV channel, who sent back a VHS copy of the article. I think it still exists somewhere in mum's boxes!

Oops, sorry Brad, how could I have forgotten to mention that.

AS WINTER BEGAN TO CREEP IN, I WAS GETTING RATHER CONCERNED FOR MY dad's wellbeing. The caravan as sleeping accommodation was fine in the summer, but was hardly appropriate for the harsh British winter. One day as we took a brisk walk to the local pub, I broached the subject with my dad.

"It's funny you should mention that, I was only thinking the other day that it was getting a bit nippy out there. It's time I looked for a place of my own." He said.

And so it was that my dad moved out, to a flat on the edge of Winshill, the suburb where Ziggy and I bought our house when we got married. Winshill, where all the roads on the council estate were named after a city within the British Commonwealth, was also the place where my parents had spent much of their working lives when I was a child.

As an extension of my grandmother's corner shop business, my mum and dad drove a mobile shop around that estate five days a week for many years. This was why, for the most part, I was brought up by my grandmother Doris. When I was about nine or ten years old I used to love going with my mum and dad during school holidays on a Thursday, because this was their 'early finish' day, returning home by 7pm. I would meet loads of kids who used to race to the familiar Radford's green van to spend their pocket money on Lucky Bags, 4-for-a-penny Black Jacks and Fruit Salad chews, or my favourite Flying Saucers (edible paper filled with sherbet). It was only when I was about thirteen that we discovered that while the 'travelling shop' as we called it, was doing a roaring trade, the corner shop was not. In fact the one was subsidising the other, as my grandmother was not supervising the running of the shop efficiently.

As a result Nancy and Mev eventually gave up the travelling shop so that they could bring the corner shop back up to a profitable state, but they didn't sever links with their loyal customers in Winshill.

Five days a week my dad would deliver cases of groceries to customers on that estate. Although I had a secretarial job during the week, once I was old enough to learn to drive I would sometimes help Mev on a Saturday by driving the VW Combi (rear seats removed) so that all he had to do was nip up the garden paths with the cardboard boxes loaded with groceries for his customers. I recall that many of the customers were almost nameless, being identified on their order-books by their location, such as *Deidre Delhi, Ethel on Empire* or *Monday only, Melbourne.*

Once I'd passed my driving test there were occasions when I did the complete Saturday run alone, which gave me occasion to actually meet the customers, and one in particular known as 90 Vanc. He was a dear old man who actually had a name - Percy Fleck - and one day when I delivered a small box of groceries to his upstairs flat, he invited me in for a cup of tea. I was spellbound once inside his living room. He was a bit of an artist, and his walls were adorned with small watercolour paintings he had created.

Percy had small trays of paints like those we had as school-kids, and he would copy pictures from magazines and birthday or Christmas cards. The paintings he had on his walls were mounted on a piece of cardboard, possibly an old cornflakes packet, or even cut from one of the cardboard boxes his groceries were delivered in, if he could cut it to the right size without bending the corrugated material. Then he would 'frame' it under a piece of glass which was attached with black insulating tape.

From then on, whenever I was on delivery duty I would stop and have a cuppa with Percy. As I admired one of his pictures one day he insisted that I take it, saying it was one of his favourites. On that basis alone I refused his kind offer, but he insisted, saying that if I wouldn't take it he'd stop using Radford's services.

Then he found out from my dad when my birthday was and gave

me another painting. One day he asked me which painting I liked most of some he'd done recently. I refused to tell him on the grounds that I 'knew his little tricks', but he insisted, saying that he was giving it to someone for a special occasion and just needed my help in choosing. So I pointed out one of a sunset.

I was actually thrilled to bits when a few weeks later I found it was one of my and Ziggy's wedding presents.

All three paintings still hang on my walls, though I must confess to having since had them professionally mounted and framed as befits works of art so precious.

But hang on a minute. I was talking about something else before I got carried away by the Radford's van. (Quick check up the page.) Oh, yes, Mev moving to Winshill.

My dad told us that the place he had found was fully furnished, so he only needed to take his clothes and a few personal things with him. It was quite some time before I actually visited him in his new abode, and when I did I was horrified. It was no more than a bedsit with a kitchen the size of our lavatory, and as for ablutions, he virtually had to sit on the toilet to take a shower. It was so cramped the entire thing was smaller than our living room. The only way he had any space in his living room was if he hoisted the drop-down bed up to the wall when he wasn't sleeping in it.

"Mev, this is just awful," I said in tears, "you can't live like this!"

"Why not? I have everything I need here, and I spend a damned sight less time cleaning than I did before. It suits me just fine. And if I don't feel like going out in the car, I'm close enough to walk to at least two pubs where I know people."

As far as I was concerned there was never a problem with him knowing people as wherever he went, being an ex-publican in our brewery town, my dad knew just about every landlord worth knowing, and kept away from those who weren't.

I reluctantly acknowledged that he should stay there.

ONE OF THE OUTCOMES OF MY STINT OF WORKING AT ALLIED BREWERIES was my introduction to the world of computers, and while at the time this didn't seem significant to my life, it had created an awareness. One of the things which was happening in the UK in the late 1980s was the introduction of personal computers, or PCs, into the home market,

One day I was telling Ziggy how many people had been nagging me to write a book about our adventures in Zambia and he said, "We should buy you a computer to do it on. Did you read the latest WHICH? magazine yet? They have a report on new PCs and printers in the latest issue. Check it out. That'll give you the incentive to get going on it."

I did, and after considerable research had my list of requirements and prices to hand.

I decided to give my cousin Tony a call as he was always at the front of the queue for anything new coming out. Actually Tony was my mum's cousin, but I can never remember whether that makes me a second cousin or a cousin first-removed. Removed from what, anyway? I've never been able to figure that one out. It was Tony's mum, Aunty Ena, who used to host the letter-reading, sherry-sipping sessions for the oldies which I have mentioned previously (in *More Into Africa*, I think).

Where was I? Oh, yes, computer.

I had a lot of respect for Tony's judgment. He was a keen and very competent photographer, as well as being the person who originally introduced me to the wonders of quality stereophonic sound when I was in my teens. I decided to ask him what he thought of my intended choice of equipment.

"Have you heard about these new PC's available now?" I asked him.

"Not only have I heard of them, I've got one. It's brilliant. Why?"

"Great, because we're going to buy one too and I want to pick your brain."

I told him what I had chosen to get, and why. He couldn't believe it. The combination of PC and printer was almost identical to those he had recently purchased.

"I'm impressed that you've decided to lash out on the colour monitor instead of one of the hideous black screen/green text things.

But rather than a single floppy disc drive in your motherboard you should get one with two drives. And for software, for your purposes I highly recommend Word Perfect. You really don't want to be working in..."

"Whoa, whoa, whoa!" I pulled him up right there. Tony had a tendency to go into great technical details about things. He needed to be *very* basic when it came to explaining this stuff to me.

"What on earth are you talking about? What is software?" I hadn't a clue. As far as I was concerned I was just going to buy a PC and start typing.

A few weeks later I was the proud owner of an Amstrad 1640 PC and an Epson dot matrix printer, now all I had to do was figure out how to work the bloody things. I must confess it took some getting used to after the simplicity of an electric typewriter, but I eventually got the hang of it. However, writing a book on it was a different kettle of fish altogether.

I didn't really know where to start.

"You've got copies of all your letters, haven't you?" I nodded, "then just re-write them out in the book," said Tony.

"I have a problem with that," I responded. "When I'm reading a book I don't really enjoy ones with letters in them."

"Have you read Adrian Mole?"

"No, but I watched a couple of episodes of the TV series and didn't think much of it."

"Oh, the book is far better than the television could ever portray it," he said, "I'll lend you mine to read."

So I read *The Secret Diary of Adrien Mole, aged 13¾* by Sue Townsend and thoroughly enjoyed it, and it changed my attitude to that type of format sufficiently to give me ideas on how (27 years later) to produce my first book.

26

MOVING SWIFTLY ALONG...

People talk about having their heart broken, or experiencing 'heartache'. I had always considered these expressions as purely emotional states, but I was proved wrong. I was fully aware that I missed my life in Zambia but I only discovered just how much when I was watching television one day.

There was a wildlife documentary being shown. I didn't even notice which country it was in, but there was the familiar setting of the African bush. The scene focused on a pride of lions who had clearly fed recently as they were totally ignoring nearby impala, and some warthogs were happily snuffling round about them. But in the background I heard an oh-so-familiar call.

"Where's FAther, where's FAther, where's FAther." On hearing that bird I got such an ache in my chest, it physically hurt. It was like someone had planted a lead weight where my heart should be, and I so yearned to return to Africa. *In your dreams, Ann, in your dreams!*

After much discussion, um-ing and ah-ing, we decided to take the bull by the horns and go for a career change which we knew we could do successfully. We'd buy a pub.

This decision was not based on a whim which many naive pub owners took on blindly as their 'dream come true'. We knew exactly what we'd be letting ourselves in for, which is why I had refused to consider such a possibility when Ziggy had suggested it way back in the days before he took the contract in Zambia. The one thing I had been concerned about then was the effect it would have on the children, as I knew it meant working during hours which should be spent more fully with them. But now we were running out of options, and as the children were older and more capable of understanding situations we felt we could all handle the challenge.

At that time in Burton on Trent, being a big brewery town, there were over 100 pubs operating within the town. (Many years before, there used to be one on almost every street corner, and many in between if it was a long street!) The majority of these pubs were tenanted, i.e. the property was owned by the breweries. They were rented by a publican who then fully owned the business, though was contracted to sell *that* brewery's products (before the Monopolies & Mergers ccmmission put a stop to that).

As we would have much of the proceeds of the sale of our house to invest, we decided to opt for what was known as a 'Free House', where the publican owned the property as well as the business and could sell whoever's ales he wished. Preferably it would be a country pub with the potential to expand. We decided to begin our search for a suitable establishment some miles away, in Wales.

Leaving the kids once again in my dad's charge, Ziggy and I spent a long weekend visiting places for sale. I will never forget that drive home through a rare snowstorm as we skirted Birmingham. After viewing several possibilities we discussed how only one had come vaguely close to requirements. Much more searching would be required.

The following week we had an appointment to see a firm of accountants in Burton to establish the financial procedures required for running the business. I won't say this was another bomb to shatter our world, just a minor explosion this time.

On meeting with the expert he strongly recommended that we did *not* follow the Free House route, but said we'd be far better becoming tenants of a pub and putting the proceeds of sale of our house in a good savings or investment plan.

"The way things stand at the moment, you'll get a far better return on investment that way," he said.

So back to the drawing board. We decided to first approach the brewery whose beer Ziggy preferred, Marston's. I wasn't so sure about this. He was supposed to be selling the stuff, not drinking it! But I conceded to Ziggy's demands that you had to believe in what you were selling (she says with raised eyebrows). But there was no doubt that the then small league Marston's brewery could brew a damn good pint.

It just so happened that my great uncle George was pals with one of the Marston's directors, so I asked him if he could 'put in a word'. We got an appointment to see an appropriate person on Thursday of the following week. Okay, so now things were moving.

On the Tuesday morning I was sitting sewing a dress for Vicki when the phone rang. Ziggy was doing something in the kitchen so I answered it.

"Hello," said a distant voice, "can I please speak to Mr Ziggy Patras?" There was something strikingly familiar about her accent.

"Yes, may I ask who's calling please?" I enquired, using my best office voice.

"Mr McClane from Zambia would like to speak to him," she replied. I called Ziggy.

"Hello? Oh hi, Rob, how're you doing?"

Now I knew Rob McClane, and was fully aware that he wouldn't be calling Ziggy all the way from Zambia for a social chat. I stood behind Ziggy and pressed my ear up beside his head as I tried to listen to the other half of the conversation, without a lot of luck as Ziggy kept elbowing me away for being a distraction.

I caught odd words… 'Germany'; 'Kafue'; 'acid plant'; 'flight'. WHAT WAS GOING ON?

"Okay, yes, thanks Rob, I'll wait to hear from you."

By the time he put the phone down I already had his suitcase packed!

Well perhaps not physically, but mentally I did, and had him halfway to the airport.

"What did he say? What did he want? Tell me! Come on!" I whined.

"He wants me join him at a meeting in Frankfurt on Thursday. Apparently the Germans are funding the refurbishment of the acid plant in Kafue, and Chemimex have got the contract. He wants me to be at the meeting in Germany with the possibility of my working on the project."

"In Zambia?"

"Yes of course in Zambia."

"Woohoo! Yes please! Yeahhh!"

I continued to skip and dance around with a big fat grin on my face for oh, goodness knows how long, at the mere thought that we might be moving back to Zambia.

With not too much reluctance I cancelled our appointment at Marston's for the Thursday and instead, on that day, I took Ziggy to East Midlands airport for his flight to Frankfurt.

The good news was that after long and detailed discussions at the meeting, Ziggy was appointed as the Engineering Administration Manager on the forthcoming project. The bad news was that his contract was single status.

"But don't worry," he said, "once I get over there I'll be able to sort it out for you and the kids to join me."

"You'd bloody well better," was my reply.

In the meantime we still had the house-sale problem: the buyers of our house in Saxon Street were still waiting. Thank goodness they hadn't been in too much of a rush.

During the couple of days that Ziggy had been in Germany I had noticed a For Sale sign outside a property just two hundred metres around the corner from the bottom of our street. I told Ziggy about it on his return. It was a large, three storey, end-of-terrace Victorian house. We arranged with the estate agent to view it.

Walking in through the entrance porch revealed a long passageway where, off to the right, first lay a large bay-windowed living room, and behind that a separate dining room. Down two steps in the passageway there was then a large pantry and following that a good-sized 'breakfast room'. At the end of the passage and down a couple more steps there was a kitchen, then a scullery and a toilet leading off. A door opened onto the rear yard of the property.

It would seem none of those rooms had been in use for years except for the front living room, which had been utilised as a committee meeting room by the owners. The association who owned the house ran a local football team and a social club, which was situated on some land beyond the rear of the property.

Returning to the front of the house, the staircase leading off the main passage was boarded in and accessed by a locked door. The estate agent unlocked it and led the way upstairs.

"Until about six months ago these upper floors were used as the accommodation for the social club's caretaker," she told us.

Turning right at the top of the stairs we found the front room overlooking the street had been made into a living room (immediately above the one on the ground floor) and next to it was a small bedroom, also looking onto the street. The room behind the living room had been the main bedroom and next came a bathroom. A door at the rear of the passage led into a huge room which had been used as a kitchen/dining room. Here a window overlooked the impressive River Trent Valley, with a backdrop of the housing, commercial and brewery buildings which comprised Burton on Trent.

Back in the passage, another flight of stairs took us to the top floor where we found two more spacious bedrooms and an ample windowless storage room.

Returning to the ground floor we were led out of the rear door leading to a narrow yard which accommodated a small flower bed and a huge single-storey prefab-type building. What on earth...?

The estate agent thought this might have been the football club's original social building. Immediately behind this structure the property was fenced off, yet had a gate in the corner leading conveniently to the car park of the larger, new and more conventional brick-built social club.

Whilst the back garden wasn't very interesting (apart from the bloody great 'shed') and was therefore limited space-wise, it would at least be pretty much Sooty-escape-proof, having high, wood-panelled fencing.

As we were re-entering the house I noticed a window at ground level below the dining room window.

"Why is there a window there?" I pointed.

"Oh, I forgot about that. Come and see."

Under the main staircase was a door which I had assumed simply led to under-stair storage space. Apparently not. The door opened onto yet another flight of steps, going down. Switching on a light she led the way.

"Here you are," she said, "two basement rooms."

They felt a bit damp and dingy, but weren't a bad size and I suppose could be used for something useful like prison cells, torture chambers or home-made beer, wine and pickle storage.

Returning above ground we were told, "Have a wander around the place if you like".

We did, and it was then we began to take in the finer features. Except for that front downstairs living (committee) room, which sadly had a gas fire installed, the other five main rooms still sported the original Victorian fireplaces, complete with perfectly ornate tiling. These could be left in place, with or without being used, as the house came with full central heating.

All the rooms had traditional deep skirting boards, and most had dado rails and moulded light cornices. This house had so much character and space, amounting to 17 rooms, excluding the passageways. It was amazing.

We told the agent we were definitely interested, subject to a surveyor's report. The agent had mentioned earlier that the owners were aware that work would need to be done on the property and had set its price accordingly. She also let slip, inadvertently I thought, that they were anxious to sell as even though the property was empty it was costing them money (insurance, rates and the like) which the organisation could ill afford.

This house was well within our price range, but it depended

greatly on what the 'work to be done' consisted of, and how much that would cost. We contacted a reputable surveyor and within the week he reported back.

There was some outside brickwork which needed to be re-pointed; a small area of damp at the rear of the property would have to be addressed; some of the original sash windows needed repair and the whole house required rewiring. We immediately got quotes for the work and found that if we could get the sellers to drop their price by a couple of thousand pounds we could do it. They did!

Things began to move very swiftly from then as everyone, including our purchasers, was more than happy to push their respective solicitors to complete.

As we began to gather cardboard boxes and pack our possessions, Ziggy got 'the call' from Zambia. All formalities having been completed by the various parties involved, they wanted him over there as soon as possible.

Personally I reckon he'd sent Rob McClane a secret message asking him to, "Get me outta here a.s.a.p." just so that he wouldn't have to go through the house-moving ritual again. But it was with heavy heart that I said goodbye to my beloved as he winged his way back to sunny Africa.

After getting a few quotes, I arranged for the services of a builder who came recommended by a friend to get stuck into the required maintenance work as soon as we took possession of the property.

Because the main kitchen would need a total revamp we decided to follow the lead of the previous owners and not use the ground floor initially. There was more than enough space on the first and second floors to accommodate us.

The kids and I were experiencing mixed feelings about the move. We had enjoyed our Saxon Street home, what little time we'd spent in it, as it had a lovely big garden (even if it did take some serious upkeep), and we would really miss our lovely neighbours. And it was the last home my mum and dad had enjoyed together.

But life moves on.

ONE OF THE THINGS WHICH WAS GOING TO BE A PROBLEM AT THE NEW house was lack of bedroom storage. For many years now we had been used to having fitted wardrobes in our bedrooms, but in the Victorian property there were none. Not one. As we weren't planning to do any home improvements to the house in the immediate future, some form of bedroom storage furniture needed to be purchased. One day I mentioned this to my cousin Jean, and she said that her ex-mother-in-law was moving out of her bungalow into a retirement home, and was selling off most of her furniture. I duly contacted Emily and made arrangements to have a look at what she had.

Due to the close proximity of our old and new properties, a mere 300 yards door to door, Ziggy had reckoned we could accomplish the move with a couple of wheelbarrows but, since the crafty bugger wasn't going to be there to push them, I thought it would be best to hire a large van. With the help of a couple of fit friends, we should be able to do the job without the need to call in professionals.

I waited until I had the use of the van before calling on Ziggy's best mate Bill to come and help me collect any suitable furniture. I had no idea what might be there, but I didn't want to have to make two trips out to the village where Emily lived, and figured there was bound to be *something* useful in the old dear's place which I could buy, so off we went.

Emily had quite a houseful of stuff. All the furnishings I was interested in were extremely old but in excellent condition, and I managed to buy two wardrobes and a dressing table for my bedroom as well as three large chests of drawers for the kids.

She had asked a very fair price for her worldly goods and as we were about to leave said, "But I wonder if you'd like to have this too. It's in very good condition, just needs a tune-up, and I'll only ask forty quid for it."

She opened her front room door and led us inside. "It" was a full-size, upright piano.

I should have said, "No" right out, but I hesitated; even confessed that I had piano lessons as a kid. BIG mistake. She knew she had me. Within five minutes I was handing over my last £40, which she could have noticed was all I had left when I'd pulled money from my pocket to pay for the furniture.

After we'd loaded the wardrobes into the van, Emily called on her neighbour to help Bill get the piano loaded. We boogie-woogie'd our way down the slight slope to the parked vehicle because Bill let the neighbour take the strain of the load while he walked alongside rattling out the strains of *In The Mood* on the piano keys. He said it was the only tune he knew how to play, but it was good enough to turn the heads of a few passers-by in the street, and had me bopping along to it.

After quite a struggle to get our last acquisition on board the van, we hurried home to continue loading items to be delivered to our waiting residence.

You would think that such a short-distance house-moving procedure would be a doddle after our previous intercontinental moves. On the contrary, it was a much more knackering experience than usual. Let's face it, I'd gone through enough house moves by now to know the score. The bane of this one was that we didn't get a break between the packing and the unpacking. The other pain was that every single item, barring the piano, had to be carted up the narrow flight of stairs to our first-floor accommodation. The piano, we decided, could stay in the otherwise empty front room downstairs where Bill could tinkle away to his little heart's content any time he visited.

Once everything was placed where it was required, we then had the disruption of the first major internal work. The entire house had to be rewired - while we were in it!

Yes, I know what you're thinking. Since the house had been empty why didn't we get it done before we moved in?

After contracts had been exchanged on the deal we were given a set of keys so that we could organise mundane stuff, like cleaning and having the central heating boiler serviced. But we couldn't start work on major repairs to the property until it actually belonged to us. Okay, we could have taken out a bridging loan with the bank for a couple of weeks, but that would have cost us a lot of pennies, so I decided we could put up with the inconvenience of floorboards being ripped up beneath our feet, accompanied by all the inherent dust it involved, for a few weeks. (I won't be doing that again!)

The upside was that the disruption caused by that experience made having repairs done to the old sash windows seem quite minor. And, of course, the external work to the property was a doddle for us, only requiring a steady stream of liquid refreshments in the form of tea, to the builders.

Within a few weeks the kids, dog and I were well settled in our new home.

27

INTERLOPERS

Ah, look at this, someone has left their laptop untended again. How about I take the opportunity to tell you a little story of my own? This is Brad speaking by the way.

I have lots of recollections of our lives during the period covered by this book, but two incidents in particular spring readily to mind:

I love horses.

There are so many happy memories of living in Zambia, and a great deal of them revolve around horsey exploits, given the social element it afforded many expats, as you'll likely have read earlier.

While most of our time as kids involved exploring the show grounds, playing out faux romances in haybale forts and making up stories of giant ghost horses, we did occasionally ride horses. We'd take lessons, which was okay, but the best was when we went on rides around the cross-country course that some adults competed on. The difference was that we rode around the giant logs they'd jump over. I always wanted to do those jumps.

Then the chance came to try out show jumping. I remember being excited and scared, but confident enough in my riding to get on with it; after all it was only five very low jumps spread around the arena.

The instructor waved me through into the paddock for my two

laps, and it was all going great - small leaps over poles I could have walked over. I was in the stride and getting used to the sensation. As soon as we cleared the fifth jump of the first lap, horsey noticed the open paddock gate, and instead of repeating the course bolted to the left, throwing me off balance and out of the saddle. Then I was hanging down on the right with my foot stuck in the stirrup, arms flailing around uselessly, with the horse's hooves thundering into the ground inches from my head. After a few seconds, which felt more like minutes, my foot finally freed itself and I rolled to a relatively safe stop. I stood up then walked off to try and find my steed, feeling half pleased with my jumps and most happy to be alive.

Of course, now I'm an expert, so at junior gymkhana a couple of weeks later I entered into the beginners' show jumping event. Surely I'm now prepared for any wayward eventuality?

So there we were again at the paddock entrance, full of confidence, and getting waved through by the marshal for my turn. Take two.

We cleared the jumps effortlessly, but as we cleared the final fence I notice some clown had left the gate open *again*! Self-preservation kicked in and I held onto the saddle for fear of death while she galloped straight through the collecting ring, heading for the stables. Being aware of the potential end result I prepared for the entrance, ducking as low as I could as she trotted in through the stable doorway.

No harm, no foul, but from that point onwards I shied away from riding things that have a mind of their own. I still love horses, but these days I'll rather sit astride a motorbike which generally does what I want it to do.

ANOTHER MEMORY COMES FROM THE PERIOD WE SPENT BACK IN BURTON ON Trent.

Summers in Burton were great. There was a small gang of us that would tear around on our bikes and explore the local woods and parks together. One afternoon we had returned from investigating a construction site and were now trying our best to destroy our back tyres doing skids in the road (as boys are wont to do), and ended up at my friend Philip's house for a glass of squash and some fish finger sandwiches.

When we went back outside to where we'd left our bikes, there was that sickening feeling as I realised mine was gone - someone had stolen my beloved BMX! We ran up and down the street looking for it to no avail, searching gardens and pathways, and eventually realised this wasn't some prank or lesson to lock up our bikes (well, technically it was).

I trudged home in a foul mood to break the news to mum and grandad, who was visiting at the time (Dad was in Zambia), and the police were called. Burton on Trent was not exactly the crime capital of the world and so the policeman who came explained this was perhaps an opportunist crime and to keep a look out for the bike. I remember thinking, "Isn't that your job?" Clearly they did have bigger fish to fry.

About a week later we were due to move house, just a short distance from where we lived. I was having a look around the new home prior to the big move and as I peered out of one of the top floor windows down into the social club carpark behind the house, something caught my eye. I recognised the chrome frame and red grips at once - and some little toe rag was cleaning my bike in the carpark behind some other houses, with his mates standing around.

Red hot adrenalin flooded through me and I sped down the stairs without much thought as to what I'd do when I got there, but in the minute or so it took me to sprint to that carpark I'd come up with a plan: Make an excuse for being there and confirm that it was in fact my bike, and then alert the authorities - I certainly wasn't going to confront this criminal gang single-handed.

I ran as fast as I could down the road and round the back of the houses, storming into the carpark in a mock panic, asking the boys if they'd seen anyone in a blue shirt who I thought was after me; they said, "No," and carried on cleaning.

Happy that this was my bike I raced back to tell mum, who called the police again and explained where this crime syndicate was operating. The local constabulary soon arrived and recovered the BMX from the local crime lords and returned it to one very happy boy. A bonus was, my bike was clean!

Delirious to be reunited with my beautiful bike I thought nothing more of it (beside going out to spend all my pocket money on a bike lock!), but about a week later we were absolutely amazed when a policeman came round and presented me with a cheque for £5 for my part in solving this heinous crime. I was overjoyed - I'd made a month's worth of pocket money profit after my lock purchase!

WELL, SINCE BRAD'S MANAGED TO FIND HIS WAY IN HERE, I GUESS I MIGHT as well take advantage of it to add a few words too. Hi, this is Leon here.

I have several unforgettable memories of the time we spent in Zambia, but two of the most memorable will be indelibly etched in my mind, and one quite literally on my forehead.

It was shortly after our move to Lusaka. Brad had his gleaming new BMX which I was only allowed to *look at* under his supervision, never mind actually ride it! I'm sure I must have ridden the prized BMX at some point as I did have a vague understanding of how it worked, such as where to find the brakes. Clearly any lessons must have been limited as this vital information proved hard to recall under pressure.

Our next door neighbours' kids were roughly the same age group as us and we sometimes hopped over the wall to play with them. On this particular afternoon we were taking it in turns to ride their bicycle up and down their long driveway. I was thrilled when it was my turn and duly set off pedalling merrily down the drive. I recall the unnerving effect of the pedals being whisked from under my feet as I started to pick up speed. It was the sort of bike where the sprocket was locked to the turn of the wheels, so once my feet lost their footing on the pedals there was just no going back without the inevitable smack on the shins you would receive if even attempting to replace said mis-positioned appendages.

Legs akimbo and handlebars a-wobbling, I continued to gain momentum. I'm not sure what exactly was going through my mind, but it certainly wasn't the location of the brakes within easy fingers' reach. As the long driveway got shorter and shorter the big black solid metal gates at the bottom got bigger and bigger. I panicked. All I remember thinking is that it's ok, I'll stop when I get to the bottom. By this time my brother and the bike's nervous owner were running behind screaming at me to stop, but clearly the actual method for doing so had escaped me.

I remember seeing their wide-eyed guard at the gate house with his arms outstretched imploring the speeding screaming kid to stop by sheer willpower. Unfortunately his telekinetic powers must have been on the fritz, as with an almighty CLANG I finally reached the conclusion of my descent.

I'm not quite sure how the bicycle handled the collision but the gate was fine, not a scratch. My forehead on the other hand was not let off so lightly. A warm sensation started to flow down my face as I staggered, blubbering back up the driveway, under the concerned guidance of my big bruv.

As luck would have it, I had managed to time this little mishap to occur five minutes *after* the local clinic had closed, so Mum had to plead for the emergency doctor to visit us to apply the obviously required stitches. I remember being laid out on the dining room table on top of a bedsheet, which was wound tightly around me to keep my flailing limbs from knocking out the on-call doctor. As mum leaned across my mummified body and held my head as still as a rock, I looked up in horror at a massive needle of anaesthetic which was to be poked into the wound on my forehead. Once it had all gone numb I was all stitched up. It reminded me of my mum repairing one of Vicki's dolls years ago.

Boys will be boys though, and the resulting stitches were proudly worn like a trophy to my stupidity. The bedsheet had to be thrown away.

My second favourite recollection centres around the Gymkhana Club. Many a happy memory persists of that wonderful place where we were allowed to create our own mischief, er, entertainment, but one of the most poignant was the building of a haybale secret hideout.

There were some stables on the far side of the grounds that were usually used to accommodate the visiting entrants during the annual show, but which were often used to store haybales during the rest of the year.

My brother was included in the crowd of the 'older kids' while my sister and I were relegated to the juniors. The old kids had figured out that they could remove some strategic haybales from the top few layers in the middle, and thereby create a depression in the centre of the stacked hay that was not visible from the outside.

This gave them a 'secret hide-out' where they could assert their dominion by not allowing the juniors in. They had even managed to create a tunnel from their hollowed-out section to the ground level by the stable entrance, quite a feat if you've ever tried to pull out a bale surrounded by others.

Not to be outdone, the juniors attempted to make their own fort in one of the neighbouring stables that had been made more accessible by the withdrawing of some bales for their intended purpose of feeding horses.

One day when we returned to the clubhouse nearing home time mum, aghast, said, "Leon, where's your watch?"

I had recently received for Christmas a lovely new maroon watch of the big hand/little hand variety which I was absolutely enthralled with. I was so proud of the fact that I had a 'proper grown-up watch', not like the digital ones favoured by most kids my age because they were easy to read. I think I was actually more upset than mother, although judging by her 'maroon' face you might not have guessed it at the time.

We figured it must have come off while I was trying to wrestle the haybales in our little fort in a vain attempt to match the impressive hideout of the seniors. It's not easy trying to search through broken haybales with a face full of tears I can tell you. Add to that the failing light and it was not looking good. The ultimatum of, "you're going nowhere until you find that watch" was not much more upsetting than the actual turmoil of losing my favourite possession.

I was beside myself. We had searched and searched and searched. It wasn't in the piles of loose straw of our failed fort. It wasn't in the senior's impressive hideout that we'd been allowed a brief glimpse of. It wasn't in the fields. It seemed like all hope was lost as I made my way reluctantly in the pending gloom to meet the inevitable doom of informing mum that the watch was well and truly gone. Then my darling brother, huge grin across his face, came trotting along with a broken-strap maroon watch clutched in his grubby hands. I could have kissed him!

I have never ever been happier or more thankful to have a big brother looking out for me, and I never wore the (fixed) watch back to the Gymkhana Club again. It was from then on a 'special occasions only' watch. Big brothers are okay sometimes.

28

ONCE MORE UNTO THE BREACH

A week into August I received the phone call I had been waiting anxiously for. Ziggy called to say he'd had permission to bring us out to Zambia and asked when did I want to fly? After the stupid "Tomorrow!" initial response, I suggested that four weeks should be long enough for me to organise the packing-up and departure. He duly arranged our flights.

The kids were thrilled to hear the news and couldn't wait to tell their friends they were going back to live in Africa. They received a mixed response ranging from sadness, to green envy, to incredulity that anyone would want to leave their beloved town of Burton on Trent.

So I was back to my favourite hobby, packing boxes! The advantage of *this* move to Africa was that I knew exactly what I needed to take! Things I hadn't used much during our previous foray stayed put.

After the experience of having tenants in our property when we moved to Zambia in 1980 I had no intention of going that route again. At least this time our furniture and belongings could be stored at our house instead of being put in commercial storage. It was cheaper for me to install a good security alarm system on the property than to pay storage fees. And they would be available for my dad's use, should he need to borrow anything. Actually, I was secretly hoping that he would move into our home, as I still wasn't happy about where he was living.

The downside to this packing business was that I still hadn't finished unpacking all the boxes since the move from Saxon Street, but I still had to go through them all to see what stuff should be directed where.

I checked out all our electrical equipment and replaced several items. This turned out to be a good move, as at least we still had a kettle and toaster to use after all our possessions had been carted off by the removals firm.

In the event, my dad did move in. Only a couple of weeks after we'd left the country, the alarm kept going off for no reason at all. Apart from annoying the neighbours, it also annoyed my dad because, as keyholder, he would receive a call from our local police station which was just across the road from our house, telling him to come and switch the bloody thing off.

Of course, he got the people who installed it to come and sort out what was causing all the trouble, but realised he might as well move in to save time and petrol money going back and forth for them. I think the fact that he missed a lot of his Stapenhill friends at the local pubs also tilted the scales.

Unfortunately after living there for quite a time he found the cost of maintaining the heating system to be very draining on his British pension; he also felt like he was rattling around in the huge place on his own. He eventually applied to the local council and was allocated a small bungalow not too far away, where he was much happier.

ONE OF THE THINGS WHICH I HAD KNOWN WAS GOING TO BE A HEART-breaking experience was parting with Sooty. It certainly wasn't feasible to take him with us, even though he wouldn't need to undergo quarantine on his arrival in Africa, but the cost of flying him out there would be prohibitive. We needed to find a new home for him, but being a fully-grown big dog, we knew this wouldn't be easy.

An acquaintance at our local pub said he would like to take him, but I had seen his tendency towards unreliability so couldn't trust him to look after our dog properly. We put the word out among our friends, to no avail. The last thing I wanted to do was hand him over to the RSPCA, not knowing what would happen to him. But as the time of our departure drew closer, with no new owner found, I eventually contacted a lady involved with the RSPCA. She said she would take him, and was sure she'd soon be able to find such a lovely dog a good home and would in the meantime keep him at her house.

On the evening before our flight out to Zambia, the kids and Sooty, complete with assorted possessions, piled into my dad's car and I drove off to the other side of town where the lady lived. As we were led into her kitchen we were greeted by three other dogs and an assortment of cats. She was clearly an animal lover, and made a big fuss of Sooty.

After explaining a few things about him to her, his likes and habits, the kids and I each said our goodbyes to him. The lady almost had to push us out of her house at our reluctance to abandon the beautiful dog we knew we would never see again. With tears streaming we slouched back to the car and bawled our eyes out all the way home.

We later learned that Sooty got a wonderful home on a dairy farm, where he was able to run around to his heart's content with their other dogs.

AND SO IT WAS ON SATURDAY, SEPTEMBER 3RD 1988 THE PATRAS/JOHNSON families once more gathered at East Midlands airport for a tearful farewell. Leaving my dad was extremely heart-wrenching. He was now on his own family-wise, apart from one brother and a few sisters-in-law (plus nieces and nephews), most of whom he saw only rarely.

After many hugs and kisses we boarded our plane with tear-stained cheeks to venture once more Into Africa.

29

INTO CHILANGA

A thankfully uneventful flight saw us land happily back in Lusaka to the customary blue skies and smiling faces, and one husband looking pleased to see us.

"So," I enquired, "have you found us somewhere to live?"

"I couldn't find us a house in Lusaka but I did manage to find us a very nice place in Chilanga."

"And where, pray, might that be?" I enquired.

"Do you remember going to Munda Wanga Zoo when we first moved to Lusaka?"

"Yes."

"Well that is Chilanga."

"I remember going to the zoo but doubt I could find it again. Roughly what direction is it in?"

"It's on the other side of town, on the road to Kafue." He said.

"Ah, very convenient," I thought sarcastically, but it was good for him given that the job he was working on was in Kafue.

"Just wait 'til you see it. You'll love it."

In the event, I did have to wait to see it due to the fact that, between the airport and Chilanga, lay the Gymkhana Club and the car simply would not go past there.

It was still quite early in the day so there weren't many people in the vicinity of the clubhouse except two or three stalwarts who, nonetheless, gave me and the kids a hearty welcome home. The kids instantly went tearing off to look for any friends who might be around, but were disappointed to find it was too early for them to be there. We strolled over to the stables and were thrilled to see most of the familiar horses were still around and delighted to meet up with the grooms who, ever friendly, gave us a warm welcome back.

We enjoyed an early beer then clambered back into the car and headed out of town. After the description Ziggy had given me whilst in the club I was eager to be introduced to our new home.

Travelling towards Kafue we were pretty close to Munda Wanga Zoo when we turned left off the main road. We drove almost a mile down a rough dirt road, passing a few large properties along the way, before arriving at our destination. Wow! I loved it.

The house was H-shaped, and consisted of a spacious lounge, dining room and a huge kitchen with pantry off. There were four bedrooms and two bathrooms on one side of the house, the master bedroom having its bathroom en suite, as well as another curious feature - a door which led out to the garden. The other side of the house featured a guest bedroom with bathroom en suite, as well as another room which I guessed could be used as an office. I quickly commandeered that as my sewing room. Each room of the house was appropriately furnished, with the bedrooms having more than adequate fitted wardrobes.

A double carport was attached to the house and there was not one, but two patios.

Glass doors led off the lounge area to the patios. The patio at the rear of the property got the sun first thing in the morning, an ideal place to sit and enjoy breakfast. The larger front patio, however, would be the preferred relaxing place.

From there, looking beyond our swimming pool set in the sloping garden, all we could see was open veld, bushes and trees. It felt like we were living out in a game park. In reality there was a house next door, about four-hundred yards to our right, but that was out of sight from where we sat. The random twinkling of a few lights at night also indicated there were other homes in the distance, but during daylight hours the properties were rendered invisible by trees. It was so peaceful and, facing west, it was the perfect place to sit with an African sundowner.

For those not familiar with the expression, perhaps I should explain that a sundowner is not a person, nor just a time of day when one watches the sun go down, but is also the drink of choice one consumes whilst watching this spectacle. In the majority of cases a sundowner consists of a large gin and tonic with plenty of ice and a slice of lemon, usually from one's own trees (just the lemons).

At any time of day, however, sitting in that awesome setting was an absolute delight. The predominant sound was the beloved cape turtle dove with its, "where's FAther" call which had caused me so much heartache when we were in England. But at sundown we had an unbelievable added bonus.

We could hear the roar of lions.

Fair enough, we knew they were in the zoo, being less than a couple of miles away as the eagle glides, but that was beside the point. Not being able to see them made it all the more magical, as if they were walking through the bush, just out of sight. It is truly amazing how their roar carries so far. This video comes the closest to the sounds we used to hear, especially the second half of the recording: https://www.youtube.com/watch?v=_22gJ5kB31k .

I just hoped that those lions were adequately penned, as the one thing which was missing from our 'perfect' house was a fence although, to be honest, I was less worried about escaped lions being a menace than I was about intrusion from burglars. However, Ziggy assured me that the agents letting the house had promised a security fence would soon be installed. Knowing Africa, the sooner the better as far as I was concerned.

The pool also needed some attention. It was some time since it had been used, and apart from being half empty the water was greener than any surrounding vegetation. Apparently there was a plug in the bottom which needed to be pulled to empty it, and the walls scrubbed before filling it with clean water from the hose. We set the wheels in motion to do that during the following week.

The property also came with a house servant named Julius, who lived in a kia at the rear of the property with his family. Also included were two rather old mongrel dogs. I wasn't too confident that they would be any use in deterring potential burglars and decided to get my own hound as soon as we had the fence erected.

While he'd been here on his own Ziggy, for ease of sociability, had spent many weekends staying with the McClanes who lived in Lusaka. They were currently looking after a Toyota King Cab vehicle belonging to a mutual friend who was travelling overseas and suggested that we might borrow it, saying "I'm sure Tony won't mind", until we had managed to find ourselves a vehicle. With Ziggy working in Kafue it was down to me to take the kids to Lake Road School in Lusaka, which was half-an-hour's drive in the opposite direction to Kafue.

The first term of the new school year was due to start the week after we arrived. Ziggy had already registered them in advance of our arrival, now my first task was to set them up once again with school uniforms. With all this accomplished we soon settled down into our renewed Zambian life.

It wasn't long before all our stuff arrived from England. We were well set up with all the nice new kitchen equipment I'd bought. My sewing room had a dedicated desk for my sewing machine and over-locker, and the wardrobe in there was perfect for storing all the fabrics and patterns I'd packed.

At the opposite end of the large living area was a lower level section with its own comfy chairs, so we made that the designated television lounge. The hostess trolley sat conveniently by the dining table, and my Amstrad computer and accompanying printer were allocated a desk in the safety of our bedroom.

The kids were delighted to have the use of their bikes, and though not really having anywhere suitable to ride them while at home, we were able to take them with us to the LGC in the back of the Toyota.

WHEN WE WERE IN THE UK PEOPLE OFTEN USED TO ASK HOW WE COPED with things like dangerous spiders and snakes in Africa. I told them I had seen hardly any snakes, and that the spiders I'd come across had primarily been the ones which were known as wall spiders, because you would mostly see them on walls. When on the move they would scurry across the wall on tiptoe, but when stationary would completely flatten themselves against the wall. They often lived behind mirrors and pictures.

Actually I was quite proud of myself with these spiders. I had been terrified of spiders since I was old enough to recognise one, and wouldn't go in a room if there was a spider in there, insisting on it being splatted and all evidence removed. When we first moved to Zambia I soon realised that I'd need to toughen up with regard to creepy-crawlies, as there were so damn many of them.

But there always has to be one, doesn't there? Let me tell you about a visitor we had:

We had just finished cleaning out the pool and were in the process of refilling it. As we worked outside I had opened the door which led from the garden to our bedroom. This gave easy access to the house, including our bathroom. This essential room was oblong in shape and, as you walked in, the shower cubicle was the first thing on the right, then came the bath before reaching the end of the room where the hand-wash basin and toilet were. There came a point during the afternoon when I needed to use the bathroom.

As I was going about my business I noticed a wall spider not 12 inches away from where I was sitting, and silently commended myself for my sheer complacency to its presence. Having completed my intentions I stood up and looking forwards, I *froze*.

Sitting there, on the face of the tiled shower tray, was the biggest spider I had ever seen in my entire life. It was the size of a tennis ball! Well, that's what it seemed like from where I was. Perhaps it was a tad smaller than that, *but not by much*!

How I hadn't noticed it on the way in I have no idea, but now I had to walk past it to leave the bathroom. Or not! At the point where the spider was, walking through the doorway would put me within inches of this monster.

I shouted for help. And shouted, and shouted. Eventually Vicki came.

"Don't come inside!" I yelled at the top of my voice as she unlatched the door. She shot backwards so fast she stumbled on a mat and finished up on the bed. As she recovered I called out, "Vicki, please go and tell your daddy to come here. Tell him it's very important."

"What's so important, mummy?"

"Well if you promise not to scream…"

"I promise."

"…or you might frighten it and it'll run to me."

"What will, mummy?"

"Slowly open the bathroom door and then look to where the bottom of the shower is," I told her.

I watched, as, slowly pushing the door open she crept forward. It was like watching a stalking cat.

Then she saw it, screamed at the top of her voice and ran off. At the same time I leapt onto the toilet (fortunately I'd already closed the lid!).

The spider stayed where it was.

After what seemed like an age, Ziggy appeared at the door.

"Now, what's all this noise ab… whoa, that's a big un, isn't it?"

"Yes. Now will you please do something about it?"

"Like what?"

"Well splatter it or something."

"Kill that? Are you mad? It's HUGE!"

"I'm fully aware of how bloody BIG it is, but it needs to go before I can leave here."

"Oooo, don't tempt me," he grinned.

"Come on, DO something. *Please*."

"Okay, I'll organise it, you just wait there," he said as he wandered off.

"Yeah, right, like I'm going anywhere," I called after him.

Next thing I heard him yell, "LEON!"

A few minutes later he reappeared, with Leon in tow carrying a Tupperware container and a fly swatter.

With a wide grin on his face, Leon chirped, "Where is it mummy?"

My fearless husband had brought his 10-year-old son to do the dirty work!

I looked Leon in the eyes then turned my stare to the spider. He followed my gaze.

"WOW, he is a beauty, isn't he?"

Well not quite the words *I* would have chosen to describe a huge, brown, very hairy spider, but each to their own.

"Don't move," he said as he crept into the room. I didn't know if he was talking to me or the spider but I kept very still, and watched.

Getting down onto his knees, with the plastic box in his left hand and the swatter in his right, Leon slowly inched the box towards the spider.

I can say that at this point I was mighty glad I was in the bathroom, as I knew I would crap myself if that spider made any sudden movement, either towards Leon or myself.

But he succeeded in placing the box squarely over the spider without a hitch.

"Pass me the lid now please daddy," he said.

Ziggy did as he was bid, with outstretched arm, standing well back.

Placing the edge of the lid on top of the little wall, Leon slid the box upwards and onto the lid until he was able to secure it shut. One *very* brave boy. One captured spider. One VERY happy mother!

We then got one of the huge Coke concentrate jars I'd acquired for winemaking and Leon put the spider in there, together with a little foliage and any insects he could catch. Next day he took it to school to get it identified. It was a wolf spider.

The kids also proudly showed it off at the Gymkhana Club as we called in there after school. It was only a few hours later after we got home that Brad advised us of a minor issue:

"Mummy, I was talking to Rob at the club and apparently he knows a lot about spiders. He said, 'You'll always find wolf spiders in pairs'. Do you think we should look for the other one?"

It was pretty obvious that like several other small species of wildlife we'd noticed, the spider had been disturbed from its resting place by the filling of the pool. After a painstaking search of the area, sure enough another one was discovered, and promptly joined its mate in the jar until we could decide what to do with them.

After many photographs were taken and a couple of days passed, we disposed of them by emptying the jar into a handy hedgerow, halfway between home and school. Unless they had very high homing instincts I didn't think we'd see them again.

To be on the safe side I made a wedge of fabric which I pressed into the gap under that outside door to our bedroom, just in case any of their brothers or sisters tried to pay us a visit.

30

BACK IN THE SADDLE

N ow that I had the kids all sorted and settled back in at Lake Road School it was time to turn my attention to what I was going to do with *my* time. There was no question that it had to involve a horse.

Once Tilly had become fully fit after we left Zambia in '86, Heather had managed to sell her to someone on the Copperbelt. I communicated that I would love to buy her back but was soon advised that the new owner had no intention of parting with her, as they were getting along famously. So I put the word out around the Lusaka horse fraternity that I was looking for a well-mannered mount. It wasn't long before I was contacted by a guy from the polo club saying he had a horse to sell. I couldn't believe my ears when I heard its name, but nonetheless arranged to go and view it.

I have learnt a few things about horses over the years. The first of my more painful memories stretched back to when I was about fourteen years old, when I had my first pony. Our school was liberating a bit, and between the compulsory seasons of hockey and rounders we were asked if we'd like to do anything 'different' during our outdoor activities period. I suggested that some of the class might like to go horse riding, and that I could fix it with the farm where I kept my pony.

They had horses and ponies for the riding thereof. I won't say it was a riding school, as that would be far too grand a description for this establishment. It was a family farm in the Trent Valley where their main interest was dairy cows, with a few add-ons like chickens, ducks and half a dozen pigs. And horses. Of course, they didn't have enough horses to accommodate our entire class, but then our entire class didn't want to go horse riding. There must have been about eight of us.

I made the necessary arrangements with the farm's family member who was in charge of the steeds and we all went along there on the designated Friday afternoon.

Allocating mounts was quite a feat in itself. It wasn't a question of who had the most experience - only half of them had ever sat on a horse before - but rather whose bum would fit which saddle. They were all ponies of various description and colour, apart from a thoroughbred horse called Rodney. Whether he ever raced was highly questionable as the only reason he seemed to go faster than the rest of them was because his legs were longer.

I led the way through the various meadows given over to riding and grazing cows (as opposed to hay crops). We walked around a bit until my classmates became bored with that and asked if we could go faster. I tried to explain to the girls how to make a horse do that, and they mostly managed it after a fashion. All except the one riding Rodney.

He must have decided it was beneath his dignity to take instructions from a beginner, and barely moved beyond a slow trot.

"Come on," shouted Barbara, "make him go faster."

Far be it from me to decline such a request, I trotted up behind him and gave him a hefty whack on his rump with my whip.

In justifiable (I see now) retaliation, quick as a flash, he lashed out and kicked me in the middle of my right shin, and it bloody hurt! But it had the desired effect and he loped off at a slow canter all the way back to the farmyard.

I helped the girls dismount, or fall off semi-gracefully, before hobbling up to the farmhouse, normally a no-go area, to see if the farmer's wife could clean up my bloody leg. After putting a plaster on it she gave me instructions to call at the local hospital to get it stitched.

Here ended my first lesson. Some horses use their feet for purposes other than walking on. And I still have the scar to prove it.

"Why is she telling me all this crap?" I hear you ask.

It is an explanation for my reluctance to go creeping up on horses now, especially ones I don't know.

The majority of the polo club's animals were out grazing in the meadow next to the polo field. They all looked peaceful and docile, but after my youthful experience I would never take a chance of getting too close to a crowd. Some have nasty streaks and can inflict damage from either end, or a tiff could flare up between them causing a mini stampede, which you definitely don't want to be in the middle of. But standing by the fence I could easily see the dark bay thoroughbred which had been described to me, and he did look very nice.

When I confirmed my interest, his owner suggested that I take him on two weeks' trial before closing the deal, which I felt was very decent of him.

After arranging temporary stabling with one of my friends, the following day I strolled from LGC to the polo grounds carrying saddle and bridle to collect my potential acquisition. Half a dozen grooms were standing around, having completed their morning duties, and watched on as the five-year-old gelding was led out of his stable.

I walked up and stroked his neck, moving my hand slowly up and around his ears and down the side of his face. Still gently holding his face I stood in front of him and leaning forward until my nose was level with his muzzle, I gently snorted into his nostrils. He breathed in my scent with a sort of curiosity and we stood softly snorting each other for many seconds. All this time the grooms looked on, completely mystified by my actions, and clearly wondering who, or what, this weird woman was. They had obviously never seen anyone do this to a horse before. Maybe no-one else does it, but it was something I had a habit of doing, especially with a horse that I wanted to bond with. I stood back and asked his groom to tack him up.

He first put on the bridle, then, handing the reins to me, hoisted the saddle onto the horse's back. As I stood at the horse's shoulder the groom finalised the tacking-up by sharply tightening the girth.

At this the nag's head whipped round and the little bastard bit me on the arse!

The grooms all fell about laughing. I realised they had been expecting this, which is why the groom had handed me the reins the way he had, to make sure I was in the right location to receive the nip, not him.

What they hadn't been expecting though, and neither had the horse, was that within an instant of it happening I swung round and punched the horse on the snout.

I have known horses in the past that have a tendency to back-bite when the girth is tightened, and wanted to nip this habit in the bud, (if you'll pardon the pun). It worked, because he never, ever, did it to me again.

I mounted up and we set off towards the LGC arena. As we walked along I knew I was going to be happy with him. He had a lovely gait, not quite as long a stride as Tilly had had, but very comfortable. We turned off the main lane into one which ran along the rear of a row of stables, but when we were about halfway down he suddenly stopped dead in his tracks. I urged him on. Nothing. I kicked his flanks some more, but this horse was going nowhere. At a bit of a loss how to shift him, other than get off and lead him which I certainly wasn't prepared to do, I kicked and urged but to no avail.

The lane we were standing in was well shaded by tall trees. I stretched over to one side and grabbed at a branch, from which I was able to break off a lengthy twig. Once more urging him forwards I slapped him on the rump with the switch. He moved. Backwards. So I smacked him again. This time he reared up. Now that is one thing which cannot be tolerated as it can be dangerous for both rider and horse, so I reacted by swishing the leaves on the end of the twig over his ears, and urged him on again. This time he walked forwards, for about eight paces. Then the entire performance was repeated until he continued to walk on as requested.

He had behaved just like a naughty little boy, but finally got the message that his nonsense would not be tolerated. From that point onwards he obeyed all commands, within reason, without need for chastisement.

I had arranged to take a stable with Penny who, for some reason, had one to spare. Our arrival there generated a lot of interest as a new kid on the block always does, and Tommy Tucker was introduced to the LGC fraternity. He was greatly admired and ridiculed in equal quantities. I mean, who in their right mind gives a horse a name like *that*? It's bad enough for a nursery rhyme, but a horse? Not surprisingly, with the sense of humour many of my friends had, his name got quite a few variations.

But odd name or not, Tommy proved to be a super horse, taking to jumping just as readily as Tilly had done, except thankfully he didn't try to do it at a flat-out gallop.

31

UNINVITED VISITORS

We decided it was time for a party. At the end of October I was about to enter the final year of my thirties and that seemed as good an excuse for a party as any. We could also combine it as a celebration of Ziggy's 40th, which had occurred in our absence at the end of July. Thankfully the Lusaka shopping facilities had improved substantially (for Zambia) while we'd been suffering our stint in England, and after receiving positive responses from all our friends I set about buying all the necessary food and drinks.

I also borrowed plates and knives and forks from the Club as they could be more readily replaced than my own stuff, should any mishaps occur. Additionally I suggested to guests that if they wanted to sit down during the proceedings it might be prudent to bring their own chairs, as there would be more people than I could seat. It was, as usual, a very raucous affair with lots of singing and dancing, finishing off with silly games, made all the more entertaining by the inebriation of most of the participants.

This was quite extensive in some cases due, we discovered later, to a slight misunderstanding. One of the guests had been replenishing his glass when the soda syphon ran dry. Ziggy suggested the guest went and filled the syphon with water from the bottle in the fridge (which was pre-boiled), while he sought a gas capsule to operate the syphon.

Unfortunately the guest performing this water replenishment must have had a different arrangement to us when it came to storing boiled water. Ours was kept in a plain, unmarked 1-litre glass bottle. The guest must have used empty spirit bottles for the purpose in his home, because instead of filling the syphon with nice, safe, chilled boiled water, he inadvertently filled it with the contents of a bottle of Smirnoff Vodka which was also sitting in the fridge.

The lucky (?) guests who were drinking whisky/brandy and soda got much more than they bargained for as the party progressed. It's the biggest wonder we didn't kill anyone.

All in all we had a fabulous time, even if it did take a couple of days to recover from this wonderful experience.

The following Tuesday night, or early hours of Wednesday morning to be precise, we were sleeping soundly when we were awoken very abruptly by someone thumping on the bedroom door which opens onto the garden.

"Who the hell would be doing that at whatever unearthly time of the morning this is?" we wondered.

Ziggy leapt out of bed and pulled on his shorts, while I fumbled around trying to re-dress in whatever clothes I'd taken off the night before (not dungarees! – see *Into Africa*). After agreeing that he shouldn't open that particular door he headed for the main passageway.

"For goodness sakes don't go outside, Ziggy," I called after him as he strode off. Of course I didn't expect him to take any notice of me. I hovered in the passage, holding the door connecting through to the living area, ready to slam the door shut if I didn't like what I saw next.

Then I could hear voices, and a very agitated Ziggy.

Eventually my curiosity got the better of me and I went through to the kitchen where the voices were coming from. Standing at the open back door I could see Ziggy in heated conversation with two Zambian Police Officers. I dashed to his side.

"What the hell is going on here?"

"It would seem we have been robbed!" Ziggy said, sweeping his arm around the kitchen.

I looked to the worktops and instantly noticed that our microwave oven was missing, as was the kettle and the toaster.

"Oh my God!"

"It would appear," said Ziggy tersely "that five men, armed with pangas, forced Julius to open up so that they could just help themselves to our property. Julius, in his wisdom, decided to WALK to the police station to alert the police to the situation. The police, of course, have no transport, so the three of them walked back here. Naturally, by the time they arrived the bastard thieves were well gone, with all our stuff!"

(The police station was a couple of miles away.)

"Julius," I shouted at him as he had already backed well away from the door, "Why the hell didn't you wake us?"

"Ah madam, it was too dangerous." (I conceded that might have been the case initially.)

"Then why didn't you go to the house next door, and ask to use their phone in this emergency?"

(Our nearest neighbours were only 400 metres away.)

"Ah sorry, madam, I didn't think of that."

"I bet you bloody didn't. Get him away from me," I shouted to whoever would listen, "before I have a go at him with a panga myself!" There was something about his demeanour which told me that Julius was no innocent bystander in this fiasco.

I stormed out of the kitchen to make sure the kids hadn't been disturbed by all this noise. Ziggy finished talking to the police officers and came to find me.

"You'd have been hard pushed to kill Julius with the panga," he said "it was nicked along with everything else."

He sat me down with a stiff drink while he explained further.

He had headed into the kitchen with the intention of getting our panga from the pantry before answering the door, only to find the back door already wide open. As soon as he entered the pantry he noticed that the panga, along with our beer crates, was missing. That's when he realised we'd been robbed.

So he got the large chef's knife from the kitchen drawer and headed towards the back door when two men appeared. At such a quick glance he hadn't realised they were police and raced towards them with the knife. They ran away very quickly..

"Police! Police, sir! We are the Zambian police!" they had shouted from around the corner.

At this Ziggy called them to show themselves, which they did, at some distance from him.

After he lowered the knife they told him how Julius had appeared at the police station and asked for help, but they didn't have any transport. They then had to wake up a colleague to look after the police station so they could accompany Julius on foot back to our place.

"So what happens next?" I asked.

"I have to go and make a formal statement at the police station and get a case number for the insurance claim," he said.

"Oh, shit!"

"What?"

"We have no insurance. You know I've been asking you for weeks to get our video equipment back from Rob McClane, which you brought over from the UK and lent to him months ago. I needed it so that I could get the model and serial numbers of the machines. That was the last thing I needed to put on the insurance forms before posting them off to England with a cheque." (We had decided that taking out insurance in Zambia was a waste of time and money.)

I will not offend your eyes by writing down the words Ziggy came out with in response to that news. I wandered through the house trying to establish what had been taken:

- **Hi-Fi** system, consisting record deck, tape player, amplifier and four speakers
- **Television**
- **Sewing machine** and **5-thread overlocker**, as well as most of my fabrics and haberdashery. They even took my tapestry frame, complete with semi-completed canvas (except they didn't take the yarn)

- **Binoculars**, which we were most upset about as they had belonged to my granddad
- **Microwave oven; toaster; kettle** and **steam iron**
- **Olympus OM2** camera with several **lenses** (So no photos of the wolf spiders.)
- 6 or 7 crates of **beer** – some full, some empty
- On top of our hostess trolley there was a box containing all the **plates** and **cutlery** we'd borrowed from the Club - they took those
- An assortment of **clothes,** mostly Ziggy's, which were waiting either to be ironed or put away
- The **curtains** off the lounge windows to carry away the takings!
- The three childrens' **bicycles**

But worst of all, they put the whole bloody lot into Tony's **bakkie** and drove off with that too!

I felt sick. In my months of dreaming of returning to Zambia when we were back in England, this was one of the realities of African life I had allowed myself to forget.

The only thing electrical they didn't take was the hostess trolley - perhaps they didn't know what it was, or maybe they simply couldn't fit it in the bakkie with everything else! Oh, and my pride and joy, my new Amstrad PC was thankfully still safely sitting on its desk in our bedroom.

As you might imagine, we didn't sleep much on going back to bed for the remaining hours until daylight, getting up when we heard the kids stirring. They were naturally very upset when they heard the news, especially when told their bikes had been nicked.

Essential items like the kettle and toaster were replaced but we didn't bother with much else at this stage. We had a very miserable couple of weeks after the event but, hey, get over it, life goes on.

One decision which was made as a result of this occurrence was that we needed to get a dog. A proper one which had more inclination to deter burglars than the two useless hounds we had inherited with the house. Conversations with friends at the Gymkhana Club led me to

290 | ANN PATRAS

a family who also lived on the outskirts of Lusaka. They had an eighteen-month-old Rottweiler/German Shepherd named Jessy who needed a new home. It transpired that their other three dogs, all pure Shepherds, did not like Jessy, and were always picking on her. Her owner said that she was an excellent guard dog and yet very gentle and friendly with family and friends. We took her.

She was the most amazing dog. With the stocky body of a Rottweiler she had the markings of a black-and-tan Shepherd, more tan than black. She took to us immediately and we adored her. The kids played with her a lot and she paid no heed when they used her as a cushion or jumped over her recumbent form as they raced around. She was also totally unmoved by the two resident dogs. However, as we still had no fence around the property we decided to keep her inside the house at night lest she should take a notion to go searching for her old home, though we thought that highly unlikely as she had settled in so well with us.

We'd had Jessy for only a couple of weeks when one night Ziggy suddenly sat up in bed.

"What was that noise?"

Amazingly I had heard nothing. Sounds in the night are usually my domain so Ziggy figured there must be 'something up' for it to have woken him. He donned his shorts and left the bedroom while I just lay in bed and pondered this unusual phenomenon. After about ten minutes he was back.

"Well, well, well! What a good dog we've got." He said, a big grin on his face. "When I reached the dining room I found Jessy standing and looking very alert. She was happy to see me too and walked towards the front door. I thought she must want to go outside to do a wee. Maybe she'd barked about that, and that's what had woken me up. So I got her lead - didn't want her disappearing into the dark - and took her outside. As soon as she was out the door she pulled me off to the right and started sniffing around below the windows, and it was only then that I noticed the curtain."

He paused for breath, "Go on, go on!" I urged.

"Part of a curtain was sticking out through a hole in the glass by the window-handle, and there was a fist-sized rock on the windowsill.

Someone must have been trying to break in, but instead of finding the window-latch they must have been very surprised to get some very large teeth instead! Jessy obviously tried to bite them and went as far as she could through the glass before letting go."

"Is she hurt?"

"Thankfully not so much as a scratch on her, but there is some blood on the curtain where the would-be thief had been. So I took her for a walk all around the house, and I let her off the leash in case she spotted anyone 'cause I didn't want to delay any attack opportunities, but there was no-one around. Surprise, that, eh?"

"I hope you gave her a treat."

"Oh yes. We now have one less piece of steak for tonight's supper."

32

LAKE KARIBA

Once we had overcome the disruption and aftermath of our break-in we turned our thoughts to Christmas.

"I've got a suggestion," said Heather.

Heather's suggestions were often found to be quite interesting.

"And what would that be?" I enquired.

"Let's go to Kariba. For Christmas and New Year."

I looked at Ziggy, who shrugged his shoulders.

"Okay, what's the plan?"

"Well actually we've done it before, with Penny and Bernie Evans and the kids. We had a great time, obviously took all our food and stuff, and the Christmas presents. And we put a few decorations up around the cabins."

"I can bring our Christmas tree to put the presents under," I said, warming quickly to the idea. The more I thought about it, the more fun it sounded.

Penny and Bernie were keen to join us and so plans were laid. We booked three cabins at the furthest end of Eagles Rest Lodge

After a bit of haggling, Ziggy managed to borrow the company's Mitsubishi L200 double-cab bakkie to accommodate our substantial kutundu, and shortly after noon on the 23rd December the McCleerys and Patrases drove south from Lusaka.

A few miles before Zambia's M15 road reached Siavonga we turned right onto the dirt road which led to our destination. One thing was for sure, that access road certainly hadn't improved in the five years since we'd last driven there from Kitwe with the McConkey/Cummins gang, between Christmas and New Year.

With more potholes than road it was appalling. It was a damn good job I hadn't managed to buy any fresh cream for the Christmas feast, as it would have been shaken into butter by the time we reached the resort of Eagles Rest.

Actually, 'resort' was rather a grand title for this place in those days as it consisted of about half a dozen chalets overlooking the lake, and only offered minimal self-catering facilities: a fridge, a 2-ring electric hob and a pair of braai tongs (the latter we suspected having been left behind by a previous visitor).

Our arrival on the Friday gave us plenty of time to properly set up camp, put up all the decorations and dress the Christmas tree. On Saturday the Evans tribe arrived from Mazabuka and, what an arrival!

I always thought we were pretty well equipped when it came to camping, although the Eagles Rest facility couldn't be classified as full-on camping (not having to use tents), but our capacity to 'leave out nothing' faded into insignificance compared to the Evanses, who arrived in a 5-ton truck.

To say it was full of everything but the kitchen sink would be no exaggeration. They had been allocated the largest of the cabins which fortunately included a pretty wide veranda. We stood open-mouthed as the family off-loaded all their week's living-worth of consumables and personal possessions, which culminated with a hefty stereo unit and speakers, and a large deep-freezer (full of provisions). The crowning glory was a comfortable three-piece lounge suite!

Talk about home from home. And I thought *we* were the ones who liked our creature comforts. We were but amateurs compared to these guys!

We had a carol-singing session on Christmas Eve before turning in relatively early, knowing that the next day was likely to be pretty hectic. Christmas morning dawned clear and bright and we hastily placed the presents round the tree. We had decided not to take any chances by putting them there the night before, in case some pseudo Santa came along and took them all away.

We actually had the same cabin as in our previous visit, and once again gave the kids the benefit of sleeping inside while we had our bed outside, on the veranda. It was wonderful to awaken to a stunning sunrise over Lake Kariba.

The walk to the water's edge from the cabins was quite steep as the lake had dropped from its highest level by about ten yards. The last time I was there I'd been told that the level *then* was so low because the company controlling the dam had, at some point, had the flood gates open for several weeks as a 'tourist attraction' and as a result lowered the dam to a crazy level, but how true that tale is I'm not sure.

Waters in certain areas of Africa can be dangerous places with threats from crocodiles and hippos. You wouldn't think those sweet-looking vegetarians could be a threat to people, but if you got in their way they could turn very aggressive and give you a very nasty bite. I once played badminton with a guy who had had an encounter with a hippo. He was one of the lucky survivors, only suffering a big chunk missing from the back of one of his thighs after being attacked.

Another problem one needed to know about in Zambian waters was bilharzia. As I believe I mentioned in a previous book, bilharzia is a disease caused by a parasitic worm. The worm, or fluke, has several different species. It affects the intestines and the urinary system preferentially, but because it lives in the blood vessels it can harm other systems in the body too, including the lungs, the nervous system, and the brain.

Millions of people are affected by bilharzia worldwide with over 200,000 deaths attributed to it during 2014 according to the World Health Organisation.

These miniscule worms are known to be prevalent in Lake Kariba, though the hosting snails tend to be confined to areas where the water is fairly still. Fortunately, the small bay overlooked by Eagles Rest is pretty well churned up by people and boats, so was purported to be safe from this parasite, which was as well because the weather was glorious during our stay and the kids spent a lot of time in the water.

I too ventured into the wet stuff on a daily basis, the most memorable of those being when I was invited to try my hand, well, all of me actually, at water skiing.

The first time I nearly drowned was when my feet were strapped into the skis and the rest of me disappeared under the water. The second time was more memorable as the water wanted to enter my lungs via a different orifice.

I don't recall ever having had an enema in my life, but at some time the procedure had been graphically described to me so I had a fair idea what it would be like. As the speed boat surged forward and pulled me along I found great difficulty in rising to a standing position on the skis and, as a result, squatted behind the boat travelling at a great rate of knots, with my backside feeling like someone had inserted a high-pressure hose into my rectum.

I reached the point where I was sure water was about to come spraying out of my ears when one last push of my legs sent me on a 180° arc. That was my third near-drowning as I landed face down in the water before letting go of the tow rope.

I declined all kind invitations to give it another shot.

And if that incident wasn't enough to make the holiday memorable, another experience is indelibly imprinted in the minds, hearts and souls of the entire family. It involved the world-famous singer Neil Diamond.

Penny Evans, it would seem, was a big fan of his and the inclusion of their hi-fi set on the holiday was to prevent her from suffering Diamond withdrawal. Alas it meant the rest of us had to suffer ND overload.

With the rare inclusion of other artists' songs, we heard *Cracklin' Rosie*, who was *Forever in Blue Jeans*, making *Love on the Rocks*, in *America*, while a *Song Sung* (too many times) *Blue* for everybody's favourite *Sweet Caroline*, more bloody times than you could shake a stick of biltong at.

It reached its peak one evening towards the end of our stay when Ziggy, somewhat loudly, advised Penny, "*I am ... I said*, absolutely sick to the back teeth with Neil Bloody Diamond's not-so-*Beautiful Noise*, and if I hear him just **once** more I will be playing frisbee with your bloody LPs in the direction of Lake Kariba!"

I think Penny took the hint, and at the same time the rest of us breathed a sigh of relief.

To this day, none of the Patras clan can hear the first notes of a Neil Diamond song without being transported back to Lake Kariba DOHM DOHM DOHM or in Ziggy's case, immediately pressing the *OFF* button.

33

HERE WE GO AGAIN

A couple of weeks after we had recovered from our Kariba holiday, Ziggy returned from work looking a little distracted. I waited until we were back in Chilanga and the kids had gone to bed before I asked him what was on his mind.

Apparently some new 'men at the top' of the company he worked for had been having fun, slowly but systematically firing people who had been hired by the original bosses at the beginning of the project. Ziggy, in his wisdom, had decided to jump before he was pushed, and resigned from his job.

Oh, no! Not again! I could not believe he was doing this to me yet again.

One thing, dear reader, that I didn't mention when I told you about Ziggy announcing he would no longer be working for Mutende, which sent us winging our way back to England in 1986, was that this was not the first time he'd quit a job right out of the blue.

When I first met my (to be) husband in 1969 he was coming to the end of an apprenticeship with a large mechanical engineering company. His final year was spent in the drawing office and he was finding work in small-parts engineering rather tedious, so he decided to find work elsewhere. He got a job with Conder, a local company in the mechanical construction field who built things like offices, clinics and school buildings. By the time we got married he had progressed through the drawing office as Section Leader before moving on to become a Site Engineer.

In October 1976 I gave birth to Brad. He was five weeks premature and needed the care of the Burton General Hospital's Special Care Baby Unit. Having decided to breastfeed I needed to be there with him, so was living in the hospital facilities when one evening Ziggy came to visit us and announced that he had a new job. I thought he meant he was working on a new project for Conder. Silly me.

With the possibility of a future partnership, he was going to work for two blokes who owned a business building - wait for it - pigsties and swimming pools.

It's a bloody good job that I was sitting on the bed when he told me this, and that I wasn't holding the baby at the time!

"Tell me you're not serious." I said.

"No. It has great potential."

The hell it had! During the previous weeks I'd had plenty of time on my hands, having finished work when I was seven months pregnant, and could not recall hearing about a crazy rise in demand for pork or bacon which would cause a surge in the need for pigsties.

As for the pools - England hardly had the weather to encourage people to spend their hard-earned cash on having swimming pools installed in their back gardens! So I found it difficult to believe that there would be sufficient demand for either pools or pigsties to the extent that it would keep three grown men, plus the labourers who would actually build the bloody things, gainfully employed.

Yet my husband of over two years, now with a non-income-generating wife and a babe-in-arms, had given up a permanent, well-paid job, complete with company car, for this.

My dear old dad was renowned for his favourite expression 'the mind boggles!' which he would use at situations such as these, but mind-boggling didn't even touch the sides of what was going through my head at that moment.

If memory serves me right, the job only lasted a matter of months before he quit and got a 'proper job' with another local firm of structural engineers, before eventually moving on to the company he was with prior to our move to Africa in 1980.

But back to Zambia.

Before he had chance to say anything further on the subject, I told him, "If you think I'm going back to live in cold and cloudy England you've got another think coming! I refuse point blank, so you'd better start thinking of somewhere else."

"Fair enough," he responded, "I guess I was expecting that. What about South Africa?"

When we had visited South Africa back in 1982 we had been very impressed with the place in general. Of course we weren't so impressed with the apartheid practices we'd seen, but were aware that things were on the change. We guessed it wouldn't be long before SA was forced to give up their racist laws and the country would 'settle down'.

The more I thought about it, the keener I became to move south, for various reasons.

Zambia was in the grips of an AIDS epidemic. We were aware of it of course, although we didn't realise the extent of it at that time. What we *did* realise was that it put us at risk should the need arise to use the services of the Zambian health system, which at the time left a lot to be desired in the way of hygiene.

[Apparently, Zambians known to be infected with AIDS in 1985 stood at 36,707 but by the year 1990 the figures had risen to a horrific 293,881. Five years later that figure had almost **trebled**, and trebled again by the year 2000, where statistics indicated 15% of the population was infected.]

A further point in South Africa's favour was that just about everything imaginable was available there at a price more commensurate with one's salary.

On second thoughts, perhaps it wasn't such a bad thing that Ziggy had quit his job.

And so the slog began.

BACK IN 1989 THERE WAS NO JUMPING ONTO THE INTERNET TO SEE WHAT jobs were on offer in various cities within the borders of South Africa. South African newspapers didn't appear on the streets of Lusaka, and the Times of Zambia barely had a situations vacant column for its own towns and cities, never mind SA's. The only way Ziggy was going to find a job in South Africa was to fly down there.

Before he could do that we first had to make accommodation arrangements for me and the kids, as I most certainly was not willing to stay alone with them in the remote countryside of our Chilanga house (which still had no fence around it). After discussing the situation at the LGC, my friend Penny very kindly offered for us to stay with her and her husband and their daughter Sarah.

In a couple of suitcases we packed our clothes and a few of the kids' toys (they didn't have many these days). My precious computer still had its original boxes for transportation so that, and what few other things I didn't want to risk losing, accompanied us too.

The remainder of our stuff was left at the house and Julius was threatened with very grim consequences should any of that disappear in our absence. But what to do with Jessie?

Even though we'd only had her a relatively short time we had come to love that animal; she was such a faithful and trusting dog that I was loath to leave her to a loveless life at an empty house, though it was clear we couldn't take her with us to Penny's. It was also obvious we wouldn't be able to take her with us to South Africa if Ziggy got a job there, so we were really looking for a loving permanent home for her.

In the event, our stay with Penny didn't last very long as her husband wasn't so enamoured with the arrangement. But we weren't without friends and hearing of our need to move on, the McCleerys immediately offered us space at their house.

This arrangement worked well as being a larger property we weren't under each other's feet, and the kids were delighted at being able to wander around the farm. Then the rain set in, and did it ever cause some disruptions! For two days we were actually unable to leave the property. The road leading from the McCleery's farm down to the main road crossed a donga. Normally any water in the donga would pass through a pipe under the road, but with the amount of rain we were getting it had breached the road to the extent that we couldn't cross it. Thankfully this happened over a weekend so at least the kids didn't miss school.

As the water level dropped we were able to risk driving through this temporary ford, so long as one didn't linger long enough for the water to get up the exhaust pipe.

Unfortunately I was a little over-zealous in my driving to the extent that, unbeknown to me at the time, I drove so fast that the force of the water pushed the turning fan up against the radiator which, in turn, got damaged. Of course, the radiator then lost its water, which we didn't notice as there was already so much of the wet stuff on the ground, until after a few days the engine ground to a halt.

Great. As if we didn't have enough complications in our lives, we were now without transport. As David and Heather's place was on the opposite side of town to the kids' school, and they were both busy with their own commitments, we were in a bit of a pickle.

But not for long. As soon as our latest dilemma hit the Gymkhana Club, Lorraine and Rob Chalcraft leapt into the breach and offered to put us up. They lived a few miles further down the road from Lake Road School, so would easily be able to drop off and collect the kids as they went to and from work. Perfect.

34

OUT OF ZAMBIA

Rob and Lorraine had only been married for a couple of years and as yet had no kids, and their housing situation was quite unique. They lived, you see, in a very large garage.

Some people they knew were having a house built on the outskirts of Lusaka. It looked like being quite a large, modern house, but it was taking some time to build. We are talking Africa here remember. Any property left untended would soon find itself minus anything removable, like roof tiles, windows, doors and door frames (firewood), any exposed plumbing, and probably the bricks as well.

About a hundred yards from the house being built there was another large building intended for garages and storage. Part of that building had been sectioned into rooms and consisted of a bedroom, bathroom, kitchen, large lounge and another large room off the lounge. There was enough space to accommodate the five of us sleeping in that room.

When I told the kids that we were going to live with Lorraine they wouldn't believe me. Right up to us having all our luggage and my computer brought to the Gymkhana Club by Heather, they still thought I was pulling their legs. Only when they saw me talking to Lor about loading our things into her Volkswagen combi did they take it in.

I have never seen such well-tanned kids turn so pale so quickly. They were all still terrified of Lorraine and the thought of now having to *live* with her scared them shitless. (My apologies, but I really can't think of a more perfect way to describe it.) I never heard a peep out of them as they sat in the back of that VW on the way to The Garage.

The next day at the club Penny told me that she received a call from Ziggy, who had no idea that we'd moved on. Penny gave him a brief outline of the situation and told him she would get hold of Lor's home number to give to him the following day so that he could then contact me there. Remember, we were still a few years away from cell phones at this time too.

The following night I gave Ziggy the lowdown on everything that had happened. His first concern was to get the car back in working order. He asked me to get details of the garage where it had been taken to and he would talk to them about it, which was a great relief for me.

It turned out that they needed numerous spare parts which weren't available in Zambia, so Ziggy took full details and arranged to buy them in South Africa. For his part, Ziggy already had two job offers under his belt and was going to a second interview for a third job the next day. It was hoped that he would be able to return to Zambia on the next available flight after that.

In the meantime we had settled well into life with the Chalcrafts. As some attempt at repayment for their kind hospitality I offered to cook all meals during the course of our stay. At the time neither Lor nor Rob were much into cooking, apart from braai-ing or frying up a couple of steaks. I was more than happy to add a wider variety of dishes to their menu for the duration of our stay.

Naturally this meant I spent a lot of time in their small kitchen. One of the downsides of this was a problem they were having with cockroaches. Whenever I opened a cupboard to retrieve a plate or something, hordes of them would scuttle off in all directions. They weren't huge, but could still leave behind evidence of their presence on the dishes, which then had to be rinsed before being used. As horrible as this situation was, I eventually accepted this as part of life in Africa. In fact, contrary to popular belief, cockroaches are not just attracted to dirty places. They can live off small crumbs, soap, paint particles or small droplets of water. They can be found in sparkling-clean homes because, if cockroaches once get in, they will find a way to survive. In fact the Chalcrafts had a housemaid who frequently cleaned out the cupboards, but eradicating the roaches was virtually impossible.

Anyway, there was more than enough equipment for me to work with, though I soon retrieved from Chilanga a couple of cookery books and my kitchen scales.

Being in the era long before digital scales, when we had first set up home I had chosen to buy a set of balance scales for accuracy in my kitchen. Three weeks into our stay with Lor and Rob I was about to measure out something when I noticed that the weights tray and ingredients dish were not equally balanced; the weights tray was actually resting on the base of the unit - most odd. I turned the scales this way and that, trying to figure out why this was. It was then that I noticed the small plate attached to the underside of the weights tray. It would appear this contained tiny weights which are used to fine-tune the scales. I noticed something slip out of there as I upturned the scales.

Using a small screwdriver I carefully removed the fine weight-plate to discover scores of baby cockroaches milling around amongst the tiny weights. No wonder the scales were out of kilter! After a clean up and dousing down with Killerspray, I got stuck into the cooking.

As for the kids, it was amazing how well behaved they could be, frightened of doing anything to cross Lorraine, although I think Brad was on the receiving end of Lor's wrath a couple of times over something relatively trivial, but which would result in a very loud reprimand.

When Ziggy returned from SA we had quite a houseful, as apart from seven humans there were also seven dogs and seven cats. And no, we weren't all going to St Ives!

Talking of dogs, our problem of a home for Jessy had quickly been resolved. Lor asked her sister-in-law if she would like to take her. We were absolutely delighted when she agreed, and so Jessy was transported to her new home. It shows what a wonderful dog she was, because despite experiencing the trauma of change of ownership to us only a few months earlier, she soon settled into a happy life with Rob's sister Heather and her family. I have since heard that they too loved her to pieces and Jessy lived a long and happy life.

Something which made staying with Lor and Rob quite homely, despite living in The Garage, was that along one wall of their living room were the two large wooden wall units they had bought from us when we left Zambia the first time, together with many of the books upon them.

IMMEDIATELY UPON HIS RETURN FROM SOUTH AFRICA ZIGGY TOOK THE parts to the garage for our car, but we weren't expecting any overnight recovery of the vehicle bearing in mind the Zambian pace. In the meantime friends rallied round to transport Ziggy where he needed to go to finalise all things for our departure. He also dropped his next bomb.

Unbeknown to me, after we had the break-in Ziggy had refused to pay rent on our house (and therein lies another tale, I'll tell you in a minute) until the perimeter fence, which had been promised when he took on the rental, had been erected. We were now four months down the line so quite a lot of money was involved, and whilst he'd saved it, Ziggy had now used much of that money for his flight to SA.

The agents handling the house rental for the owners didn't agree with Ziggy's idea of *no fence, no rent* and so placed a lien against our car for the amount of rent outstanding. Once it was fixed the car would have to be sold (whether we had wanted to sell it or not) and their 'entitlement' taken out of the proceeds of sale before we received any balance left over. What a stuff up!

It also came as no surprise when another one of Ziggy's earlier cunning plans backfired on him too.

As mentioned earlier, when we returned to Zambia, by now being fully aware of what was or wasn't available in the country, I had shipped a mass of stuff to follow us. When our freighted possessions arrived Ziggy performed his normal miracles when it came to import duty. Talking to the right official, in the right way, with the right amount of money, he had managed to bring our stuff in without paying any import duty. This was all well and good, but it meant that we had no proof that we had brought it in, therefore on taking it out were now bound to pay export duty, which could amount to a fair sum.

While we wouldn't be taking anywhere near as much out as we brought in, I did want to take our clothes and most of our remaining household items with us, though a few things would be sold.

Yes, now about the house rental: All this time I had been under the impression that the company was paying the rent, but it appeared that they hadn't strictly agreed that Ziggy's contract would be changed from single to marital status. They agreed to pay for our air tickets from the UK to Zambia only, but Ziggy would be given a housing allowance equivalent only to single accommodation for himself. Any extra required to accommodate his family was for his own account. Mr Patras had failed to mention this minor detail to me.

Now back to the possessions: Ziggy came up with a bright idea for getting our stuff out of the country without paying duty.

He went to a shipping agent and told them we were going on extended leave to South Africa and that once there we would be camping, therefore we needed to have many things which we couldn't take with us on our flight. These would be packed in cardboard boxes and shipped to Johannesburg to await our arrival there.

"And we'll be bringing it all back with us when we return," he lied to them.

Even by our camping standards, we wouldn't be expected to take *that* much stuff out, even for a camping trip lasting a couple of months, so he went round to every shipping agent in Lusaka with the same story, arranging to send two or three boxes out with each one.

While he was doing all this I was getting help from kind friends to visit the house in Chilanga to collect the remainder of our possessions, which we packed for transportation.

One of the things which was sold was the kids' Lego train set.

Although very rarely used, Brad in particular was heartbroken when I told him we couldn't take it with us, but I simply couldn't justify the expense of exporting it. In fact to this day he still admonishes me for disposing of one of his favourite toys. But I didn't dispose of all the Lego. I kept a couple of boxes full of basic pieces. In fact 30 years later I still have it tucked away in a wardrobe and, one day, when I think he's grown up, I might let Brad take it to *his* home.

Another upsetting sale was, of course, that of Tommy Tucker. He was a beautiful horse and had already won a couple of rosettes in the local shows we had entered, and he'd exhibited great potential in all events. I had no trouble finding a buyer for him. A teenager, a newcomer to the club, was very keen to take him on and was totally undeterred by the fact that he kicked her one day as she tried to catch him in a small paddock. She got my vote (and my horse).

And so our life in Zambia drew to a close.

By this time we were all (except Ziggy) in a state of flux, torn between sadness at leaving Zambia, our animals and friends, and the excitement and trepidation of embarking, once again, on something new. The one consolation was that there was more chance that our pals might visit us in South Africa, as many visited there annually for one reason or another.

We were given a great send-off at Lusaka airport, arriving there well before the required time complete with cool boxes containing snacks and drinks. Someone even baked a farewell cake.

To say that our departure was emotional would be a gross understatement, as once more hugs and kisses were exchanged and tears were shed.

To mess up the words of that wonderful crooner Frank Sinatra, cue music... ♪♪ ♪♪

https://annpatrasauthor.com/audio-video/

And so, the end is near
and we all face this last departure.

Once more we move away
from all our friends, here in Lusaka.

We've had so many homes,
That I am feeling like a nomad.
If I pack one more box,
I think I'll go mad.

Mistakes, we've made a few,
in fact too many here to mention.
We've broken lots of rules,
but got away without suspension.

We've travelled far and wide,
hit every pothole on the highways.
Oh yes, we did it all,
but did it our way.

Yes there were times, along the way
When there was far less work than play.
And if we ever had a doubt
We locked the doors and just went out.
We drank the beers and all said "Cheers",
We did it our way!

We've been to lots of parks,
both near and far. Gone on safaris,
We've seen the lion's kill,
and heard the call of the Grey Loeries.

We bought the very best
of tasty steaks, done in the braai way,
Oh yes, we cooked them all,
and did it our way.

We've made many friends we hold so dear

And we'll be sad not to be near.
Without their laughter and the fun,
We'll miss our pals, yes every one.
But now's the day, to fly away.
And go on our way.

We're going on our way.

IF YOU ENJOYED MY BOOK

I would be incredibly grateful if you could see your way to putting a review on Amazon or Goodreads, or anywhere you fancy actually. (Though preferably not on public walls or toilet doors).

Reviews are very important to us authors and are always much appreciated. MANY THANKS

And I do love to hear from my readers, many of whom have now become friends, so feel free to email me on annpatras.author@gmail.com

Also, check out my website/blog for photos and stuff.
Damn silly things still seems to happen to the Patras family so you'll often find more tales on my www/blog about our crazy antics, past and present.

WEBSITE: http://www.annpatrasauthor.com
FACEBOOK: https://www.facebook.com/AnnPatrasAfricaSeries/

WHILE I STILL HAVE YOUR ATTENTION I would like to recommend that you join the Facebook Group, We Love Memoirs. It is the Friendliest Group on Facebook and puts readers who enjoy memoirs in touch with the authors who write them. I can personally highly recommend many books produced by author members.

ACKNOWLEDGEMENTS

Finally, big thanks must go to Celia Burnett, Pauline Armstrong, and also Victoria Twead of Ant Press for their invaluable assistance in making this book fit for human consumption.

The fabulous illustrations were all down to me. 😃

ABOUT THE AUTHOR

Ann Patras was born and raised in Burton upon Trent in the English Midlands. Ann has always had a lot of interaction with people, initially through her family's busy corner grocery shop, then her parents' popular pub and later through her own varied careers. She started her working life as a junior legal secretary and ended it as a gallery curator with lots of other stuff between, including a spell as police reservist!

After raising three kids, countless dogs and living in Africa for thirty one years, Ann and Ziggy, over 45 years married, now live in Andalusia, Spain and have absolutely no intention of moving again.

ANT PRESS BOOKS

AWESOME AUTHORS ~ AWESOME BOOKS

Ant Press

If you enjoyed this book, you may also enjoy these Ant Press titles:

MEMOIRS

Into Africa with 3 Kids, 13 Crates and a Husband by Ann Patras

More Into Africa with 3 Kids, some Dogs and a Husband by Ann Patras

Much More into Africa with Kids, Dogs, Horses and a Husband by Ann Patras

Chickens, Mules and Two Old Fools by Victoria Twead (Wall Street Journal Top 10 bestseller)

Two Old Fools ~ Olé! by Victoria Twead

Two Old Fools on a Camel by Victoria Twead (thrice New York Times bestseller)

Two Old Fools in Spain Again by Victoria Twead

Two Old Fools in Turmoil by Victoria Twead

Two Old Fools Down Under by Victoria Twead (NEW)

One Young Fool in Dorset (The Prequel) by Victoria Twead

One Young Fool in South Africa (The Prequel) by Joe and Victoria Twead

Fat Dogs and French Estates ~ Part I by Beth Haslam

Fat Dogs and French Estates ~ Part II by Beth Haslam

Fat Dogs and French Estates ~ Part III by Beth Haslam

Fat Dogs and French Estates ~ Part IV by Beth Haslam

Simon Ships Out: How One Brave, Stray Cat Became a Worldwide Hero by Jacky Donovan

Smoky: How a Tiny Yorkshire Terrier Became a World War II American Army Hero,

Therapy Dog and Hollywood Star by Jacky Donovan

Smart as a Whip: A Madcap Journey of Laughter, Love, Disasters and Triumphs by Jacky Donovan

Heartprints of Africa by Cinda Adams Brooks

How not to be a Soldier: My Antics in the British Army by Lorna McCann

Moment of Surrender: My Journey Through Prescription Drug Addiction to Hope and Renewal by Pj Laube

One of its Legs are Both the Same by Mike Cavanagh

A Pocket Full of Days by Mike Cavanagh

Horizon Fever by A E Filby

Cane Confessions: The Lighter Side to Mobility by Amy L. Bovaird

Completely Cats - Stories with Cattitude by Beth Haslam and Zoe Marr

From Moulin Rouge to Gaudi's City by EJ Bauer

Fresh Eggs and Dog Beds 1: Living the Dream in Rural Ireland by Nick Albert

Fresh Eggs and Dog Beds 2: Still Living the Dream in Rural Ireland by Nick Albert

Fresh Eggs and Dog Beds 3: More Living the Dream in Rural Ireland by Nick Albert

Don't Do It Like This: How NOT to move to Spain by Joe Cawley, Victoria Twead and Alan Parks

Longing for Africa: Journeys Inspired by the Life of Jane Goodall. Part One: Ethiopia by Annie Schrank

Longing for Africa: Journeys Inspired by the Life of Jane Goodall. Part Two: Kenya by Annie Schrank

South of Barcelona: A New Life in Spain by Vernon Lacey

A Kiss Behind the Castanets: My Love Affair with Spain by Jean Roberts

FICTION

Parched by Andrew C Branham

A is for Abigail by Victoria Twead (Sixpenny Cross 1)

B is for Bella by Victoria Twead (Sixpenny Cross 2)

C is for the Captain by Victoria Twead (Sixpenny Cross 3)

D is for Dexter by Victoria Twead (Sixpenny Cross 4) - coming soon

NON FICTION

How to Write a Bestselling Memoir by Victoria Twead

CHILDREN'S BOOKS

Seacat Simon: The Little Cat Who Became a Big Hero by Jacky Donovan

Morgan and the Martians by Victoria Twead

ANT PRESS ONLINE

Why not check out Ant Press's online presence and follow our social media accounts for news of forthcoming books and special offers?

Website: www.antpress.org
Email: admin@antpress.org
Facebook: www.facebook.com/AntPress
Instagram: www.instagram.com/publishwithantpress
Twitter: www.twitter.com/Ant_Press

Printed in Great Britain
by Amazon